Behind the Scenes at Special Events

Behind the Scenes at Special Events

FLOWERS, PROPS, AND DESIGN

Lena Malouf
CSEP, AIFD, AAF, PFC-I

John Wiley & Sons, Inc.

New York • Chichester • Weinheim • Brisbane • Singapore • Toronto

Copyright © 1999 by Lena Malouf. All rights reserved.
Published by John Wiley & Sons, Inc.
Published simultaneously in Canada.

This publication is designed to provide accurate and
authoritative information in regard to the subject matter
covered. It is sold with the understanding that the publisher is
not engaged in rendering professional services. If professional
advice or other expert assistance is required, the services of a
competent professional person should be sought.

Library of Congress Cataloging-in-Publication Data

Malouf, Lena.
    Behind the scenes at speecial events : flowers, props, and design /
Lena Malouf.
        p.   cm.
    Includes index.
    ISBN 0-471-25491-6 (cloth : alk. paper)
    1. Hospitality industry—Management—Handbooks, manuals, etc.
    2. Promotion of special events—Handbooks, manuals, etc.   I. Title.
TX911.3.M27M25   1998
647.94'068—dc21   98-17815

Printed in the United States of America

10 9 8 7 6 5 4 3 2 1

Contents

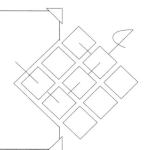

Chapter 4   The Power of Color   53

Chapter 5   Innovative Design and Decor   63

Chapter 6   Theme Creations   77

Foreword

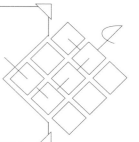

Lena Malouf is legendary. Like many other legends, she has left a legacy for those who will follow her and from which others currently can benefit. One part of her legacy is her perishable art sustained in photographs and her many training classes across the world. The other part is this book.

Lena's brief biography of herself in the Preface provides historical fact that this person has had it together from an early age. Starting from a basic foundation in her parents' retail business, Lena entered into the floral business and unconsciously set about sharpening the leadership skills that would drive her to the top in all her endeavors.

The book that you hold in your hands today is written from a designer's perspective. But, the designer has gone beyond just the final environment. She definitely provides the reader with an education on the use of color; innovative design and décor; design principles; and the elements of art, themes, flowers, and tabletop. However, she also puts on her Certified Special Events Professional (CSEP) hat and takes it further to encompass the management of events—a 12-point management plan and event essentials. Then, she tops it all off with case studies of events from around the world. This book is filled with information, illustrations, and handy planning, design, and organizational tools that will delight the novice and the seasoned professional alike—and it provides all special events industry professionals with a unique resource not previously available to them.

Having said all that, what is most obvious to me in this book is Lena's willingness to share as much of her knowledge and experience as possible with her readers. This is so like her. She's been doing it all her life. So, read on, dear reader. You're in for a treat.

Carol F. McKibben, CSEP
President, The International Special Events Society (ISES)
President, McKibben Communications

Preface

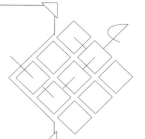

Uncountable hours go into writing a book of this size but once completed, the author feels not only a sense of relief but a real sense of personal achievement. In this book, I happily share with you the systems, formulas, and checklists that work, as well as the sophisticated styling, innovative ideas, creative concepts, proven formulas, and systems that work for me. The field of special events is a fantastic profession and I love every minute of it.

The events industry is comprised of many facets and it is essential to be knowledgeable about all of the parts that make up an event. I have had a lifetime of study in the specialized discipline of flowers. The special event is a complete extension of this art as it involves the lighting that makes it magical, the sound that brings it to life, and the decor that turns it into fantasy.

Through the many lectures and demonstrations that I have given in both Australia and the United States, I have met hundreds of people searching for good books that will serve as a springboard for creative ideas in the field of special events. *Behind the Scenes at Special Events* is such a book. It covers the smallest of details from transporting flowers or trimming a napkin, to the inspirational creation of all the components of a themed event which meets the client's most demanding expectations.

The 12 Point Management Plan discussed in Chapter 2 is highly informative and will guide you in dealing with clients. Event Essentials (Chapter 3) explains the responsibilities of the contractors involved in planning a special event.

The storyboard technique of theme building with its step-by-step formula is clearly shown in the highly distinctive color plates within the book and the truly amazing conceptual art of Freddrik Campioni Garcia.

At this point I can only reflect on where it all started for me . . .

I was born in the small country town of Canowindra in New South Wales, Australia, 250 miles west of Sydney with a population of 2,500. My father and mother, Nicholas and Rose, owned the big general store where you could buy anythng from a horseshoe to a hairpin, candy to a comb. It was a store that offered an enormous range of products.

At a very early age I was conditioned to provide service. At the age of seven my brother Doug would put me on the back of his bike to deliver the eggs or the ketchup while the eldest of the family, Carl, would bribe both of us with sixpence to help him weigh the sugar or potatoes. At eight I was serving in the shop alongside Dad and at 10, elevated to the office stool to file his invoices.

In addition to school and working/playing in the store, I had lessons in dance, singing, violin, painting, sewing, and there was no way I could go play cricket with the boys until my two hours of piano practice was finished. I can only recall happy days and family love. Indeed I was very fortunate.

Aside from all of this however, Nick and Rose instilled in us trust and integrity, the belief being that if you had these values, the rest would take care of itself.

Unbeknownst to my loving parents they were also teaching us such important management techniques as marketing the business, gaining product knowedge, using positive telephone techniques, applying problem solving skills, selecting the right team, and encouraging feedback. While not realizing it at the time, we learned these techniques and applied them subconsciously.

My parents marketed their grocery haberdashery, toy, and hardware store by having open house after Sunday Mass and serving coffee and cake. They let the mix of established and potential clients come together. Nick believed that the old, but happy, customers were walking testimonials. Product knowledge was embodied in the statement "Taste the honey. If it's not right, we'll return it." In regard to telephone technique, problem solving, and feedback, the approach was very uncomplicated. "Talk to the people." Finally, in regard to team building it was well known that if you worked with Nick and Rose you were there for life and most employees were!

After 44 years of trading, Nick and Rose sold the

family business and in the early 1950s we moved to the city of Wollongong, on the coast 50 miles south of Sydney. School finished, certainly, but education didn't.

I was never quite sure of what I had really learned from these child-into-teen years until I was out there doing it by sheer instinct, sheer gut feel. Going into business now seemed inevitable and I opened my first flower shop in 1957. Carl went into building and Doug opened his first real estate office. Nick and Rose were supportive in every way.

The 1970s proved to be an important decade in my professional development. I attended Sydney Technical College and Sydney Teacher's College, began training florists throughout Australia, and most importantly earned my Diploma of Teaching. Over the next two years, I appeared on national television with close friends, and well-known Australian culinary celebrity Bernard King. This was certainly fun, as well as being a learning experience.

In 1982, I was accepted into the prestigious American Institute of Floral Designers, as well as the American Academy of Florists and the Professional Floral Commentators International. Lectures, demonstrations, and the release of many articles with Cenflo Publications in Chicago followed and still continue today. The influence of my American colleagues catapulted me from floral retailing to specialization in floral and party work. Study continued along with major presentations in the United States which kept me learning and provided many creative challenges.

In the late 1980s, I met Angelo Bonito of Floral Events Unlimited, Silver Springs, Maryland who asked me to start an Australian chapter of the International Special Events Society (ISES). After considerable coaxing, I decided to accept the invitation. We were formally chartered in 1992 and today we boast over 200 members and 3,000 special event professionals worldwide. This international society, headquartered in Indianapolis, is closely linked with George Washington University in Washington D.C. and the recognized accreditation of Certified Special Events Professional (CSEP) enhances any event person's professional reputation. The Society encourages lifelong education and self-development.

At this point I look at where I am at today. I feel as driven today as I did at the age of 20 and I attribute this to the fact that I absolutely love what I do. Fortunately, my eye for detail has never wavered and my close friend Marge Hayes of Sydney who is an Ikebana Master, reminds me to look deep and look often. I feel constantly energized as I strive for excellence in my field and therefore constantly excited with life.

I look forward to meeting you in Australia, the United States, or someplace else around the world. Happy reading!

With Sincere Thanks . . .

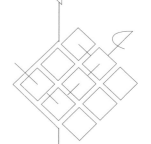

When **Mr. Harry Noe** of Culinary & Hospitality Industry Publications Services (CHIPS), Kingwood, Texas, reviewed the chapter outline of this publication he referred me to Claire Thompson Zuckerman, then senior editor at John Wiley & Sons, Inc., New York. On that recommendation I left the United States knowing that I was a Wiley author.

To the Synopsis contributors:
Richard Dutton, Malaysia; **Janet Elkins,** California; **Lech Sobecki,** Melbourne; **Pamela Wheat,** Sydney; **Romaine Periera,** Sydney.

To my American suppliers for their support:
Tom Coulouris and team from Rose Brand, New York, NY; **Knud Nielsen Co.,** Evergreen, AL; **Jim Marvin Enterprises,** Dickson, TN; **Creative Candles,** Kansas City, MO; **Smither's Oasis,** Kent, OH; **Design Master Color Tool,** Boulder, CO; **Lion Ribbon Company,** Chester, NJ; **Lomey Manufacturing Corp,** Asheville, NC; **Zucker Feather Products,** California; **BBJ Boutique Linens,** Skokie, IL; **Something Different Linens,** Wallington, NJ; **Encore Studios,** Clifton, NJ; **Flower News Magazine,** Chicago, IL.

To **Dr. Joe Jeff Goldblatt** of George Washington University, Washington D.C., who constantly waves my flag and has encouraged me to put words on paper.

To **Alison Harriman,** color consultant, Sydney; **Margaret McAlister,** proofreader, Wollongong; **Harry Koponen,** Memo, Melbourne; **David Ferguson,** stage manager, Syndey; **James Michaels,** Distinctive Events, Sydney.

Jerry Astourian of Astourian Lighting Design, Los Angeles, CA, has contributed very generously in Chapter 3 in regard to lighting knowledge. Jerry is a professional technician who shares his skills generously.

To **Julie Sidie-McIntyre,** my personal assistant of many years. I call her "Jewel" for short and that she is in every way. Her expertise and efforts have always been invaluable. I just love her—we have lots of laughs.

Freddrik Campioni Garcia, creative art director, San Antonio, TX, is an amazing events man and an outstanding conceptual artist—as evidenced throughout this book. Freddrik is a close, dear friend and associate of mine over many years.

To **Eda Michelle,** a fashion guru and very close friend of many years. We meet early each morning for a power walk in the park with our Golden Retrievers. Creative thoughts are continually exchanged—some become a reality, while others blow with the wind.

Doug Malouf, my brother, is a motivational speaker of international repute—next to him I am a novice. To him, writing has become an art form and it is just great having such a resource person in the family.

Finally, anything I do seems to involve a cast of thousands and takes more resources than the movie *Titanic,* but the four movie stars in my life are my daughter, **Sharon,** my two sons, **Gregory** and **Brett,** and my lovely daughter-in-law, **Michelle.** Their expressions of interest in my work and their constant love has allowed me to achieve.

Special Acknowledgment

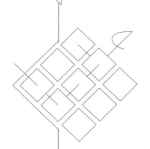

To Mr. Ray Williams, A.M.

Sydney, Australia

In business life we are occasionally fortunate enough to meet the ideal client. When I was called into HIH Insurance, Sydney, Australia, to discuss their events, I had no idea what an enormous impact Ray Williams, and later his family, would have on my life.

Because of his faith in my ability, I have been able to create and develop enchanting schemes. We have worked on an exciting range of events with spectacular results and it has been a wonderful working relationship. My professional achievements are a result of his trust in me.

Eight years and some seventy events later, I am now publicly saying *thank you* to an extraordinary man who is not only a supportive client, but has become a friend and adviser to both myself and my family.

Ray,

My thanks,

Lena

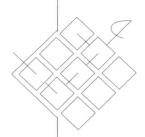

Chapter 1

The Secrets of Superb Organization

At any given moment, all over the world, there are crowds of eager people walking through the door of some special event—a glittering awards night, a wedding, a product launch, a sports championship celebration. The list of reasons to celebrate is endless, but you can be sure of one thing. Everyone who arrives at one of those events is hoping for something special that will give them a night to remember. Something that will cause their mouths to drop open as they gaze around them in awe.

Events that deliver on the hope of something special are not just happy accidents. They are the results of months of meticulous planning and brilliant teamwork. They require the efforts of dozens, maybe *hundreds,* of specialists to pull them together. Most of all, they require commitment and creativity from the team that plans and manages the event. Event planners have to be tacticians, business professionals, creative designers, artists, and amateur psychologists.

So you've won the contract—what now? After wiping champagne from the lips and peering into the future, there is the tendency to feel overwhelmed at the enormity of the task ahead. There is so much to do and so little time!

Your job as event manager will be to combine people and resources and, in a given lead time, produce an event that achieves its objectives and meets your client's expectations. To achieve this you will be concerned with the following four concepts:

Managing the Event

1. **Resource Management**—Involves managing time, people, and income. A successful resource manager is a clever administrator. The timing of the event, budgets, and lead time all affect how an event is organized.
2. **People Management**—It takes many people to produce a successful event. All of their personalities, tastes, and levels of expertise will help shape the personality of your event.
3. **Responsibility Management**—In dealing with people a great deal of responsibility is laden onto the event manager. An appreciation of legal issues and an understanding of risk management principles are crucial.
4. **Production Management**—This concept relates to organizing all the tangible elements of the event—everything you can see, touch, hear, or taste at the event including décor, staging, catering, and entertainment.

---

1. Resource Management

An event manager has three resources to manage: time, money, and people. To organize and implement an event, a series of actions or tasks needs to be carried out. In essence, an event manager needs to be a clever administrator of these component parts and resource management is the integration of people, money, and tasks within a given time frame to achieve this objective. These elements need to work in harmony to produce a well–organized event.

All events begin with an objective, otherwise known as a mission statement. For example:*

> The mission of ISES (International Special Events Society) is to educate, advance, and promote the special events industry and its network of professionals along with related industries. To that end, we strive to . . .
>
> - Uphold the integrity of the special events profession to the general public through our "Principles of Professional Conduct and Ethics"
> - Acquire and disseminate useful business information
> - Foster a spirit of cooperation among its members and other special events professionals
> - Cultivate high standards of business practices

An event manager will *prioritize, delegate, schedule, implement,* and *liaise* to make sure all tasks are completed within the given time and budget allocated to the event. Before discussing this, let's look at an Organizational Chart. (Figure 1.1).

Prioritizing Tasks
In order to fulfill the mission statement, sets of actions or tasks need to be carried out. Some tasks will be more important or require more attention than others and the art is to prioritize and allocate time and preference to those tasks.

Proactive and Reactive Differences
All tasks are either proactive or reactive. Proactive tasks help bring a special event to completion. Reactive tasks, while important, do not necessarily help bring an event to completion.

As a rule of thumb, a special event organizer should spend 80% of the time being proactive, and 20% reactive. Knowing the difference between these

*Courtsey of The International Special Events Society

3

Security	Technical	Entertainment	Decor	Staging	Venue/Caterer	
Schedules	Light	Feature act	Themes	Platforms	Site	Serving stations
Contacts	Sound	Speakers	Floral	Requirement	Menu	Ramps
Access	Briefs	Bands	Wall features	Briefs	Budget	Exits
Parking	Quotes in	Sight acts	Ceilings	Quotes	Waiters	Lifts
Entrances	Photography	Repertoire	Floor options	Draping	Beverages	Restrictions
Exit	Video	Contracts	Stage plans	Rostrums	Crew meals	Breakout rooms
Fire codes	Special effects	Travel and	Stage apron	Podiums	Tables	Toilet facilities
Staff/officer	Follow spots	Transfers	Designing	Steps	Chairs	Air conditioning
	Pin spots	Accommodation	Task sheets	Ramps	Dinnerware	Heating
	Stage light	Rehearsals	Purchase goods	Elevations	Glassware	Venue costs
	Power availability	Costumes	Tablecloths &	Signage	Cutlery	Venue
	Intelligent lighting	Breakout rooms	covers	A/V needs	Bars	restrictions
	Speaker equip.	Schedules	Napkins &	Trussing		Liquor liability
	Special effects	Mirrors	trims	Scaffolding		
	Mirrored balls	Racks	Invitation	Scissor lifts		
			Guest & table			
			list			

Marketing	Legal	Transport	Staffing	Administration	Financial	Miscellaneous
Prospect invites	Insurances	Load in	Our Team	Time lines	Budget	Printing
Film video	Permits	Load out	Volunteers	Emergency and	Cash flow	Signage
Take photographs	Licenses	Truck rental	Contractors	Key contacts	Invoicing	Programs
Editorial & articles	Contracts	Limousine	Committee	Contingency	Statements	Banners
Direct mail	Trademarks	Bus/Taxi		Travel bookings/	Accountant	Posters
Promotion	Copyright	Air Transport		accommodation		Corporate
Advertising				Post event		gifts
Pledges				Management fee		
Sponsors				Stationery extras		
Aim/objective				Phone & fax costs		

Figure 1.1. Organizational chart for an event in general. This chart guides you through the elements that may be required to produce your event.

tasks can help the event manager prioritize. Here are some examples of proactive and reactive tasks:

Proactive Tasks	Reactive Tasks
Booking venue	Crew meals
Booking staging	Writing reports
Briefing contractors	Writing thank you
	letters
Site inspections	Bookkeeping
Budgeting	Filing
Calling for quotes	Invoicing
Executing the event	Post evaluating the
	event

Delegating

The bigger the event, the more likely it is that many tasks will be farmed out to contractors. However, delegation of a task is not a relinquishment of responsibility; the event manager must ultimately be accountable for every aspect of an event's organization.

Scheduling

By prioritizing and delegating tasks the event organizer is faced with a logistical problem. There is only so much time available and some tasks may not be able to be carried out simultaneously, or are not possible to achieve until another task is complete.

The art of scheduling is arranging a set of tasks in a sequence, taking into account the priority of the task. On completing a schedule, the event organizer has created a time-line that is realistic and achievable. Figures 1.2 and 1.3 show sample schedules.

Wednesday, 6th December

0900 hrs   Designer to commence table decorations in Jim Crack Room (breakout room)
Exhibition hire company delivery arrives in Jim Crack Room
Stage manager's assistants set up room dividers to cordon room area ×3
(Dancers & Singer) and Lena's preparation area
AJC to provide tea, coffee, and soft drinks for working crew ×6 pax
AJC to provide telephone in Jim Crack Room

Thursday, 7th December

0900 hrs   Décor team continues to set up in Jim Crack Room
AJC to provide tea, coffee, and soft drinks for working crew × 8 pax
AJC to provide telephone in Jim Crack Room

Friday, 8th—Schedule Involving Staging and Lighting

0100 hrs   Stage Manager to arrive
AJC to clear Shannon room of all tables, chairs, and staging

0200 hrs   Décor team to commence set up in the Shannon room with crew ×6
Lighting company to commence load in and set up with scaffolding towers crew ×12
Staging to commence load in and set up of rostra and stage with crew ×12
Décor, carpenters, and set makers to commence set up of township décor with crew ×7
AJC to provide tea, coffee, and soft drinks for crew ×38 pax
AJC to provide telephone in the Shannon Room

0500 hrs   Event Planner has catering provide breakfast ×38 pax

0600 hrs   Sound company to commence set up of sound with engineer

0700 hrs   Décor & carpenters to conclude set up of township
AJC to position dance floor ×105 pieces

900 hrs   AJC to position tables

0930 hrs   Position and dress chairs on stage for:
*Main band   *Support band   *Feature artist's band (Total = 17)

1000 hrs   Staging to conclude set up
Motorola 4 × 2-way radios arrive for Producers at AJC function center reception
Chairs to be covered
Dancers to commence rehearsals on dance floor (duration 2 hrs)
AJC to provide coffee, tea, and soft drinks for artists × 22

1100 hrs   Main band commence load in and set up (duration 1 hr)

1200 hrs   Light and sound set up including light focus to be completed
AJC to provide lunch for crew ×16

1300 hrs   Décor to have completed dressing of room
Dancers to continue rehearsal
AJC to provide tea, coffee, soft drinks, and water for artists × 25

1400 hrs   Set up band's dressing room in Vice Regal room
Set up of dressing room area for site performers on Mezzanine level

1430 hrs   Main band commence sound check (duration 1 hour)

1530 hrs   Feature artist and band to commence load in and sound check (duration 1 hour)
Lena to check Panorama Room and route to Shannon Room
Cocktail tables in Panorama Room to be dressed

1630 hrs   Support band to load in and sound check (duration 1 hour)

1700 hrs   Video company and photographer to arrive

Figure 1.2. Advance scheduling—a comprehensive time and action work schedule leading up to the event.

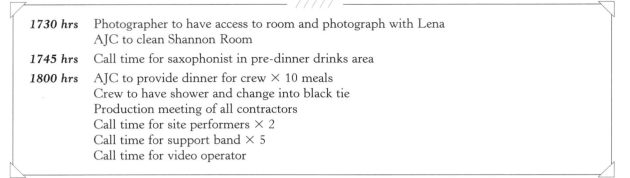

1730 hrs   Photographer to have access to room and photograph with Lena
AJC to clean Shannon Room

1745 hrs   Call time for saxophonist in pre-dinner drinks area

1800 hrs   AJC to provide dinner for crew × 10 meals
Crew to have shower and change into black tie
Production meeting of all contractors
Call time for site performers × 2
Call time for support band × 5
Call time for video operator

Figure 1.2. (cont.)

Friday, 8th December

1825 hrs   Trio to commence playing in the Panorama Room

1830 hrs   Guests arrive
Cocktails are served in the Panorama Room

1900 hrs   Doors open to the Shannon Room
Site performers: Saloon Madam and Chief Sitting Bull on standby
Support Band commences on stage (duration 25 minutes)
Drinks are served as guests are seated

1925 hrs   Guests are seated
Support Band breaks (taped music played as they depart stage)
Main band quartet takes position on stage and remains on stage during Act One Dancers

1930 hrs   Act One Dancers (wild west segment) commence accompanied by 5-minute backing tape

1935 hrs   Act One Dancers conclude
Entree is served
Main band quartet commences (duration 35 minutes)

2000 hrs   Commence clearing entree

2010 hrs   Entree is cleared
Main band quartet breaks (taped music as they leave the stage)
Saloon Madam features with upright piano number (duration 7 minutes)
Support band takes position on stage and remains on stage during Act Two dancers

2017 hrs   Act Two Dancers commence (accompanied by backing tape: duration 3 minutes)

2020 hrs   Act Two Dancers conclude
Support band continues (duration 50 minutes)
Main course is served

2100 hrs   Commence clearing main course

2110 hrs   Main course cleared
Support band breaks (taped music as support band leaves the stage)
Feature artist and band on stage and remain on stage during Act Three Dancers

2115 hrs   Act Three Dancers commence accompanied by 3-minute backing tape

2118 hrs   Act Three Dancers conclude

2120 hrs   Feature Artist performs on stage accompanied by her seven piece band (40 minutes)

Figure 1.3. Evening schedule—a precise time and action sample schedule for the client's event.

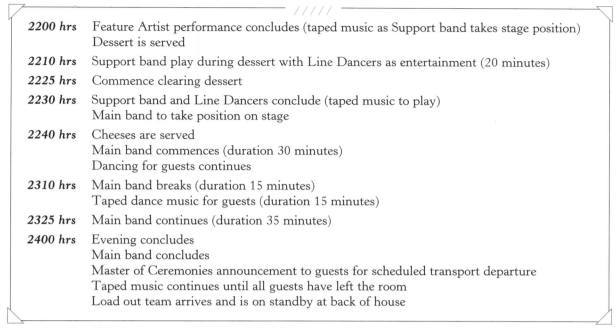

2200 hrs	Feature Artist performance concludes (taped music as Support band takes stage position) Dessert is served
2210 hrs	Support band play during dessert with Line Dancers as entertainment (20 minutes)
2225 hrs	Commence clearing dessert
2230 hrs	Support band and Line Dancers conclude (taped music to play) Main band to take position on stage
2240 hrs	Cheeses are served Main band commences (duration 30 minutes) Dancing for guests continues
2310 hrs	Main band breaks (duration 15 minutes) Taped dance music for guests (duration 15 minutes)
2325 hrs	Main band continues (duration 35 minutes)
2400 hrs	Evening concludes Main band concludes Master of Ceremonies announcement to guests for scheduled transport departure Taped music continues until all guests have left the room Load out team arrives and is on standby at back of house

Figure 1.3. (cont.)

Note the precision timing and detailing. The smaller the job the simpler the schedule. Before detailing a schedule such as that shown, all key contractors must supply the event manager with all their lead-in, set-up, and load-out requirements. Only then can the producer coordinate the full schedule.

Venables Creating Entertainment, my producers of "A Night in the Wild West," created this schedule which is meticulously detailed for an event that catered to 700 guests. Nothing is left to chance. The set-up is done over a two-day period due to the work load of all the event components. Staggering the various teams is essential even for much smaller events. A smooth flow of tradespeople must be maintained throughout the set-up period. Note the refreshment breaks given to the working crews. These short breaks are necessary and always appreciated.

While arranging varied aspects and tasks within the given time frame, the event manager must always have an eye on the "bigger picture." Naturally, producing an event in the off-season and producing an event on a national public holiday will dramatically impact on scheduling production, budget, and availability of desired venue space and equipment. Dr. Joe Jeff Goldblatt's book, *Special Events—Best Practices in Modern Event Management,* 2nd Edition, pages 142–152 discusses this.

Liaising with the Team

An event manager communicates well with contractors. This includes the ability to present a brief that gives a general overview of the event. All parties in the event need to know where they fit in the scheme of things. Refer to Figures 1.4, 1.5, 1.6, and 1.7 on the following pages for simple yet effective ways of liaising with contractors in the early stages of planning. These figures show samples of Quote Requests for Production, Technicals, Light and Sound, and Entertainment, respectively.

There are several methods of liaising including production meetings, telephone, E-mail, and fax, but there is nothing like face-to-face communication.

An event manager will recognize the importance of a comprehensive contact list that can be distributed and used by all members of the team. Figures 1.8 and 1.9 show contact samples.

The Importance of Money

Planning an event is akin to running a business. At the end of the day you will be left with a profit/loss statement that lists the event's income and expenses. The event manager needs to be sound in their approach to financial management.

An event income is derived from the client, box office/registration, even sponsorship, or all of the above. Being able to forecast your expenses accurately and quote accordingly will be the key to running a viable and profitable event management company.

Again, budget expense items are similar to tasks in that they need to be prioritized, delegated, and scheduled for payment. Conscientious event managers build a contingency into their budgets to cover unforeseen expenses, which always seem to occur when working on a job.

Written Quote Request for Production
From: Lena Malouf Events Pty. Ltd.
Fax: 61-2-9388 7911 Mob: 0418-239757
Email: lenmal@maloufevents.com.au

To: _____   Company: _____

Fax:_____   Ph:_____ Mobile: _____

Would you kindly quote on the following:

Job:_____

Place: _____

Date: _____   Time: _____

My specific requirements from your company are:

_____

_____

_____

_____

_____

_____

_____

_____

_____

_____

_____

_____

Set-up time for job: _____   Dismantle time for job: _____

Please fax back your written quote by: _____ am/pm _____

With the approval of this quote, deposits will be forwarded.

Figure 1.4. Written quote request for production. This is a sample of what to send to obtain a quote.

Written Quote Request for Technicals
From: Lena Malouf Events Pty. Ltd.
Fax: 61-2-9388 7911 Mob: 0418-239757
Email: lenmal@maloufevents.com.au

To: _____   Company: _____

Fax:_____   Ph:_____ Mobile: _____

Would you kindly quote on the following:

Job:_____

Venue: _____

Date: _____   Time: _____

My specific requirements from your company are:

_____

_____

_____

_____

_____

_____

_____

_____

_____

_____

_____

_____

Set-up time for job: _____   Dismantle time for job: _____

Please fax back your written quote by: _____ AM/PM _____

With the approval of this quote, deposits will be forwarded.

Figure 1.5. Written quote request for technicals. This is a sample of what to send to obtain a quote.

Written Quote Request for Light and Sound
From: Lena Malouf Events Pty. Ltd.
Fax: 61-2-9388 7911 Mob: 0418-239757
Email: lenmal@maloufevents.com.au

To: _____   Company: _____

Fax:_____   Ph:_____ Mobile: _____

Would you kindly quote on the following:

Job:_____

Venue: _____

Date: _____   Time: _____

My specific requirements from your company are:

_____

_____

_____

_____

_____

_____

_____

_____

_____

_____

_____

Set-up time for job: _____   Dismantle time for job: _____

Please fax back your written quote by: _____ AM/PM _____

With the approval of this quote, deposits will be forwarded.

Figure 1.6. Written quote request for light and sound. This is a sample of what to send to obtain a quote.

Written Quote Request for Entertainment
From: Lena Malouf Events Pty. Ltd.
Fax: 61-2-9388 7911 Mob: 0418-239757
Email: lenmal@maloufevents.com.au

To: _____　　　　Company: _____

Fax:_____　　　　Ph:_____ Mobile: _____

Would you kindly quote on the following:

Job:_____

Venue: _____

Date: _____　　　　Time: _____

My specific requirements from your company are:

_____

_____

_____

_____

_____

_____

_____

_____

_____

_____

Set-up time for job: _____　　Dismantle time for job: _____

Please fax back your written quote by: _____ AM/PM _____

With the approval of this quote, deposits will be forwarded.

Figure 1.7. Written quote request for entertainment. This is a sample of what to send to booking agencies.

Job Name: _____

Contact type: _____ Contact Name: _____ Co. Name: _____ Address: _____ _____ Phone: _____ Fax: _____	Contact type: _____ Contact Name: _____ Co. Name: _____ Address: _____ _____ Phone: _____ Fax: _____
Contact type _____ Contact Name: _____ Co. Name: _____ Address: _____ _____ Phone: _____ Fax: _____	Contact type: _____ Contact Name: _____ Co. Name: _____ Address: _____ _____ Phone: _____ Fax: _____

Figure 1.8. Sample contact page—An important sheet to be completed for any function. It should be copied to all suppliers involved in your special event. This accessible list will save time and money.

Fire:	000	
Ambulance:	000	
Police:	000	
Local Hospital	_____	
Emergency Service:	_____	
Power:	_____	
Weather:	_____	

In an Emergency Contact on Site:

Venue Manager	(Name)	(Contact No)
Venue Security	(Name)	"
Producer	"	"
Decorator	"	"
Technical	"	"
Hire Supplier	"	"
Entertainment Agent	"	"
Caterer	"	"
Piano/Other	"	"

Figure 1.9. Emergency contact number page. This is a vital page and should be kept on hand by all those working on-site.

If you are not very experienced, the petty cash/check page is an asset to be maintained carefully during the set up of the event. Cash is then not being handed out carelessly. Checks should also be written out precisely with suppliers' invoice numbers on the check stubs and check numbers recorded on the appropriate incoming invoices to avoid double payments. Figure 1.10 shows an on-site *petty cash and check used* sample sheet.

Moving People and Plant

Events are always held *somewhere*. The event manager needs to know how to assemble all the parts required for an event and how to get them there. This often requires booking travel and accommodation for artists, performers, and contractors. Logistics of moving people and plant can range from city to city, country to country, hotel to hotel, warehouse to off-site space.

Contingency

Sometimes things just do not go according to plan even when the plans are carefully laid out. There can be a change in weather, a power strike, cancellation of artists due to illness, etc. Astute event managers

Check No. or Cash Out	Date	Amount	Supplier	Item

Figure 1.10. Petty cash/check listing. This enables you to keep a current tally of monies expended for the event. It is handy to take on the job to record any emergency out of pocket expenses or purchases.

will make contingency plans for this type of scenario by compiling an emergency contact list, for example. Planning for contingency is the art of identifying circumstances out of everybody's control and providing solutions should these circumstances arise.

The Art of Being Professional

Event managers form business relationships with their clients and suppliers which need to be carried out professionally. This means briefing contractors in writing following any discussions or meetings, receiving proposals and quotes in writing, and entering into written agreements or confirmation of acceptance. If things do not go according to plan later or if a personality conflict develops, the paperwork provides confirmation.

Decisions made over the phone should be confirmed in writing immediately. Minutes should be taken at all meetings and distributed to all involved parties. Continued communication with all those working on the project is a safe and sure way to have a successful event.

Name:_____ Position: _____

Area of Expertise: _____

1. Did you feel the event worked? Why / why not?
   _____

2. What part of your tasks did you find difficult?
   _____

3. Is there anything that could have happened during the event to make your working role more effective?
   _____

4. What did you learn from this event?
   _____

5. Was the working schedule informative enough? Please explain answer.
   _____

6. What were the advantages / disadvantages regarding load in and load out?
   _____

7. Did the production meetings meet your expectations? Please explain.
   _____

8. What did you like the most?
   _____

9. What did you like the least?
   _____

10. Where do you think improvements could be made?
    _____

Other Do you have any specific comments you would like to make?
   _____

Figure 1.11. Team post event evaluation. This questionnaire allows you to recognize the positive and negative aspects of the event.

This professional business relationship will form a paper trail which presents two advantages: (1) It reduces the possibilities for misunderstandings and (2) if a contractor or a member of the team is unable to continue on the job, a good paper trail will bring the new person or team up to speed quickly.

Post Event

An event is not over at the conclusion of the occasion. A debriefing approximately a week after the event is an excellent way of learning how to manage your resources better the next time around.

Often event managers will write a post event report to the team as Figure 1.11 shows. These become valuable resource tools for events that occur on an annual basis. Let us move on to . . .

2. People Management

Organizing events can become a delicate balancing act of skills, egos, and creativity. The ability to motivate, communicate, delegate, listen, advise, and make decisions are the key elements required for transforming a stressful experience into a unique, creative, and fun occasion.

While event managers need a good understanding of all the disciplines required in event production, contractors are the *specialists* in their particular field. While it is important to choose the *best* contractor for your event, it is essential to choose the *right* one.

Many contractors are creative people in their own right and have their own sense of what is aesthetically pleasing and practical. For example, no two caterers or decorators are alike. While they may be able to present similar menus and décor styles, ultimately they will invest their own personality into the food they present or the sets they create. The event manager's job is to marry the right contractor to the concept and requirements of the event.

Instilling team spirit into the selected group of contractors is an essential that brings success. The entire team must head in one direction, be focused on the company's objective, and aim at doing the best they can possibly do.

The Art of Briefing

A good event organizer will present a full written brief to the contractor as shown in Figure 1.12. Typically, a brief will include date of the event, client, objective of the event, concept of the event, venue, services/products required, delivery times, access times, and possibly a request for quotation.

If more than one quote is required, another approach is to:

- Prepare an outline of the brief
- Select the companies or contractors you prefer
- Set aside a morning and arrange their individual meeting times
- Have a face-to-face meeting with contractors
- Request a return fax or letter by the requested date
- Make comparisons being sure to check the quality of equipment used or hired, weighed against the labor content of the quote.

This approach works well for me because the personal contact is a plus all the way around.

Committees and Events

Event managers sometimes have to deal with committees. Like contractors, committee members will have their own tastes, ideas, and subjective opinions, but unlike contractors you will not be able to choose your committee members. Committee members are often representatives of the community and their skills may not lay in any of the event disciplines so it is important when dealing with willing committee workers, to explain clearly why you have made certain decisions and how wrong decisions will affect an event.

A committee's function is to provide guidance, support, and make major decisions. However, they are not an *executive* decision-making body.

The committee's responsibilities are generally to:

- Choose the venue
- Determine the event's objectives
- Allocate the total budget amount
- Approve the event concept
- Decide key activities (e.g., opening ceremony)

From: Lena Malouf Events Pty. Ltd.
Fax: 61-2-9388 7911 Mob: 0418-239757
Email: lenmal@maloufevents.com.au

To: _____

Company: _____

Would you kindly quote on the following General Overview of the Event and return by
Deadline date:_____

Style of Event: Client Dinner

Pax: 500   50 tables of 10

Venue: _____   **In:** Grand Ballroom

Date: _____   **Time:** _____

Stand-by time/Operators: Sound check 1 pm on the day

My specific requirements from your company is for provision of:

☐ light   ☐ sound   ☐ staging   ☐ hiring of _____
☐ entertainment   ☐ catering   ☐ staffing

Figure 1.12. Written quote request and brief. This example of a complete job brief gives your contractors full information in regard to event requirements.

General Overview of the Event

Theme: _____

Color: _____

Prefunction/Drinks Area: _____

Entrance Decor

Outside/prefunction: _____

Inside the room: _____

Wall Decor
Pair of columns on opposite wall to stage to match pair at either side of stage
End walls feature columns of florals

Table Linens
50 tables of 10 guests
Double cloths to be used—floor length cloth in cream with green overlay and napkins

Tabletops
The flowers will consist of: _____
The colors will be: _____
The shape is circular in two levels.

Stage/Staging
Stage 40′ × 20′ × 3′
Steps either side
Back wall of cascading foliage with fairy lights
2× columns either side of stage
Masking for stage (black)
Heavily-dressed stage apron
Tiered seating including handrails and steps
Black drapes around room, including stage wings
Dance floor 36′ × 36′

Entertainment

- "Markel String Quartet"—2 violin, viola, and cello. Provide pre-function music in foyer and then on stage with additional flute for band breaks.
- Feature Band: "The Look Band"—12 piece. Joined by vocalist at end of night.
- Feature Act: "The Swinging Singers" accompanied by band—20 min. bracket between entrée and main course
- "John Michaels Quartet"—piano, guitar,

drums, bass, trumpet, and vocal. 45 min bracket between dessert and cheeses.

Light and Sound desk
A black facia surround must be provided to give this area a good finish. Positioned inside and right of the main entrance doors to ballroom.

Sound

- No reinforcement for quartet in foyer
- Amplification for the band, quintet on stage and "John Michaels Quartet" will be required with foldback
- 6 × vocal mic ("Swinging Singers" (4); John Michaels; extra vocalist)
- Vocal mic at sound desk
- CD for incidental music
- Plug boxes for music stands (22)
- 6 station talk back

Light
Soft lighting required throughout the room, pin spots would be an advantage with this particular scheme. The stage lighting can go into rather creative bands of light for effect. 16 sections of décor will require lighting around the room. One follow spot for the featured artist with color changes for the show.

Operator Attire

☐ Lounge suit   ☐ Black tie   ☐ All black

Load in time
From 6 PM the previous evening

Load out time
1 AM immediately after function concludes

Producer/Stage Manager for this event
John J. Smith & Co.

Quotes and Invoices
All quotes and invoices to Lena Malouf Events *by the requested deadline* otherwise, your quote will be unable to be considered.

I look forward to your response,

Lena Malouf, CSEP

Figure 1.12. (cont.)

The event organizer's decisions/activities are to:

- Choose and hire contractors
- Design production schedule
- Distribute the event budget
- Brief volunteers and event personnel
- Report to and advise committee on big decisions
- Style the event
- Obtain speakers or entertainment
- Produce the event (usually) or provide production management
- Organize load-in and load-out

Volunteers

Volunteers can be one of an event's most important resources. Without volunteer support, producing some events and/or fundraisers might not be financially possible.

In dealing with volunteers, it is important to develop a good relationship with the head of the volunteer organization. Volunteers need to be fully briefed, so they understand their function within the event and it is good form to provide recognition for their services. This brings us to . . .

3. Responsibility Management

Responsibility management is concerned with legal, moral, and ethical business practice. Event managers are concerned with the principles of *risk management,* the importance of *written contracts,* and *quality management concepts.* They understand that sometimes *licenses and permits* are required for an event.

Risk Management

Risk management is more than just purchasing public liability insurance. Responsible event managers are concerned about safeguarding people and equipment. They are also aware that peoples' reputations are at stake. *An event manager organizes an event in a way that is not negligent* by recognizing potential risks and acting to prevent and minimize these risks.

Event managers need to develop systems to ensure the work they do is not negligent. They may use checklists, develop work practices, or build risk management procedures into their tasks.

For example, when hiring a contractor an event manager might request:

- Evidence of public liability and workers' compensation insurance
- Evidence of relevant qualifications and permits
- Names of references
- A history of any previous claims made against the contractor

- A quality assurance statement
- A written quote with all of the above attached

Quality Management

While risk management takes a "wholistic" approach to organizing the event, quality management is *customer focused.* A quality assurance statement is a written description of exactly how the event manager plans to achieve the high standard of excellence required by the client.

Quality management is more than saying "I'll do the best I can." Like risk management, quality management means using a systematic approach in organizing events. This might involve using checklists and designing double-checking mechanisms. An official policy of carrying out a detailed site inspection for every new contract is an example of quality management.

Contracts and Agreements

An agreement is simply the terms and conditions that define the business relationship between two or more involved parties. It is wise to have an attorney write or check all written agreements.

An agreement might be one page or several. Only one written agreement can exist between the involved parties. All the parties must sign the agreement in the presence of a witness. Typically, an agreement can include:

1. The names of the legal entities entering into the agreement
2. Name of the client
3. Name of the event
4. The date of the event
5. The times of the event
6. The venue
7. An exact description of services carried out by one party
8. An indemnity clause
9. Payment terms
10. Access times
11. Cancellation clause

Licenses and Permits

It is negligent practice to overlook any necessary permits or licenses required for the event or by your contractors. If you are unsure exactly what licenses or permits you or your contractors need, find out by asking the contractor (and their competitors), or seeking advice from your attorney or your local, state, and federal authorities.

There are so many rules, regulations, and laws that vary from country to country, city to city, and state to state that it is difficult to keep track of them, and because every new event is often very different from the last one, there might be a new aspect that requires a permit. When in doubt, ask!

A Note on Notifying Authorities

When organizing an event that deals with the general public, an unusual venue, or requires a permit, make it part of your risk management policy to notify the police, fire department, ambulance, and any other relevant public department. You might be surprised to find that these departments will sometimes offer free assistance and advice in organizing your event!

Business Ethics

When you run a business in the highly charged and competitive field of special events, you need several special attributes:

- Adaptability to relate to people of different backgrounds
- Creativity to take that event into a special realm, and
- A high standard of ethical behavior.

You're likely to come up against sharp operators of one kind or another, whether they're clients, contractors, or artists so it's essential that you have a clear understanding of what is acceptable when it comes to decision-making and behavior.

- Ethics concerns the **values** and **principles** of what we do and how we respond to situations and people
- The course of action we choose has a direct influence on the long-term business relationships we are trying to foster
- People in business appreciate being respected and trusted
- Ethics is about:
  What we are prepared to commit to
  What we decide to defend; and
  How we will conduct ourselves in order to achieve our goals and objectives in business

The International Special Events Society (ISES) Principles of Professional Conduct and Ethics (see above right) is an excellent list for event organizers to adhere to.

---

4. Production Management

Production management is the integration of venue, décor, entertainment, catering, staging, audio/visuals, and all the tangible elements of an event. These will be discussed further in Chapter 3, Event Essentials.

ISES Principles of Professional Conduct and Ethics

1. Promote and encourage the highest level of ethics within the profession of the special events industry while maintaining the highest standards of professional conduct.
2. Strive for excellence in all aspects of our profession by performing consistently at or above acceptable industry standards.
3. Use only legal and ethical means in all industry negotiations and activities.
4. Protect the public against fraud and unfair practices and promote all practices which bring respect and credit to the profession.
5. Provide truthful and accurate information with respect to the performance of duties. Use a written contract stating all charges, services, products, performance expectations, and other essential information.
6. Maintain industry accepted standards of safety and sanitation.
7. Maintain adequate and appropriate insurance coverage for all business activities.
8. Commit to increase professional growth and knowledge, to attend educational programs, and to personally contribute expertise to meetings and journals.
9. Strive to cooperate with colleagues, suppliers, employee/employers, and all persons supervised, in order to provide the highest quality service at every level.
10. Subscribe to the ISES Principles of Professional Conduct and Ethics, and abide by ISES Bylaws and policies.

The Venue

The venue has to be able to accommodate the event concept and all the elements that go together to produce the concept: the staging, décor, and technical requirements.

One of the event manager's first tasks is to conduct a site inspection of the venue. This is more than just a look around the room to see if it "feels right." You will be on the lookout for such things as access, height of walls and ceilings, and sight lines.

Risk management and quality management policies will also come into play. Potential bottlenecks, steps, slippery floors, and the quality of carpet, fittings, and facilities will determine whether the room is fit for your event.

Decor

Decor refers to the furnishings and decorations to be utilized in your event. An event manager will typically hire an event designer to design, build, and hire the décor required for the event. (See Figure 1.1).

The *type* of event will influence the *focus* of your décor. For a corporate dinner, it is best to start designing your décor from the table tops and radiate out. After all, your guests will be spending most of the night at the table. Décor for a product launch will most likely be focused on the product itself and the stage where the product will be launched.

Theme

Theme is closely related to concept. In creating a high tech light show, for example, you might create a theme based on *Star Wars, Saturday Night Fever,* even a *video arcade.* Theme ideas are only limited by your imagination and the following pages explode with creative concepts.

Florals

Floral décor always adds a finishing touch to any event. It can put the elegance into dinner, add romance to a wedding, and grandeur to a ball or make a statement for a gala event.

Floral décor is a sensitive art best left in the hands of experts. Florals will deteriorate over a period of time, so careful planning is required in their purchase and display so they can be seen and appreciated at the peak of their beauty. Therefore highly experienced or skilled florists affiliated with the American Institute of Floral Designers (AIFD) association should be sought out.

Walls, Ceilings, and Floor

The walls, ceiling, and floor of your venue form the basis of the event environment so take note of their dimensions, fittings, and colors and determine whether there are adequate rigging points for technical equipment. Dramatic decisions such as whether to "black out" the entire room should also be made. Figure 1.13 shows how props and flowers are marked on such a plan. This immediately gives the technical team an awareness of the placement.

Stage

Some venues come with a stage. Make sure it is the right type, height, width, and length for your event and be on the lookout for microphone jacks and power supply. However, to glamorize the plainness of the stage modules, refer to Color Plate 1. This 40-ft length of stage backdrop is hung either on the light

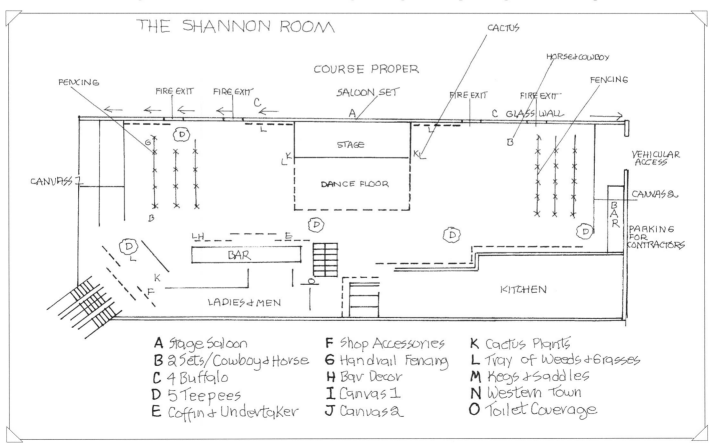

Figure 1.13. Layout of props. This floor plan shows the positioning of decor props for the Wild West Night in the Shannon Room. Decor layout such as this is essential for technical contractors.

trussing or on the push-up poles, and is very effective. It becomes a feature of the room.

Tables and Chairs

Hotel banquet rooms or other well-established venues will come supplied with tables and chairs. One of the first things an event designer will check is whether they are standard sizes because table linens and chair covers are often rented and will need to fit properly. So prior to booking any linens, visit the venue and check the fit of the tablecloths and chair covers offered. Your event guests might also be seated for hours so the level of comfort is a major concern.

Accessories

Accessories are items such as place mats, nametags, and programs that complement and form part of the décor. Paying attention to event accessories may seem a minor detail, but it is attention to these details that distinguishes a professional.

Staging

This sounds obvious, but what will the stage be used for? Is it to accommodate a band or a speaker? A dinner with a high entertainment component might need a significant stage. A cocktail function might not require a stage at all.

A stage will almost invariably need to accommodate lighting and audio equipment as well as décor. Décor might include elaborate props or simple draping. The stage is a focal point of the event, so careful consideration must be given to sight lines, elevation, and quality fittings.

Access onto and off the stage from both back stage and the auditorium is an essential requirement. Depending on who will use the stage, you might need to consider treads (steps) or a ramp. Figures 1.14, 1.15, and 1.16 show the floor plan of the Australian Jockey Club and the necessary detail that is required to produce the event.

Technical Organization

Technical production is a highly specialized field in the event arena. It is also one of the most important. Discordant audio/visual product will take the credibility out of your event and your reputation as an event manager. Putting yourself in the hands of an accredited or professional specialist in this technical area is critical to the success of the event.

Lighting

The effective use of lighting will enhance the theme of your event, add mood and atmosphere, and help direct your guests' attention to the elements you want

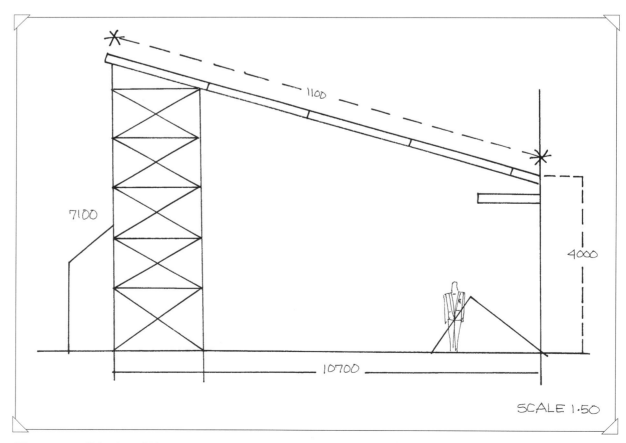

Figure 1.14. Side view of Shannon Room. This sectional view of the function room gives the available ceiling height and width allocations.

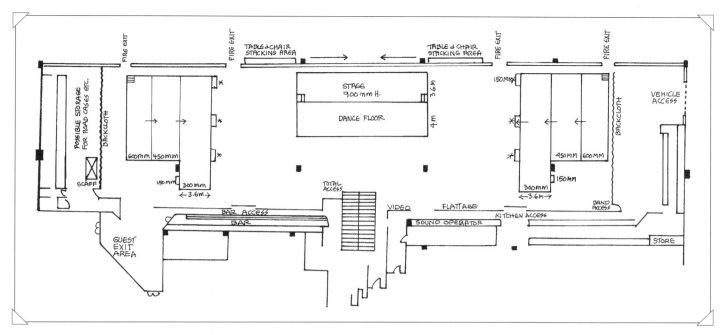

Figure 1.15. Shannon Room full room layout. This layout allows all contractors to identify various areas, accesses, and exits together with positioning of structures within the available floor space.

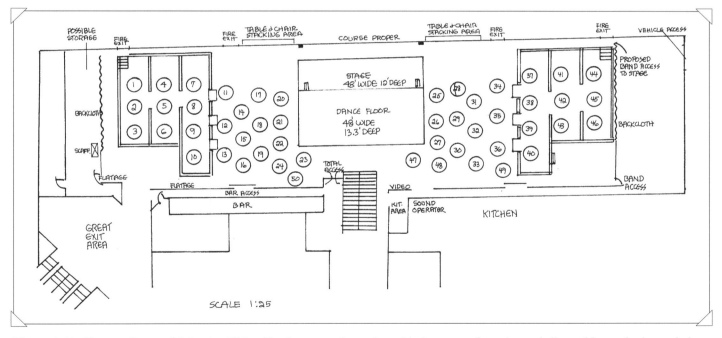

Figure 1.16. Shannon Room table layout. This table placement plan assists with the set up of catering and client table numbering and place-card setting.

to emphasize. A lighting designer will often be hired and will work with the event designer so that the lighting complements the theme and décor of your event. See Color Plate 2 where, on the stage, five huge pedestals have been created with flowers and fabrics—but the real features here are the swirls of light created by a lighting designer. Lighting such as this moves through various patterns or light tem-

plates (known as "gobos") and at various speeds according to the requirements.

There is a huge range of lights that add color, ambience, and effects including theatre lights, pin lights, fairy lights, star curtains, follow spots, strobes, UV lights, intelligent lighting, and the ancient candle! Apart from lighting the room and stage, lighting is used to feature items such as tabletops, décor, stage

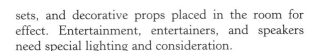

sets, and decorative props placed in the room for effect. Entertainment, entertainers, and speakers need special lighting and consideration.

Sound

Sound can create the worst nightmares for any event manager. It is crucial to have a skilled sound engineer on your team. It is soul destroying, gut wrenching and deflating when the microphone cuts out during a keynote speech or if there is terrible feedback. More than once, a famous singer has not been provided with adequate feedback and consequently has sung off key.

Video and Photography

Video and photography are used to document and/or promote your event and create publicity. Legal and ethical issues are also involved. For example, you often need to have written permission to electronically record live entertainment.

Special Effects

Special effects such as pyrotechnics, stunts, or magic can be used effectively to create a lasting impression of your event. They can surprise and delight your guests, but again there are risk management legal issues involved. These always need be checked in regard to permits and licenses.

Entertainment

Booking entertainment requires careful thought and strategic planning. Entertainment might include a *feature act, a band,* and *sight acts.* It is good management practice to secure a written booking contract with your entertainment. It is advisable to book bands and artists through a registered entertainment agency.

Feature Act

The preferences of the audience attending your event is important to the success of your feature act, so it is important to have a good grasp of the demographics and tastes of the people involved. A feature act might consist of any of the following:

- A high profile Master of Ceremonies
- Featured singer
- High profile orchestra
- A comedian
- A theatrical presentation
- Group of dancers

Bands

A band is a group of musicians who will perform at your event. Bands could well be the feature act or simply provide background music. Booking a band well in advance is advisable because good bands are in high demand.

Your first point of contact should be a registered booking agent. A fee will be negotiated and the agent will also request repertoire, access, production, parking, and sometimes a rider (a legal brief from the band listing their requirements).

Sight Acts

Sight acts could include wandering magicians, street theatre, stilt-walkers, clowns, living statues, jugglers, and fire-eaters and can be an excellent method of entertaining your guests.

Repertoire

Using entertainment in repertoire can be a cost-effective way of filling in an entire day or multiple days of an event especially when you have a fluid, constantly changing crowd which is unlikely to see the same act twice.

A Note on Contracts/Booking Confirmations

Every entertainer you hire must sign a written contract. When using a registered agency, you may need to enter into a contract with them as they act on your behalf. The contract will include:

Contract Requirements

1. The name of event
2. The names of the parties entering into the agreement
3. A billing clause
4. A cancellation clause. (An absolute must!)
5. The fee
6. Payment terms
7. The venue information
8. The date of event
9. Call times through brief sheets
10. Other clauses required by entertainer or organizer
11. Personal requirements of the entertainer
12. Travel arrangements and transfers
13. Accommodation
14. Any special requests

Travel, Transfers, and Accommodation

Sometimes you may be required to arrange airfares and accommodation for entertainers, especially if you are booking acts from out of state. In this case, transfers and accommodation costs, and possibly additional security, need to be included in the budget. It is essential that these details are included in the written contract.

Rehearsals

Scheduling adequate rehearsal time is an exact science. In a very short period of time, staging, décor, and audio/visuals need to be loaded in and rehearsal time also needs to be scheduled. Theatre companies solve this problem by using rehearsal rooms that feature a mock up of the stage design. Event managers often don't have the budget for this luxury, so adequate rehearsal time needs to be built into the production schedule.

Costumes

Costumes might form part of the overall theme and design of the event. You might decide to put entertainers, waiters, security, crew, or everyone attending the event in costume!

Costumes are either rented or custom made. Either way, you will need accurate measurements of the people you plan to costume and be prepared for emergencies, should costumes rip or not fit.

Facilities

Entertainment facilities include dressing rooms, green rooms, and catering. Before and after your band and speakers entertain your guests, they need somewhere to *go*.

Entertainment Schedules

The entertainment agent and each entertainer should be given a schedule specifying not only what time to perform, but also who their key contact is, where they can park, how to find the venue, when they can rehearse, and their stand-by time.

Catering

The quality and appropriateness of the event's catering will either make or break an event manager's reputation. When choosing a caterer, check their accreditation and their references. Ask for a taste sample. Be precise in what you require and take the advice of your caterer. Ascertain exactly what they are and are not supplying. It is wise to present a series of menus for the client to select, together with the accompanying wines.

Menu

The menu should require the client's final approval. Budget, theme, number of people, and the type of event should all be taken into account when selecting a menu. Also, there might be added requirements such as a vegetarian or kosher menu.

Beverages

Not only do you have to budget for beverages but also enough waiters to serve them. There is nothing more annoying than being at a function and not being able to get a drink. When serving alcohol, you might need a license or permit and be required to police the consumption of it.

Waiters

Waiters are a highly visible element of your event and they are even more visible when they can't perform their task professionally. Waiters are often hired through the caterer or an agency. Again, the correct number of waiters is essential, so that your guests are not left pining for their food.

Crew Catering

It is good form to provide refreshments and catering for your crew because they often need to work long hours at a stretch to achieve your production schedule.

Site

You will need to make sure your venue can accommodate your catering requirements. Look for such things as cooking equipment, running water, access to the kitchen, and room layout. Figure 1.17 shows a useful checklist for site inspections.

Event Management Concept

The event management graph shown in Figure 1.18 shows the step-by-step flow of an event as it actually happens. Initiated by Harry Koponen of MEMO Sydney Australia, it specifically shows the concept itself, as well as the necessity of collating every task that's required to prioritizing those tasks. Step four shows the delegation which leads into schedules and ultimately managing a successful event.

Job Sheet

Figure 1.19 is a simplified version of a job sheet that can be used for a function. Paperwork is a must, but it need not be complicated, especially if you're new in the industry or not as experienced as an event manager or producer.

Venue
Name/Address _____

_____

Contact: _____

Position: _____

Phone: _____   Fax: _____

Measurements
Length of Room: _____

Highest Point: _____

Pillars: _____

Other: _____

Width: _____

Lowest Point: _____

Arches: _____

Other: _____

Access
Entrance: _____

Fire Exits: _____

Stairways or Elevations: _____

Elevators: _____

Exits: _____

Contractors' Access: _____

Escalators: _____

Other: _____

Kitchen
Kitchen Position: _____

Bar Positions: _____

Restrictions: _____

Power
Power Availability: _____

A/V Equip Availability: _____

In-House
Air conditioning: Yes / No

Platforms: _____

Rostrums: _____

Steps: _____

Ramps: _____

Dance Floor: _____

Tables   Type: _____   Size: _____

Chairs   Type: _____   Size: _____

Coolroom Facility: Yes / No

Coat Check: _____

Number: _____

Number: _____

Contractors' Access
Their Parking? _____   Times: _____   Passes needed?   Yes/No

Breakout Room Position: _____   Need to create?   Yes/No

Load In & Out Information (important for props)
Service Lift Management: _____   Height: _____ Width: _____ Depth: _____

Service Corridors: _____   Height: _____ Width: _____

Load in times: _____   Load out times: _____

Figure 1.17. Sample site inspection checklist—an excellent page to take with you on site inspections. It helps answer any questions and avoids relying on memory after the visit.

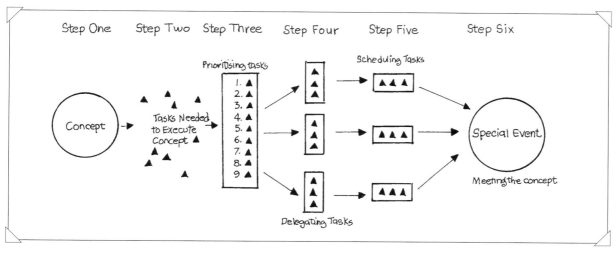

Figure 1.18. Event management concept. This easy step-by-step guide allows you to bring form and sequence to the initial idea of the event. The tasks you would list here would be those gleaned from the Organizational Chart shown in Figure 1.1.

Date	Job	Action by	Notes	Done

Figure 1.19. Sample job sheet. This simple sheet saves you doubling up on tasks and ensures that, once completed, you have not allocated staff unnecessarily. Use in duplicate—one copy for the staff member, one for office use.

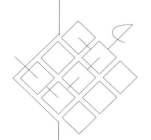

Chapter 2

The 12-Point Management Plan

1. The Initial Meeting with the Client

Be Well Groomed

First impressions are critical. This is a cliché, but with much truth! Cultivating the correct image is a prerequisite for the events person. A professional image is critical in influencing the client's immediate perception of you and it can open the door to a rewarding partnership, whereas a poor initial impression can lose business before it begins.

Professional attire will need to be considered in the context of the client and their environment, but there is no place for jogging suits, running shoes, and other purely casual garments. A business suit is the obvious choice because it offers formality, flexibility, and a timeless style.

When you walk through the door for that initial meeting, your client will be appraising you, consciously or unconsciously. If you look and feel as though you are ready to go places, then chances are you will!

Take time to work out what style best suits you, then plan your corporate wardrobe around that. A mix and match approach certainly is appropriate for an events person, and can be based around the business suit already mentioned. A simple change of jacket or accessories allows the basic ensemble to be dressed up or down as desired. Flexibility is the key! How many times have you spent hours on location, only to find that there is not enough time to get home to change? This approach to dressing professionally will also allow you to pack more lightly, a big benefit for out of town trips.

Choose classic color schemes that do not go out of style. Consider black, navy, or gray for darker tones. Beige or ivory work well for a lighter look. Bright colors should be confined to accessories on appropriate occasions. Jewelery should be minimal with perhaps only small earrings, a fine chain, or a subtle brooch. Junky or colorful items should not be considered. Leave them at home for the party!

A wardrobe for men is much simpler to plan. A classic dark suit, or blazer with slacks is ideal. Bulky objects should be removed from the pockets so the classic line of the garment is not distorted. A tie should normally be worn, and men should either be clean shaven or keep beards and mustaches well groomed.

Organize the Briefcase

Carry only items that are relevant to the meeting. This will minimize clutter. Bulky handbags should be avoided. Consider a slim attaché or traditional briefcase which can hold the client's brief and your professional profile, along with a notebook, pens, calculator, and business cards. Women can also include a mirror and lipstick for last minute touch ups!

Profile of Work

The profile of work is the events person's major tool in an initial meeting. It is a record of your achievements, experience, and skills. The field of event planning cannot be described effectively via numbers and figures, so events professionals must demonstrate the value of what they offer in a more subjective fashion.

The profile of work should include photos of previous events, showing the breadth and variety of your work and themes. Try to portray the events from more than one viewpoint. Overview shots should be combined with detail shots to provide the client with different aspects of the services you can offer. It is very distracting at an early meeting to have these items in disarray. They should be neatly presented, in the correct order, in a black leather display book.

The standard display book is 24 in. by 18 in. with black reversible pages. It is easily accessible, yet displays photos and rendering beautifully. Alternatively, enlarged, laminated photographs with or without a ring binder allows visual material to be readily stored and viewed. These also can be blown up to an impressive size for client viewing. One can also use what is called a "storyboard" (see Color Plate 3). The storyboard clearly shows the client the component parts and/or decorative units that will be used throughout the room.

The professional profile should include:

- Career achievements in precise point form
- Professional memberships with associations and organizations
- Brochures of your professional services
- Photographs of current work
- Testimonials from clients
- Potential client fax back sheet (Figure 2.1).
- Business cards

Listen More Than Talk

Clients usually have firm ideas of what they are seeking. Active listening will allow you to determine these needs. Enter a meeting with a conscious commitment to listen to every word the client says and never speak over the client!

Following the introductions, outline your services in a succinct overview. Do not ramble! Then encourage the client to discuss their own requirements, needs, and expectations. You can determine from this information the manner in which you will pursue the business (or if you will pursue it at all!)

The four "W"s that the event planner will require are as follows:

What the client needs
Why they need it

When they need it
Where it is to be produced

If the client has staged events previously, inquire about the staging, budget, and style. All such information is important. Listening is the essence of winning clients. It allows valuable feedback and establishes trust and rapport. An important point to remember is that the client's time is precious! Be conscious of this, and do not overstay your welcome.

When you leave, ensure the client retains a copy of your profile, or a promotional kit. A positive final comment is . . . "I look forward to working with you and your company."

2. Calling for Quotes from Subcontractors

Importance of Deskmanship

"Paper recyclers would fare better if they raided desktops in office buildings rather than collections of old papers from the local shopping centre." Michael Le Boeuf's quote, taken from the book *Work Smarter not Harder* by Jack Collinsmith, illustrates a common vice of many businesspeople. The author goes on to tell us that

a desk is not a storage depot for food, clothing, and umbrellas, a place to stack items you want to remember, or a place to display awards and trophies. Some guidelines for the use of your desk are:

* Have one project at a time on your desk.
* Keep items off the desk until you're ready to use them.
* When you complete a task, clear it to the out basket, check priorities, and move to the next task.

There are many other useful tips provided in this small but valuable book.

With a clearer view to the importance of our immediate working environment, we can begin the preparation of the client proposal.

We must approach the various subcontractors required and start to gather together the necessary resources for the event.

Selecting the Contractors

The event professional must be selective regarding the contractors providing services and equipment for the event. The obvious question is "What do I look for when selecting a contractor?" The answer is "Select and work with professionals"—preferably members of the International Special Events Society

**Fax Back to
Lena Malouf Events Pty., Ltd.
02–9388 7911**

Yes!
We are planning a special event.
Can we discuss the following with you . . .

My Name: _____
Position: _____
Company: _____
Address: _____
_____ P/code: _____
Phone: _____ Fax: _____
Our Special Event is: _____
_____
Date: _____
Venue (if known): _____
Number Attending: _____
I would particularly like to talk about:
_____
_____
Please contact me on:
ph: _____ mob: _____
☐ As soon as possible, or on
Date: _____ Time: _____

Figure 2.1. Fax back sheet—a very handy sheet to be included with your company profile to prospective clients. It allows them to contact you immediately with little fuss.

(ISES). ISES is a group of events professionals with close to 3000 members, in chapters across the globe. Accreditation with this organization is proof of excellence in the field. If you are able to draw on accredited contractors, it will give you a feeling of confidence and the hope of a successful partnership. If it is not possible to hire accredited contractors, it is important to rely on local knowledge, personal experience, and feedback from professional peers.

The initial brief should be provided to several contractors in each specific field in a checklist format and should include the specific products and/or services required of the contracting company whether it be lighting, sound, staging, entertainment, hire supplies, catering, or décor.

This style of brief should give the contractors

both an overall impression of the event and the specific points of detail as stated in Chapter 1.

The initial brief should include:

- Deadline for return of fax
- Number of people attending
- Venue address and specific room
- Standby time
- Operator dresscode
- Theme
- Load-in/Load-out
- Vehicle access

Then, according to specific discipline, include:

- Decor, color
- Tabletops, linens, accessories
- Light and sound specifics
- Stage and dance floor
- Stage manager and production managers

This format saves time when briefs are sent to several companies. Contractors can indicate their acceptance or non-acceptance to quote, and have sufficient information to prepare quotes. Additional information should not be required if this brief is prepared correctly.

Avoid procrastination when requesting quotes because once the quotes are returned, the information must be read, collated, and compared. This is a time-consuming process. The successful quotes must then be incorporated into the client proposal with other relevant information. Never present a quote at random. Assume nothing until the arithmetic is done.

3. The Contractors—Building Your Team

Once the contractors have been selected, a production meeting of all contractors needs to be organized. It is important to have an agenda ready for this meeting in order to keep it brief and to the point. Contractors are also busy people. Often, early morning or evening meetings may fit into peoples' schedules more effectively.

I have found that a centrally located 7:30 breakfast meeting with the lure of bacon, eggs, pancakes, and syrup seems to produce fantastic rates of attendance and builds team rapport. It is money well spent!

After discussing the specific requirements for each discipline the following points should be addressed:

- The importance of teamwork and the emphasis on "we" rather than "me"
- Instruct all contractors that any invoices or

further information pertaining to the event should be addressed to you as the coordinator. Direct contact with the client should occur only through the coordinator.

- A file of contact numbers for each contractor involved in the event (with phone, fax, and mobile phone included) should be distributed at the first available opportunity.
- Inform all contractors that no extras can be added unless requested and approved in writing. Likewise, any changes requested by the client or yourself should be passed on to contractors and confirmed in writing.
- Always take minutes of production meetings to ensure that responsibilities are fulfilled at a later date.
- The confirmation of an event basically creates a formalized working agreement.

4. The Creative Proposal

The following information is to be included when writing a proposal:

Proposal Requirements

- Client name
- Type of function
- Number of people
- Theme/no theme
- Date, place, time
- Financial formula—terms and conditions of payment
- Specific requirements
- Specific deadline
- Services you are providing which can include technical requirements, entertainment formats, production outline
- RSVP confirmation deadline date

5. Presentation to the Client

The presentation to the client is a critical feature in the 12 point process. The proposal needs to sell your ability to meet the client's needs on many levels, and while it should be as succinct as possible, it should incorporate elements of sight, sound, touch, and smell. These are the mediums with which we work, and we must employ them as effectively as possible in the proposal. Once you have prepared your proposal, use the following tips in its presentation:

Presentation Tips

1. Determine the date, time, location, and duration of your presentation. Do not run late for your appointment and do not run overtime in your presentation.
2. Find out how many people plan to attend the presentation and make sure you have enough copies of documentation.
3. Have your photos, renderings, or conceptual art in sequence so that you can move more smoothly through the presentation with your supporting visuals. Involve the clients regularly by directing attention to visuals.
4. When table linens, chair covers, or other fabrics are presented, have samples available. This involves the client through touch.
5. A few flowers (particularly roses!) introduce the smell component.
6. Leave nothing to chance. Have your props available to help answer any questions.
7. Choose your words carefully to avoid ambiguity.
8. Turn off your cellular phone or leave it at the office.
9. Take someone with you to record comments and feedback from the client throughout the presentation.
10. If changes are requested to your proposal, do not become defensive. Make the alterations as required and return them to the client within 48 hours for approval. Then be sure to advise your producer and the contractors to avoid any miscommunication.

6. Approval of Budget and Proposal

Once the proposal has been approved, the next step is to formalize a written quote. The client should furnish a purchase order to act as the basis for the final invoice. Now is the time to continue with or begin using the Event Manager's Décor Checklist (Figure 2.2) and the Contractors' Checklist (Figure 2.3) to keep all components flowing smoothly through to the conclusion of the event.

7. Time Lines

Create a time line grid for the event. See the grid shown in Figure 2.4 for an eight week project. It is important to adhere to these time lines. Also see the one week out A-Z event time line (Figure 2.5).

8. Call for Deposit

No job is firmed up until a financial commitment has been made by the client; normally a standard 50% of cost of the event applies. This enables the event manager to confirm with the selected contractors and forward a deposit of 50% of their quote. Preparation then begins in earnest.

9. Confirmation of All Elements and Contractors

Written notice needs to be provided to the contractors. It should refer to the briefing documents and quotes incorporated in the proposal as well as any amendments made to the original quote. No further changes can be made unless approved in writing.

10. Purchasing Stock and Making Props

As stock arrives, compare it against the invoice as it is unpacked. Begin making the decorative units if these will be done in-house. If the props are made outside your studio, supervise the construction to ensure that they are according to your specification. Constant review of sets and props is important to avoid a crisis on the day of the event. Finally, file the invoice for payment or forward it to your office for processing. See the Manifest of Goods Sheet (Figure 2.6).

11. Creating Work and Task Schedules

Creating these schedules is the responsibility of the producer with input from the entire team.

The first step is to call a meeting with your team and have someone present to record and brainstorm the group. If the work schedules are to run smoothly, the component parts must be put together in an orderly fashion. Refer back to Chapter 1 for scheduling details. The staging company is **usually**

☐ Received client brief
☐ Sight venue
☐ Create the concepts for selection by client
☐ Send proposal to client
☐ Prepare staff action
☐ Prepare time lines
☐ Send quote to client—call for deposits
☐ Confirm or cancel venue
☐ Received contract from venue
☐ Deposit received from client → send deposits to contractors
☐ Commence purchase of goods
☐ All goods purchased
☐ Order invitations
☐ Invitations received → send to clients and invoice out ☐
☐ Brief florists
☐ Brief set dressers
☐ Brief "go-fors"
☐ Brief load in and load out staff
☐ Book trucking
☐ Book travel
☐ Book accommodation
☐ Book crew meals
☐ Organize parking
☐ Working schedule completed
☐ Function running schedule completed
☐ Final invoices and extras received from: ☐ Light ☐ Production
  ☐ Sound ☐ Entertainment
  ☐ Staging ☐ Other _____

☐ Final invoice sent to client
☐ Payment received from client→ now pay contractors
☐ Get testimonial from client
☐ Breakfast to brainstorm post event

Figure 2.2. Event manager's décor checklist. This is a vital list to keep the job on track and assures that elements are not missed. It also assists your staff to see the current status of the job at hand.

☐ Sight venue with light/sound/staging/production/other | ☐ Received quote from other _____
☐ Book meeting with venue operator | ☐ Deposit sent to light
☐ Brief lighting | ☐ Deposit sent to sound
☐ Brief sound | ☐ Deposit sent to staging
☐ Brief staging | ☐ Deposit sent to production
☐ Brief production | ☐ Deposit sent to entertainement
☐ Brief entertainment | ☐ Deposit sent to other _____
☐ Brief other _____ | ☐ Final payment to light
☐ Received quote from light | ☐ Final payment to sound
☐ Received quote from sound | ☐ Final payment to staging
☐ Received quote from staging | ☐ Final payment to production
☐ Received quote from production | ☐ Final payment to entertainment
☐ Received quote from entertainment | ☐ Final payment to other _____

Figure 2.3. Contractors' checklist. Use this list to ensure that you have completed the necessary steps to secure your contractual suppliers.

8 Weeks Away from Event							
Week 8	Week 7	Week 6	Week 5	Week 4	Week 3	Week 2	Week 1

Count-Down Week to Event						
7 Days	6 Days	5 Days	4 Days	3 Days	2 Days	1 Day

Figure 2.4. Sample time line grid. This allows you to plan ahead, avoid the rush, and ensure you are working smoothly toward the event date.

A. Meet with client and all contractors
B. Check client for final numbers
C. Prepare table lists
D. Prepare table layout
E. Confirm number of guests with caterer
F. Check linens, cloths, covers, and napkins
G. Check on trucking
H. Check on drivers and time availability
I. Buy any required stock
J. Remove labels from any stock purchased
K. Buy candles if required
L. Pay out any appropriate deposits
M. Use checklists to organize

N. Check on staff uniforms
O. Recheck on any ordering for end of week
P. Pack goods and label each item
Q. Check that signage is completed
R. Check scheduling of load-in team
S. Check scheduling of load-out team
T. Arrange any crew amenities
U. Pick up any necessary keys
V. Check for ladders that may be used
W. Pack corporate gifts for delivery to site
X. Check car and crew parking arrangements
Y. Touch base with venue security
Z. Double check that all information is given out.

Figure 2.5. The one week out A-Z event time line is important because it allows you to recheck any elements and gives you extra time to complete if necessary.

Item	Goods Required	Firm/Supplier	Delivery Date

Figure 2.6. Manifest of goods sheet for a themed party. This sheet allows you to keep track of goods required. It also provides a handy list should you need to contact suppliers or firms in case of nondelivery, incorrect delivery of goods, and returns if necessary.

the first group of workers in the ballroom or event location because of the scaffolding or push-up poles required to erect the black velvet ceiling to floor drapes (room blackout). Staggering the teams means not restricting the use of scissor lifts or cherry pickers.

The light and sound team follows. The ceiling must always be a consideration because decorators may have swagging of fabrics, mobiles, or huge baskets to hang. For this reason, staging should always be coordinated with sound and lighting, and the decorators have a responsibility to work with the core group. Lighting of the props depend on the shades, tones, and hues through colored gels and shaded light washes that pick up and enhance the decorative piece. Coordinating these components of the team gives the contractor an overview of the event itself.

The working schedule simply creates a running order of the event components and the people putting it together. It differs from the event schedule. Whether the event entails 50 or 500, the order of activities must be set down on paper to ensure a smooth flow. List every task that is connected to the event along with the number of contractors involved. A round table production meeting will determine who should arrive first and in what order thereafter. Unless those details are confirmed, your event may turn out to be non-profit because labor costs will exceed the budget allowance.

12. Producing the Event

Finally, based on the highly detailed event schedule, the event begins. If the upfront planning has been done correctly, putting the plan into action will provide your guests with a truly wonderful event.

Summary of the 12-Point Management Plan

- Initial meeting
- Call for quotes
- Select the contractors
- Prepare proposal for client
- Present to client
- Budget approval from client
- Prepare time line for purchases & staff action
- Call for client deposits
- Confirm all elements and contractors
- Purchase the stock and make the props
- Create task analysis and working schedules
- Produce the event

A Management Overview That Brings Success

Operating Principles

- Live by your company's philosophy
- Put the client first
- Find out the client's needs and how to meet them
- Endeavor to meet the client's desired outcome
- Constantly review your own performance
- Have zest for life and enjoy work

Methods Employed

- Lead by example
- Encourage the team to learn and develop personally
- Look for new and better ways to improve skills
- Ask for client feedback to monitor performance
- Be willing to change and show flexibility in all facets of the event
- Encourage your key staff to participate with the company involvement and improve their own individual skills

Self-Training and Development

- Initiate group sessions between key personnel to monitor work performance, methods, cost saving ideas, new promotional and design aspects
- Encourage key personnel to take responsibility and delegate authority
- Attend national and international conferences to absorb new ideas and to challenge your own theories and creativity
- Be willing to share what you have learned (both good and bad) to those wanting to progress and grow in their chosen industries.

Essential Elements in Approaching Clients

- Enjoy client company and remain enthusiastic
- Develop and build trust through honest negotiations by doing what you promise and giving the client your best advice suited to their needs and individual company image
- Be punctual. Don't change appointments
- Meet quotes and design format deadlines
- Follow up on all areas to assure client and instill confidence
- Don't tear down your competitors. Recognize that the client chose you for a particular reason—identify it for the future reference.

Staff Training and Development

- Ensure that staff training not only covers skills but encourages individuals to become more personally fulfilled. This, in turn, will reflect a healthy attitude towards the client because self-development builds confidence, inspires creativity, and helps people to think on their feet.

Overview of Other Aspects of the Event

Opportunities

- To create a positive impression and develop client loyalty for repeat and referral business
- To design and create a concept that is new, different, and original
- To provide the client with a "wish list" of wants whether on a restricted or open budget. This can be done by using special effects, unusual costumes, fantastic entertainers, or any element that brings a feeling of excitement.

Secrecy of the Event When Requested by Client

- Maintain close communication and involvement with the client
- Style the invitation as a formal function without disclosing the theme
- Liaise only with the chairman and his/her personal assistant regarding any special event
- All correspondence sealed and marked "To be opened by addressee only"
- Ensure that service, security, and ground staff on-site are fully aware of the secrecy

Challenges

- To maintain the event's element of surprise for the guest
- To give attention to every detail of the event
- To develop a sense of theatrics throughout the evening
- To negotiate successfully with all hire services involved (light and sound technicians, caterers and staffing services, entertainment agent, rental company, photography and video company)
- To create maximum visual impact as guests enter the room and to continue this impact into the venue itself via design and decoration
- To design and decorate the venue so guests "live" the atmosphere
- To strive for continuity of theme and concept throughout all visual elements that guests experience
- To combine the element of acting with a representation of the chosen theme (i.e., hire people capable of dual roles if called for)
- To remain in a positive revenue situation relative to scale of event.

Passionate Attention to Detail

- After researching books and videos on the subject, every idea is collated. Brainstorm with the teams. Workable ideas are held while others are discarded: the team should know what *not* to use as well as ideas that can be expanded into a real theme. Every effort made to focus on the total concept.
- Conceptual art brought into play so the client can visualize the evening's event
- The display team also visualizes the theme and can begin producing props. This task analysis also creates a working schedule for all involved so they can successfully and accurately integrate with the events program.
- Develop a task analysis for team leaders of every job that has to be done
- Develop conceptual art for client approval and for use as a working design model for the event
- Design table centerpieces and decorations which represent the theme
- Constantly review costs of materials used and time involved in production. First plan the work to the budget, then work the plan.

Constraints

- Keeping the theming of the event a secret from the client's staff and/or guests prior to the function
- Maintaining total confidentiality in all correspondence with client and suppliers
- Limited set-up periods
- Inadequate kitchen facilities, staging, dressing rooms, parking, and technical support requirements (light and sound) typical of off-premise jobs
- Secrecy of theme to be maintained while pre-dinner drinks are served in an area separate from the function

Creating a Sense of Theatrics

- Hire professional actors when sight performers are required
- Utilize professional dancers for interpretation or other related entertainment segments
- Create special effects via light, sound, and audiovisual material

Negotiations

- Request quotes on requirements from highly reputable contractors in catering, staffing, light and sound, and entertainment. Select the most cost-efficient supplier without sacrificing quality.

By taking the time to think about these challenges, you will dramatically increase the likelihood of a successful event.

Finally let's look at some of the Do's and Don'ts of succeeding in business as shown in Figure 2.7.

Do	*Don't*
• Be willing to try new ideas and critically examine your current practices	• Decide to stick only to what you already know and feel safe with it because it is repetitious
• Be willing to take *calculated* risks	• Be so afraid of what's new that you stagnate and die
• Continue to listen to and learn from those who know what it takes to succeed in business	• Reject new management and leadership practices by detaching yourself from peers and industry involvement
• Set goals and formulate a mission statement	• Spend all your energy on staying afloat
• Be prepared to abandon current practices if they are shown to be at fault	• Stubbornly hold on to practices that are outdated or not working because that's the way it's been done for years
• Spend time on developing a clear-cut structure for you and your staff which encourages growth and responsibility at all levels	• Stifle yourself or your staff by not giving people responsibility and not encouraging them to learn and grow
• Encourage feedback to the top from all levels (and all contractors)	• Make all the decisions based solely on your view of the situation, which can be seen as tunnel thinking
• Take the time to understand the flow of finance in the business, and to have efficient systems in place for invoicing and purchasing	• Spend your life playing "catch-up" with contractors and clients through lack of organization and procrastinating on the paperwork that's involved
• Educate yourself in people skills: understand different personality styles and how to work with them	• Be so autocratic that people hate working for you, or such a pushover that people take advantage of you
• Keep your eyes open for signs of change, and plan to flow with it	• Assume that just because it's always been that way, it's going to remain that way
• Network within your industry and with your clients, and subscribe to industry journals and texts, to make sure you have a healthy idea of who your clients are, what they want, and how you might best provide it	• Put off networking and reading because you're too busy to spend time keeping up with clients or new developments in your industry
• Provide appropriate levels of staffing to run your business effectively	• Work your staff like slaves or have them put in impossible hours
• Aim for a better product, better customer service, and a healthy profit. Repeat business is the goal.	• Cut costs, cut quality, and run a shoestring operation that will affect the quality of the event for the client.
• Aim for continuous improvement and progress. Search for options that will work	• Stand still because you have fixed budgets and therefore fixed standards

Figure 2.7. The do and don't chart. I find this is a great chart to keep my mind focused on the job at hand. It will also help your business to be efficient.

Chapter 3

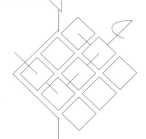

Event Essentials

What exactly is a special event? This term actually encompasses a handful of specialized disciplines which are managed and conducted by a range of talented professionals—organizers, producers, caterers, service personnel, decorators, and technicians (see Figure 3.1). Together, they bring light, sound, color, and movement to the event. In many ways it resembles a theatrical production with the performance staged in the space controlled by the venue operator.

Figure 3.1. The event disciplines. This simple chart gives you the main elements required in events.

The Conference Organizer

The conference organizer is the executive arm of the conference committee or client. His or her job is to:

*   convert decisions into action
*   keep the project on schedule
*   report to the committee or client
*   offer consultative expertise and
*   coordinate suppliers.

This job description can also come under the umbrella of Professional Conference Organizer (PCO), Meeting Planner, or even a Project Manager. Many companies or organizations have their own in-house conference department. The meetings and events industries have now developed industry accreditation and training opportunities to meet professional standards and they are bound by a code of ethics. Usually training for conference organizer and event planner is obtained through residential or professional development courses through ISES. Programs are offered in January in the United States for special events.

The requirements for this service depend on the size and complexity of the event. Goals, objectives, and budget are allocated by the client.

The Meetings Industry Association of Australia, based in Sydney, has an excellent booklet available called Professional Management of Meetings, Conferences, and Events. Its 12 pages are packed with professional tips.

The Conference Organizer's Checklist

*   Research and recommend venue
*   Negotiate rates with venue
*   Book and manage space and equipment
*   Handle travel requirements
*   Coordinate venue personnel
*   Coordinate food and beverage
*   Advise on effective program structures
*   Prepare schedule for program
*   Devise suitable social events
*   Coordinate special events
*   Liaise with speakers and performers
*   Procure all conference accessories
*   Supervise and coordinate all external suppliers
*   Carry out all aspects of on-site management
*   Deal with contractors
*   Prepare budget according to client brief for approval
*   Prepare pre- and postevent costs and budget report
*   Arrange for gifts, signage, programs, satchels, or client requests
*   Manage overall staging and audiovisual production to ensure it integrates into the business and social programs
*   Administration of the event.

The Producer

The orchestration of any type of event is usually stage-managed and if it is *not, it should be!*

This orchestration can only succeed when each individual contractor is in place. What follows is similar to the choreography of a stage show.

Large event companies usually have their own production people in-house, but in some cases event companies utilize the services of a freelance producer, depending on the size of the job.

This production component is totally dependent on the requirements, size, and budget of the function.

During the performance of an event, whether it is a launch, gala ceremony, VIP dinner, convention, or barbecue, the guests are aware of the flow of the function, but should be *unaware* of the work that goes on during the event or behind the scenes.

The producer/director is responsible for coordinating these separate disciplines to give you the final product. This smooth interrelationship of décor, technical expertise, show, catering, and service is the result of professional training and experience, not haphazard planning.

The stage manager, the producer's second-in-command, must also have a working knowledge of all disciplines, be a decision-maker, and know when to pass a problem on to the producer.

The Producer's Checklist

- Choose stage manager
- Compose the program schedule
- Do a site inspection
- Check fire exits in venue
- Check technical facility
- Consult with security regarding limousine arrival/departure
- Check contractor's access
- Meeting with staging crew
- Meeting with technical staff
- Meeting with caterers
- Contact with band
- Contact with entertainers
- Arrange for vehicle/guest parking
- Check insurances of crew/guests
- Copies of schedules
- Arrange directional signs
- Arrange a same-day meeting with all crews
- Registration desk if required
- Coat check

Technical Production—Light

Appropriate lighting is essential, and good lighting is best when subtle. This technical component can make or break the setting.

Atmosphere, mood, and ambience are set through detailed lighting which enhances the entire production. The lighting company and/or designer becomes part of the working team to produce the integrated whole. This should be predetermined at production meetings.

It is important to understand that the primary function and importance of room, stage, and floor lighting is visibility. The guests must be able to see and hear speakers and entertainers without the hindrance of too much or too little lighting. The stage itself—generally set with backdrop and/or two- or three-dimensional sets—should give the impression of a still-life picture: beautifully lit but waiting to be brought to life by either orchestra, site performer, entertainer, or show.

Various effects and moods are created through the use of colored gels. If blue and mauve are introduced, for instance, a cool and expansive effect is achieved. White is always light and luminous; reds and purple give the impression of heaviness and exotica. Yellow and orange bring warmth and vibrancy to any set, while contrasting pink sets a soft, romantic mood.

Go into a lighting studio or factory and look at the options available. This will increase your own knowledge but don't be afraid to rely heavily on your light and sound professional. This will allow the lighting professional to give the best possible design within the limitations of budget and equipment.

See the section "More about Light and Staging" and Jerry Astourian's contribution on lighting design later in this chapter for further information.

Technical Production Checklist

- Lighting for stage, dance floor, or floor
- Scenic stage sets
- Decorative room props
- Orchestra music stands
- Entrance of guests
- Steps to stage or platforms
- Show feature artist
- Table centerpieces
- Feature artists
- Professional speakers
- Corners lit or shadowed
- Ceiling or suspended feature
- Lectern and air conditioning
- Projection usage
- Microphone
- Radio two-way microphone
- Check sufficient power
- Pre-dinner lighting
- Table pin spotting
- Piano and music stand lights
- Ambient room lighting
- Special effects
- Registration area
- Back stage lighting
- Fairy light usage

The Venue and Site Operator

Events are now produced in a number of locations. This opens up quite a few options, and the right location for your event is essential.

On-Premise (within a venue)
- The 4- or 5-star hotel
- Convention centers
- University and function space
- Art galleries
- Historic homes
- Public buildings
- Specific parkland areas
- Private clubs
- Museums

Off-Premise (at an outside location)
- Specific parkland area
- Beachside areas or beach clubs
- Museums
- Marquees
- Large gardens
- Railroad stations
- Zoo function centers/space
- Private homes/grounds
- Warehouses
- Race tracks
- Sporting facilities/stadiums
- Airport hangars
- Cruisers, boats, or ferries
- Harbor islands
- Hokkas or marquees
- Shipping terminal

The Venue and Site Operator's Checklist

- Room size vs. guest numbers
- Facilities for parking
- Facilities for load in and out
- Access times
- Inquire about any restrictions
- Kitchen facilities
- Bathroom facilities
- Look for beverage area
- Check electrical outlets
- Check lighting facilities
- Check audio facilities
- Check pre-function work space
- Check if any pre-function costs
- Check breakout rooms
- Phone list for taxi returns
- Arrange limousine company
- Periods when service elevators are busy
- Portable toilet facilities
- The highest point of the ceiling
- The lowest point of the ceiling
- Power distribution board
- Facilities for invalids/disabled (ramp, toilets, elevators)
- Parking for crew
- Professional greeters
- Pathway lighting

The Staffing Service

The type and cost of food and beverage service depends on many elements:

- the **venue** where the function will be held
- the **clientele** that is to be served
- the **time** allocated for the event
- the type of **meal**—breakfast, lunch, cocktails, or dinner

The style of service can range from table service to assisted service and everything in between: buffet, self-service, silver, or specialized service.

Buffet Set-up and Layout

If you decide on a buffet, there are critical items you need to consider which will have a direct relationship to the speed of service.

Take a careful look at the room configuration and the actual serving space, and estimate the ratio of "guest-served" foods to "attendant-served" foods.

Look at the availability of staffing for the number of guests, the service standards required, and the ease of service for both guests and attendants. A "high-style" buffet will require one attendant for each 10 guests.

Staff/Service Checklist

- Ratio of waiters to guests
- Waiter access to and from kitchen
- Power availability
- Kitchen facility
- Style of dress
- Style of service
- Menu creation
- Beverage control
- Beverage service
- Beverage: alcohol/nonalcohol
- Food service
- Type of beverage
- Style of food
- Method of service
- Equipment required
- Linen and tableware
- China and glassware
- Floor service
- Billing method
- Outdoor service
- Staff training
- Function administration
- Function organization
- Interpersonal skills

The Caterer

The caterer's involvement in any event is of primary importance because the entire event can be judged on the quality of food that is served.

Never assume that the caterer will take care of everything. You must set up a meeting and provide a written list of all the requirements.

It is extremely important to hire a professional caterer for any function. Experience counts, especially if the event is to be staged off-premise or in a difficult or unusual venue. The caterer is then completely versed in the set up and service details from portable kitchens.

An established caterer is also familiar with insurance, liquor licensing, and health regulations and uses only experienced waiters.

If you are responsible for menu selection, ask the caterer to provide food tastings for you. Give the client the option to make changes to the menu or choice of wine prior to the function.

It is essential to know the exact number of guests, where the function is to be held, and the food cost per person, as well as whether the service is formal seated style or buffet, and whether the meal to be served is a breakfast, lunch or dinner. Vegetarian choices must always be an option. Dr. Joe Jeff Goldblatt's *Art and Science of Celebration* is an excellent source of information.

The Caterer's Checklist

- The style of event
- The number of guests
- The menu
- The budget
- The beverage
- Access time
- Load out time
- Table signs
- Table linens
- Type of table service
- Menus to print
- Waiters per table
- Waiter uniforms
- Coat check
- Name tags
- Style of floral centerpiece
- Type of table china and glasses
- Type of cutlery on table
- Napkin fold or trim
- Arrange checks if C.O.D.
- Check electrical outlets
- Power availability and amps
- Extra kitchen requirements
- Beverage bar access
- Side service tables
- Time stop on beverage bar
- Schedule
- Crew meals
- Band meals
- Work and storage areas
- Changing rooms for entertainers
- Vehicle parking
- Waiters on stand-by at specific time
- Lights, fan, refrigeration
- Level ground for work area
- Access to water and sinks
- Rubbish & waste disposal every day

Entertainment Agency

Every events company should have a registered, highly specialized agency which represents entertainers for performances that can be staged for conventions, VIP gala events, fund raisers, and private occasions.

This professional agent becomes part of the working team and develops and understands your style of show and your expectations. They advise and provide the appropriate entertainment for the specific event. They also know how to locate international talent. The agent also has the ability to screen talent prior to the event therefore avoiding a poor choice.

This same agency can advise you on the right orchestra, backing band, comedian, or sight performer. They submit the artist's repertoire and work on changes. Your agency can make sure you get the type of entertainment you had in mind. It is always wise to work with a professional.

For large events it may be essential to hire two bands. It's well worth spending the extra dollars on continuous music to keep the dancers on the floor tripping the night away.

It is advisable to find out the general age group of the guests since this will probably dictate the choice

The Entertainment Agency's Checklist

- Assistant to help
- Coat racks
- Free-standing mirrors
- Booking in written form
- Deposits paid
- Request artist biography
- Request artist repertoire
- Request artist's requirements
- Arrange artist's refreshments
- Arrange breakout room
- Request written confirmation
- Request written changes
- Forward event schedule
- Arrange rehearsal time
- Number of bands required
- Disc jockey option
- Duo, trio, or quartet option
- Musical options
  - jazz combos, steel bands
  - pianist, flautist, violinist
  - strings
  - cabaret singers
  - sight performers
  - guitars and accordion
  - western/Latin/rock band
- Arrange for someone to greet performers
- Arrange a brief meeting with performers
- Reconfirm the schedule
- Have all contact phone numbers on hand

and style of entertainment. Is it to be sleek and sophisticated, or casual? The entertainment budget also plays a large part in the type and extent of entertainment program chosen.

The Staging

Staging offers versatility. The size and height depends entirely on the size of the event, the number of guests, the style of show or entertainment, and dance floor(s) option.

The floor of the stage may be a level surface or risers and/or platforms can be used to create a two or three step effect. It can be a very impressive sight when musicians are seen on various elevations.

Wings can be created on each side of the stage to give a good visual appearance, but allow room for feature artists to make an entrance. Steps must be positioned to give easy stage access to the band members and performers.

The *apron* is the front face of the stage itself. At any event, it always looks better if dressed with florals or fabrics. The *thrust stage* is an extension often used for big orchestras and shows of larger size.

Elevated platforms are ideal for audience viewing. If the ballroom is of generous size rostrums can be styled into the room. For example two levels are created for the Casablanca party as seen in Color Plate 16.

A level of rostrums extend across the width of the walls and is raised 20 inches high and holds six tables. The lower level of rostrums is at a 12 inch height with more guest tables. The remaining tables are arranged on the floor. This gives all guests an excellent view of the stage.

Staging Checklist

- Room size essential
- Entrance and exit awareness
- Fire exits and signage
- Ceiling measurements high and low points
- Ceiling facility for hanging props/mobiles
- Side walls facility
- Stage floor surfaces (carpet, vinyl)
- Building of wings
- Proscenium style and use
- Stage height, width, and depth
- Room access time
- Load in & load out facility required
- Required rigging
- Rostrum measurement
- Rostrum availability
- Rostrum timber/steel
- Flat panels in wood or foam core
- Plaque reveal (e.g., building dedication)
- Carpet and flooring
- Lecterns and plinths
- Available fabrics for ceiling and stage
- Black, blue, or green cord velvet
- Drill starcloths or fiber-optic cloth
- Chiffons, satins
- Calico, cotton, or cheesecloth

Set and Decor

The room decorations set the mood, create the environment, and bring surprise to the guests.

The professional decorator is therefore faced with the great challenge of transforming the ballroom or football stadium into a night in the Sahara to an Australian outback party, to a golden gala.

Decor and/or room dressing has come a long way over the past ten years. Today's client wants more than a venue which simply looks lovely. They want the excitement of a fantasy look created especially for them. They want their guests to walk into a room that will carry them beyond their expectations.

The contribution of the theme designer, set maker, display dresser, and floral artists can transform any four walls, whether it be a hotel ballroom or an off-premise establishment. Scenic art, stage sets, fabrics, beautiful linens, and flowers are used to delight the guests.

When working on- or off-premise the working area should be organized. See Figure 8.9 for an example of an effective workroom layout. Note the location of the fresh floral, nonperishable and administration desk. Each function has its own space.

Set and Decor Checklist (On-Premise)

- Select the venue
- Room length, width, and ceiling height
- Request floor plans & sizing
- Check power and access to it
- Check back of house access
- Loading/dock area and sizing
- Lift/elevator location and sizing
- Ceiling height in loading dock
- Types of tables and diameter
- Check in-house dance floor
- Check chairs (with, w/out arms)
- Available ceiling hanging points
- Available in-house staging or rostrums
- Available in-house technical support
- Availability of scissor lift
- Availability of ladders
- Check breakout rooms
- Check wall and floor color
- Source pre-work space area
- Available floral refrigeration
- Arrange crew refreshments
- Request access to venue canteen
- Create floor plans
- Carry portable work bench
- Check uniforms for teams
- Contractors parking
- Available water
- Available sinks

Rental Suppliers

Many companies in the events industry base their business on the rental and supply of the necessary components required for a small, large, or mammoth special event.

These items include staging, marquees, hokkas, and tents, catering requirements such as refrigeration, ovens, and working bench facilities, waste disposal, port-a-johns, and technical requirements such as generators.

Other companies specialize in candelabras, racks, mirrors, pedestals, lecterns, stanchions and chain, garden, market, and sun umbrellas. Tables also come in varying sizes. All table appointments such as linen, dinnerware and silver come in a variety of types and brands. Chairs come in a variety of wrought iron, wood, padded tops, or plastic in different sizes and shapes.

Rental Supplier Checklist

- Request catalog of rental equipment with costs
- Check type and size of tables, chairs, and other equipment such as pedestals
- Confirm all orders by fax and retain transmission receipt
- Confirm contact name and phone number of person delivering the goods
- Have space allocated at the venue for goods
- Designate load out time for rental supplier company
- Check type and style of dinnerware, cutlery, and glasses.
- With generator rental, have on hand additional fuel or a local carrier on stand by
- In out-of-the-way destinations allow 5% additional product. Once on site you may not be able to get more.
- Have someone check off a list of incoming deliveries and returns.

Transport

The travel arrangements and transfer of clients for a conference or event is always an important consideration. Travel can include a number of ways to arrive at the destination.

Types of transport include:

Sedan
Limousines
Vintage car
Commuter buses
Bus coach
Private train carriage
Ferry
Cruiser
Horse and carriage

Transport Checklist

- Detail name of client and pickup address clearly by formal fax
- Stipulate requirements for the client
- Provide umbrellas in case of emergency
- Have a meet and greet MC if budget permits
- Alert venue operators to external travel requirement
- Large numbers of guests should be programmed according to specific areas

More about Light and Staging

Lighting for Stage
What are the requirements?

Broadcast quality. Is there a requirement to archive speeches, (for example, a financial institution requiring a record of correct advice). As a requirement for future use, correct broadcast quality lighting is essential. This can be achieved without losing theatrical flair.

Theatricality. Is there a dramatic element to the evening? Often the use of specific lighting in conjunction with a performance can evoke a particular mood or style which enhances the overall theme of an event. Another, often forgotten, aspect of lighting is the art of not lighting particular elements until the appropriate time to achieve an element of surprise. In these cases, less ambient light from other areas makes it easier to hide such pieces.

Moving lights. Technology has brought many advances to stage lighting in recent years not the least of which is Varilights, known in the industry as waggly/mirrors. This form of illumination has good and bad points which the event organizer needs to be well aware of. Moving lights can add a stunning visual effect to a particular stage look but basically they are a useless addition to the budget if they do not achieve their basic aim.

It is advisable to work out beforehand what to expect from these illumination wonders. Are they intended to light presenters or performers in an interesting and artistic way? Each requires its own approach as well as an understanding, well versed lighting operator to distinguish between the different requirements for the event. Above all, the requirement of any lighting design is to provide flexibility in view of any changes. Lighting formats require the operator/designer to facilitate this in a practical and creative sense. Programming time needs to be allowed in the production schedule for specific show cues in addition to experimenting with more scenic looks once the room is set with the props, sets, and flowers.

Dance floor. If dance floor lighting is required, there are a few basic rules of thumb to consider, including:

- The age group of the audience
- Subdued lights or blinding, flashing lights
- Are the moving lights a substitute for or an element of the entertainment presentation or speeches?

Stage Set Pieces. Scenic elements need to be lit according to their specific requirements. For specific lectern camera shots it is imperative to have a suitable backdrop for the camera to register against. Sometimes a simple scenic flat can accommodate this.

Lighting Scenic Elements

Tables. The classic pin spot on the table top provides a reliable standard. More interesting table pieces can result in budget blowouts and frustration, but the results of a well planned (and battery tested!!) table centerpiece can be very rewarding.

Room decorative pieces. The secret to good lighting in these situations is to make the luminaire as unobtrusive as possible while maintaining some degree of integrity to the focus on the subject. Often this can be achieved by using the correct lighting device for the job, for example a dichrioc lantern capable of focal point projection can quite easily replace bulky 650w units and quite as often as a result of their size do a better job.

Guest Entrances/Exits. Due to the extensive use of blackout curtains for backdrops, it is important to be aware of regulations that govern fire exits. These regulations may vary but the general rule of thumb is to ensure that all fire exits are unblocked and are clearly marked or illuminated where necessary. Entrances can be used as part of the set or as a set piece by themselves, for example laser tunnels or set tunnels which can be lit in an illusory way.

Staging

Masking. Masking, as mentioned before, is required to conform to acceptable standards but also to mask all unwanted elements such as banqueting and technical debris.

Rigging. If there is no house rigger available, it is advisable to have a qualified rigger place all trussing and scaffolding. Not only is this a legal requirement in many instances but the advice of a good rigger can often save time and money.

Set up/Dismantling. Access times need to be established early to enable contractors to plan arrival of staff and materials. Scissor lifts or manlifters loading dock facilities need to be checked to facilitate this.

Lighting Design*

You can have the most beautiful flowers, yards of elegant fabrics, and dozens of talented musicians at your event, but it is the use of shadow and light that ultimately creates the ambience for a special evening. The lighting designer's job is to build a series of light levels that direct the guests' attention to the areas and activities being brought together to create the event. Using a variety of lighting instruments in varying degrees of intensity, theatrical gels to add color, and gobo patterns to project silhouettes of texture, the lighting designer sculpts color, shadow, and light to bring depth and dimension to the design.

On the following pages you will see a lighting design that I submitted to Lena Malouf for a 1950s theme party she produced for a corporate client in a very large venue. Lena had given me a brief outline of the decor and entertainment that was scheduled for the event. I suggested a special effect time tunnel for the entrances, alternating colors and textures for each entertainment section, and perimeter colorplay for the themed buffet areas. Lena has a wonderful sense of color and designs with strong theme statements. I knew the lighting would also have to be strong to balance the visual element. A strong lighting statement reflects a style that uses a small but vivid color palette and requires as much shadow as it does light.

*This section is a special contribution, courtesy of Mr. Jerry Astourian, Astourian Lighting Design, Los Angeles, California.

The Design

Entrance to time tunnels. The entrances to our '50s fantasy are marked on the foyer side of the doorway with two bubble machines, each backlit in hot pink. The interior ballroom side of the doorway has a time-released smoke machine placed on the ground and positioned to send its smoke toward the open doorway. One ceiling mounted intellibeam is focused back at the doorway with a pattern of dots swirling in sky blue to create the time tunnel effect.

Entrance Equipment (based on 2 guest entrances)

4 bubble machines
4 par 46 (200s) med—on floor plates
2 smoke machines (time released—water based juice)
2 intellibeams (these will be included within the side ceiling plot)
Bubbles—#339 broadway pink
All gel colors are Roscolux

The tunnel effect needs to come out of total darkness to be effective. Bubble up lighting and existing lighting in the pre-function area would be focused away or toned down near the doorways to assist in the tunnel presentation. Bubble machines are to be moved from the entrances after everyone has arrived and brought to the side stage area for Little Pattie, the feature artist. Please keep bubbles away from dance floor for safety.

Diner facades. The diner facades that surround the perimeter of the room will be uplit in a cross coloration of hot pink and bright orange to emphasize the architectural elements within each setting. A little bit of the orange and pink gel should be pulled back to allow a small amount of white light to play onto the facades as well. A little bit of white light within the colorplay will keep the orange and pink bright and true to color. Clusters of trees flanking the stations will be uplit in lime green with sky blue accents to give them a sense of depth. Down lighting of the actual food service should come from ground supported pipe and base butted up against the sides of the buffet tables. Additional lights are added to the pipe locations and will be focused across nearby props and signage to assist in their colorful illumination.

Diner Equipment (Based on 6 × 16ft diner stations)

12 12ft pipe and base
24 sandbags (2 per base, draped in black)
48 par 46 (200w)—med (4 per pole, 2 focused on buffet, 2 for props and color)
24 par 56 (500w)—med/floor plate (4 per station for facade and tree uplights)
Buffets—#33, no color pink
Trees—#86 pea green and #69 brilliant blue
Facades—#19 fire orange and #339 broadway pink

Please note: diner lighting is designed to be "hot"—no dimming required.

Drive-in. This area of the ballroom needs to be carefully focused to keep all unwanted light and reflection away from direct contact with the movie screen. The drive-in look in this section is created with uplights in deep zephyr blue installed along the ballroom walls to wash up the walls and streak across the floor to create the perimeter of the drive-in area. To create moonlight specials in this area, four source 4's project palm leaf patterns onto the prop cars. The source 4's are paired with one palm leaf pattern in zephyr blue playing over the same pattern in pale amber gold to give the effect of a shadow through the leaves. The pale amber gold projections will need to be dimmed down so they do not overwhelm the soft blue palm leaf pattern that partners the effect.

Drive-In Equipment

12 par 56 (500w) med/floor plates (6 wall uplights, 6 floor washes)
Wall and floor—#84 zephyr blue

Please note: all blue uplights are designed to be "hot." No dimming required. Amber palm patterns should be dimmable and most likely set at 60% for a soft general presentation. Zephyr blue palm patterns to remain "hot."

Stage design. The stage backdrop will be outlined in white stringer lights in a random pattern that "drips down" the length of the 50 ft backdrop. The front stage skirting artwork will also be laced with white stringer lights. Flanking the stage front are two 10 ft truss towers (one on either end). These ground supported truss towers will each receive one par 64 lamp bar that is vertically hung from the truss to achieve side lighting for the bands. Two additional ground supported truss towers of 15 ft will be positioned at the back of the stage and out 10 ft to open up the stage visual. Each tower is outfitted with two par 64 lamp bars vertically mounted to the front of the truss to backlight the stage and band areas. All four towers are draped in white stringer lights that "drip down" their fronts and sides. To complete the stage design, seven miniature egg strobes are placed within the fabulous '50s signage. One in the middle of each four record props and one each in the letters A and O of fabulous and one in the "0" of the number 50. The stringer lights as well as the egg strobes should be on their own circuit to be used specifically to create variations to each band's look and feel.

Stage Equipment

6 par 64 lamp bars (6 1k lights each)
7 50ft runs of white (frosted) stringer bulbs
7 miniature egg strobes
2 10 ft towers of 20-inch box truss with floor plates
2 15 ft towers of 20-inch box truss with floor plates
2 smoke machines (positioned at base of each front truss tower)

Front Truss Tower (circuits paired top to bottom)

Lamps	Gels	Focus
Medium	#321 soft golden amber	Center—lead vocal
Medium	#40 light salmon	Center—lead vocal
Wide	#332 cherry rose	General wash
Wide	#383 sapphire blue	General wash
Wide	#339 broadway pink	Up stage wash
Wide	#42 deep salmon/red	Down stage floor wash

Rear Truss Tower (circuits paired top to bottom)

Lamps	Gels	Focus
Narrow	Clear	Rear star special—lead vocal
Narrow	#49 med purple	Rear special—lead vocal
Narrow	#312 canary yellow	Drum special
Medium	#19 fire orange	Horn special
Medium	#42 med salmon	General wash
Wide	#383 sapphire blue	General wash
Medium	#95 blue green	Up stage wash
Medium	#69 brilliant blue	Down stage wash
Wide	#21 amber	General wash
Medium	#86 pea green	Down stage wash
Wide	#69 brilliant blue	Upstage floor wash
Wide	#385 royal blue	Down stage floor wash

Band and dance floor design. The main ceiling position for the band and dance floor lighting will be directly across from the stage in the center of the room. Two additional ceiling positions are also utilized for support of various design effects. The main position (either free hung or from truss section) will include a series of par 64 lamp bars, intellibeams, a mirror ball, and additional effects. The lighting for each band is the core of the general ambience of the room. The lighting transitions are driven by the music. Each band will have its own look and dance floor treatment. **It is essential** that the intelligent lighting system has as much time as possible, to program a wide variety of looks to anticipate the ongoing change in music styles. The more time the programmer has, the more dramatic the whole evening will be.

Center Ceiling Equipment

6 intellibeam
1 24-in. mirror ball
4 red police beacons
2 confetti canons
4 source 4 lekos with musical note patterns
4 par 64 lamp bars

Center Ceiling (circuits paired from outside into center)

Lamp/Fixture	Gel/Pattern	Focus
Confetti canon		Over dining area
Red police beacon		Streak ceiling
Intellibeam		Column #2/dance floor
Intellibeam		Stage and dance floor
Par 64—med	#332 cherry rose	Skater's ramp
Par 64—wide	#339 broadway pink	Dance floor
Par 64—nar	#69 brilliant blue	Center stage special
Par 64—med	#383 sapphire blue	General stage wash
Par 64—nar	#19 fire orange	Dancer special
Par 64—med	#32 med pink/salmon	Stage wash
Source 4—short	n/c musical notes	Gobo on dance floor
Red police beacon		Streak ceiling
Intellibeam		Column #3/mirror ball/stage
Source 4—short	n/c musical note	Gobo on dance floor
Par 64—wide	#339 broadway pink	Dance floor
Par 64—wide	#383 sapphire blue	Dance floor
Par 64—med	#21 amber	Stage wash
Par 64—nar	#86 pea green	Dancer special
Par 64—med	#32 med salmon/pink	Stage wash
Par 64—nar	#332 cherry rose	Dancer special
24-ft mirror ball		Center of dance floor
Par 64—nar	#19 fire orange	Dancer special
Par 64—nar	#339 broadway pink	Stage wash
Par 64—nar	#312 canary yellow	Dancer special
Par 64—med	#21 amber	Stage wash
Par 64—wide	#383 sapphire blue	Dance floor
Par 64—wide	#339 broadway pink	Dance floor
Source 4—short	n/c musical notes	Gobo on dance floor
Intellibeam		Mirror ball/stage
Red police beacon		Streak ceiling
Source 4—short	n/c musical notes	Gobo on dance floor
Par 64—med	#332 cherry rose	Stage wash
Par 64—nar	#69 brilliant blue	Dancer special
Par 64—med	#383 sapphire blue	General stage wash
Par 64—nar	#69 brilliant blue	Center stage special
Par 64—wide	#339 broadway pink	Dance floor
Par 64—med	#332 cherry rose	Skater's ramp
Intellibeam		Stage/dance floor
Intellibeam		Column #4/dance floor
Red police beacon		Streak ceiling
Confetti canon		Over dining area

The Ceiling Over Drive-In
(equipment pairs are circuited together 2 × 2)

Intellibeam	Sky blue/rotating dots	At entrance doorway
Intellibeam		Column #1/ceiling/dining
Par 64—wide	#385 royal blue	Drive-in area down light
Par 64—wide	#385 royal blue	Drive-in area down light
Source 4—short	#84 zephyr blue	Palm leaf gobo—moonlight #1
Source 4—short	#84 zephyr blue	Palm leaf gobo—moonlight #2
Source 4—short	#09 pale amber gold	Palm leaf gobo—moonlight #1
Source 4—short	#09 pale amber gold	Palm leaf gobo—moonlight #2
Par 64—med	#332 cherry rose	Roller skaters room special
Par 64—med	#332 cherry rose	Roller skaters room special

Wide Ceiling—over pin ball area (circuited together 2 × 2)

Intellibeam	Sky blue/rotating dots	At entrance doorway
Intellibeam		Column #5/ceiling/dining
Par 64—wide	#385 royal blue	Pin ball area down light
Par 64—wide	#385 royal blue	Pin ball area down light
Par 64—wide	#385 royal blue	Pin ball area down light
Par 64—wide	#385 royal blue	Pin ball area down light
Par 64—med	#332 cherry rose	Roller skater room special
Par 64—med	#332 cherry rose	Roller skater room special

Pin ball area. Perimeter walls dressed with fluorescent props should receive a blacklight tube under each prop. If props are painted to look ultraviolet, par 46's in lime green cross lighting the floor and blacklighting games will give a great effect together with the royal blue downlights mentioned above.

Bursting columns. Columns will be uplit with four lights each: Two lights in pink and two lights in a cross coloration of orange and lime. The pink gels should be pulled back to reveal a tiny amount of white light. Use half gels of both orange and green on remaining lights. Letting a little white light escape through those gels would enhance the overall colorplay. Play with it, if time permits. The lighting of the columns is also a part of the intellibeam design which will help to visually transform the room when Little Pattie takes to the stage for her opening number.

Pin Ball Equipment

10 par 46 (200w) Nar/floor plates *or*
10 4 ft black lights to outline perimeter walls
    and/or uplighting props
Uplights #86 pea green

Column Equipment

20 par 46 (200w) med/floor plates, 4 lights
    each per specs—all "hot"
Column up's—#339 broadway pink/# 19 fire
    orange/# 86 pea green

Please note: all uplighting is designed to be "hot." No dimming required. Please keep all lighting away from time tunnel presentation.

Follow spots. Two "long throw" followspots will be required and should be positioned on 4-ft risers flanking the center diner station with a "clear shot" of the stage front. Followspots must also be able to hit the mirror ball and roller skater's entrance ramps.

Equipment required consists of 2 1k long throw followspots.

Please note: the following 5 gel colors are to be installed within each spot:

#32 medium salmon/pink and #332 cherry rose—front crosslights for Little Pattie

#19 fire orange: mirror ball special to back up intellibeams

#317 apricot and # 33 n/c pink to crosslight any speeches or presentations

The Finished Effect

The Cadillacs: band 2

The look: High energy/multi-colored, very *Happy Days*

Stage notes: General stage washes. All side and rear lights sequencing. *No stage string lights.* Follow spots to "bally hoo" room at guest entrance in #332 pink and # 19 fire orange

Dance floor: Pink and blue washes, mirror ball in white and hot pink

Intellibeam: Polka dots and squares all over the room and dance floor.

Little Pattie: feature artist

The look: Very hot pink/orange and red or lime/purple and brilliant blue. Pattie always in pink. Slow and sexy transitions . . . add bubbles!

Stage notes: Presentation of stage stringer lights with intro of Little Pattie. *Light band with back and rear specials only.* Pattie always front lit with hot pink follow spots. Add front pink stage washes to fill. Bring in bubbles to stage sides (keep bubbles away from dance floor) from entrance doorways.

Dance floor: Understated dance floor. Hot pink washes with static musical note projections.

Intellibeam: Use rotating abstract patterns in red on existing columns for entrance look. If guests are not dancing yet, keep them on columns for entire set and change colors when appropriate.

Buddy's Back: feature artist

The look: Very intense intellibeams—all colors will work. Lots of beams and smoke. This is the band that will get them dancing.

Stage notes: Big opening with pulsing rear and side lights. *No stringer lights.* Most *active* stage visuals of any group.

Dance floor: Rotating colors and patterns—anything goes! (Save beacons and confetti canons for roller skater entrance)

Intellibeam: Show 'em what you got! Broad sweeps/pulsing patterns machine gun room with nonstop color, texture, and movement

Hollywood Horns: main band

The look: Lush and sophisticated. Wild and wonderful. Play the crowd. Open with stringer lights. Use black-outs between songs. Police beacons and confetti canons for roller skaters introduction. Rock 'n' roll specials for dancers.

Stage notes: Give every song a beginning, middle, and end. Keep adding specials, work the color combinations—less is more. Use followspots for color washes when not on vocals.

Dance floor: *Less is more* with romantic songs. *More is better* with up-tempo.

Intellibeam: Sweeps of giant stars at intro. Watch audience—don't overpower slow songs. Use every trick in the book for fast ones.

Chapter 4

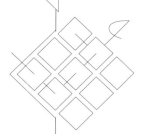

The Power of Color

How drab everyday life would be without color! Every time we see a rainbow, a garden bursting with spring flowers, or a ceiling swathed with hundreds of yards of brilliant color, we feel a surge of pleasure but we rarely stop to think why. Color not only brightens the days but commands attention visually and physically in almost every sphere of life. Its magical effect can make or break any room, especially a gala event at a function center, ballroom, or banquet hall. Color determines our moods, and even dictates the texture of elements to be combined with its hues. While line and form exert a steady influence in our lives, neither plays as dominant a role as color.

Most people know a little about color, but few have a trained sense or true understanding of the theories of color or methods of color coordination. These must be learned. Anyone interested in creating a particular mood at a special event *must* understand how colors work together, and the impact they have on the people attending the function.

Rearrangement

It's not only fun to rearrange color patterns, but a wonderful spur to creativity. Once you start, you find yourself wondering *"What else can I rearrange?"; "Suppose I tried changing this pattern . . . ?"; "There must be another way to do this."* Fortunately the urge to rearrange is as much an inborn trait as our sense of curiosity. If you observe small children, you would notice that they become absorbed in piling up plastic and wooden blocks in endless patterns, happily spending hours rearranging them and anyone with teenagers can't help but notice their love of rearranging their appearance! You'll see new hairstyles, new cosmetics, and quite dramatic changes in fashion.

People often enjoy shifting around furniture to create a new look. They'll stand and think, and stare around the room, then move a chair here and a table there in an attempt to make the room more functional.

Color can be endlessly experimented with and rearranged, and by applying a few basic color principles it is possible to come up with endless combinations that will completely change the ambience of the area. If, for example, a ballroom had a neutral color such as cream on the walls, it would be quite easy to move from a regal appearance (by picking up accents with green and purple) to a totally different warm, exciting effect by replacing the green and purple with red and orange-red.

The Reversal

Color, like most other things, can be reversed. So try the "What if . . . ?" game again. *What if I reversed this? What are the opposites? If I do this, is the contrast pleasing or discordant?* When hunting for a new color pattern, always do the unexpected—turn it around!

Combinations

It pays to think in terms of combinations when you're striving for an original or more pleasing effect. What colors can be combined? What will happen if you try an assortment? Do the unexpected. So what if certain colors are not usually combined? Maybe this will give you just the effect you want. Also remember sometimes you can't tell what works from little color swatches: you have to try big dramatic splashes of color, then stand back and judge the effect from a distance.

When you think about it, the rearranging/reversal/combination method will present many alternatives for use in design.

Almost every hour of the day, we are exposed to and influenced by color. Even an untrained eye can have a sense of what color can do, but with a little effort and concentrated thought on the subject, we can learn a lot more in a very short space of time. This extra understanding can have a dramatic effect on the way you use color to achieve an overall mood at your event.

In a design, color can be the magical ingredient that really "speaks" to observers. They absorb it without thinking, not understanding why they feel sophisticated, or energetic, or wildly happy and daring. By applying a few simple principles, you become a magician!

To the beginner, decisions about color can be scary, and sometimes confusing. Yet the whole business is intriguing and enticing. Once you try a few combinations and see the results, you feel a wonderful sense of power about this magical quality that transforms the ordinary house into a home; the office into pleasant surroundings; the dining room table into a gracious setting. Even a hospital can be transformed into a pleasant and tranquil place.

Every application of color is an extension of our personality. Psychologically, our senses react to color. Many of our reactions to color are associated with nature. Red and orange are warm, exciting colors associated with fire. Blues and greens immediately bring to mind the sea, the sky, and the countryside: coolness and quiet. Sunlit yellow exudes warmth and brightness; white is associated with purity and serenity, and mauves or violets suggest mystery.

When we have some understanding of how color influences mood and how important the viewer's reaction to color is, we are far better equipped to interpret an occasion. Even though some of today's brides choose a colorful bouquet, weddings and christenings still display predominantly white blooms.

In the home and in large reception areas, warm colors are more appropriate because they have the power to create an effect by closing in an area.

Cooler shades—blues and greens—have the effect of blending in surroundings, and therefore are a good choice for smaller foyers and rooms, since they don't subtract visually from the size of the room.

Darker colors have a weight associated with them. For example, a small area painted in black, blue, or purple would create a dramatic impact if placed in a very light colored space. More impact is achieved by careful and sparing use of weighty colors than by overuse.

A good rule of thumb is to use two-thirds of a light color against one-third of a darker color. The weight makes the darker colors look larger than the amount actually used.

As you can see, color has incredible power. It's something almost indefinable that you add to shape and size to get the feel you want. Remember, all colors appear together in nature, so be adventurous!

Color

Good design is possible without hours of studying a color chart, but color gives the arrangement lift and excitement. It plays an important part in the design and decor of any event, and must never be taken lightly. You can walk into a room that is completely coordinated with carefully themed decor, but if the colors fail to create an immediate positive impact, a lot of time has been wasted.

Harmonious color patterns delight us, discordant ones grate on our feelings. Handling color can be wonderfully pleasurable to the arranger and it adds that final distinctive touch to the finished composition.

Color has been used since the beginning of time, but it wasn't until 1667 that Sir Isaac Newton showed that color evolved from light, a fact he discovered when pursuing the subject of optics. He found that if a narrow beam of white light (for example, sunlight) was allowed to pass through a slit in a prism, it would produce a beautiful band of color. We now know this as the solar spectrum. The wavelengths of the rays of light are separated into the colors of the rainbow: red, orange, yellow, green, blue, indigo, and violet.

The Color Wheel

The color wheel is one of a designer's simplest yet most important tools. By studying the terms and the combinations on the color wheel, you'll easily see which harmonious color choices will dazzle and delight and which discordant patterns are likely to disturb or displease.

It is possible to create a balanced design without spending hours studying the color chart, but good use of color gives an arrangement vitality and excitement. It's certainly worth spending a few hours understanding the use of the color wheel.

On our color chart, the so-called primary colors—yellow, blue, and red—are placed equidistant from one another. Refer to the standard color wheel to examine this principle (Color Plate 4). Now study any three colors with the same distance and watch the trio of colors work visually. The secondary colors—green, violet, and orange—are placed halfway between their parent primary colors. Green is between yellow and blue; violet between blue and red; orange between red and yellow.

Tertiary colors are accents, obtained by combining a primary color with its neighboring secondary color: yellow with green, yellow with orange, blue with green, blue with violet, red with violet, or red with orange.

As we have already discussed, colors suggest various moods and it is important to consider these when planning your event.

Yellow is considered masculine, splendid, radiant, lively, and vivid. It's a sacred color when used as gold; suggests light and sunshine and even the slightest change in hue either increases or decreases its feeling of warmth. It makes a great choice for a room that is dark or shadowy, or to create a space that is sunny and bright. It is often used in hospitals to lift patients' emotions.

Green is nature's own color, suggestive of the renewal of life, tranquility, serenity, and hope. Although it is relatively neutral in its emotional effect, it also has a soothing effect on the color red, its complement.

Blue, the color of the sea and sky, is cool and subduing. Light blue is feminine and pretty; the darker shades are considered to be masculine. Violet takes on a dark and unattractive appearance under artificial light, so make sure to include tones of lighter blue and mauve as relief, especially for night functions.

Red is a strong and emotionally compelling color with the power to attract. This color is associated with passion, courage, virility, sex, defiance, rage, strife, and danger. It can be used alone to create distinctive moods with strong impact, or used effectively as an accent color. If used in large areas it can produce mental fatigue, and creates a longing for its complement, blue/green.

Orange has warmth and vibrancy. It should be used with discretion but can have tremendous appeal. It is not a color recommended for use in a child's bedroom because it is a stimulant. By the same token, it would be most appropriate used at an energetic function.

Purple is a color which suggests pomp, royalty, and richness. Considered a soothing color, it combines the attributes of both red and blue, the colors from which it originates.

White, on the other hand, can be placed effectively almost anywhere. It is a positive, stimulating, airy, light, and delicate color suggesting purity, chastity, innocence, and truth.

Advancing and Receding Colors

Draw an imaginary line straight through the yellow and its opposite, violet. The colors on the left of the chart, around the reds and oranges, are the advancing or warm colors because they appear to be relatively close to the viewer.

Red and orange are the most conspicuous and therefore the warmest colors. Advancing colors should be used to express impact, warmth, or closeness in a reception or ballroom area, because they appear to bring the walls in closer to the guests or audience. This would be useful if you have a large room with a small number of guests. Yellow, red, and orange help close the visual gap.

The **Halloween** party photographs (Color Plates 5 and 6) are a perfect example of the theatrical use of color. If you take a look at the right-hand side of the wheel, you'll see the receding colors of blues, mauves, and violets which give the illusion of distance, space, and coolness.

Refer now to the **Casino** opening photographs (Color Plates 7, 8, and 9) where royal blue, emerald green, mauves, and silver carry this scheme through quite well. The strong blue and green is offset by soft mauve and the tones of silver gray.

Useful Color Terms

Blending
This is the gradual merging of one color into another. For example, if yellow is the main color, other tones can be blended in by using cream stocks, mid-yellow tulips, or sunshine-yellow daffodils.

Bloom
This is the name given to the powdery substance often seen on the surface of fruit such as grapes and plums. It adds a soft, cloudy delicacy to a design that includes fruit and flowers, especially when arranged on a mirror for a dining or board room table.

Neutral Colors
As neutral colors, black, white, and gray combine well with all the other colors. In event planning, as in fashion, they are timeless because of their ability to be incorporated with other colors.

Spectrum Hues
This term distinguishes the name of a color such as yellow, blue, or green. The difference between colors is a difference in hue—yellow in green, blue in violet, pink in maroon, and so on.

Tints, Shades, and Tones
A hue that is lighter than the normal color (such as light blue) is known as a tint because white has been added. A hue that is darker than the normal color (such as dark blue) is called a shade because black has been added. When gray is added to a spectrum hue, its strength is reduced and it is called a tone.

Modified colors
These are the tints, shades, and tones of the spectrum hues, all of which are found in flowers and foliage.

Value
This refers to the lightness or darkness of color— light green or dark green, for example.

Intensity
This indicates the degree of brilliance of color. Orange has greater intensity than yellow-orange or gray-orange; red has greater intensity than pink.

Color Harmony
In order to make the most of the plant materials at hand, it is necessary to arrange them according to the well-established principles of color harmony outlined below. Understand and experiment with these principles, and then use them creatively.

Analogous harmony. This is the closely related harmony restricted to any one-third of the color chart but including one primary color. It may be, for instance, red-orange, orange, yellow-orange, and the primary color yellow, which are side by side and make up one-third of the color chart.

Direct complementary harmony. Any two colors directly opposite each other on the color chart are said to be in direct complementary harmony. Suggested combinations for floral arrangements are yellow and purple irises, red carnations and green holly, blue delphiniums and orange roses, all of which are eye-catching combinations.

Split complementary harmony. This is the effect gained in a three-color plan when two colors are adjacent to the direct complement of a particular hue, omitting the complement itself. An example is blue with red-orange and yellow-orange; or yellow with red-violet or blue-violet. Refer to the chart and play with the combinations to see what sort of effects can be created by using these combinations.

Monochromatic harmony. This refers to the principle of working from the lightest tone of one color through to the deepest possible shade of the same color. It is a favorite technique in floral design, particularly for stage, exhibition, or gala work.

There are other harmonies in the world of color, but these four will be the most useful in developing your schemes. If you have difficulty in finding plant materials in the colors you would like to use, remember that you can tie in the color using a container or prop.

Lighting and Color

Lighting was discussed in detail in Chapter 3, but its coexistence with color is worth discussing here.

As color is an important element of design, so is the impact of lighting. This will make or break your design because the way you use lighting will enhance or wash out your color selections.

When choosing the color you intend to use, it is essential to check out the selection using the lighting available in the area for which the event is designed. All different lighting sources, such as the most common fluorescent, incandescent, or low voltage, have different color values and temperatures. These alter the colors of the materials you intend to use.

Fluorescent is generally a very white, stark form of lighting, but different color temperature tubes are available, including color-corrected or daylight colors, which are less harsh than the standard fittings.

Incandescent fittings (the standard domestic fittings) have a color similar to daylight, although a little yellower. They will therefore cast a yellow wash over your color scheme.

Low voltage lighting such as the small spots and wall washing fittings, usually used in retail and commercial spaces, can be obtained in numerous colors.

You can see the implications. If selections are made using one type of light fitting but a different fitting is available in the area of your event, the colors could vary drastically.

Use clever highlighting to emphasize specific areas in your layout. Highlight or spotlight accent colors or floral displays to create interest, mystery, and drama, as well as to draw the viewers' eyes from one spot to the next. This is a great way to neutralize a dead area.

Since we are unable to select the perfect space all the time, adept use of color and lighting can help to conceal dead spots or areas that are best ignored, or which cannot be hidden using other methods. (See Figure 4.1.)

Colors at a Glance

Red

- Red is a powerful color with a strong influence in design.
- Tends to bring a room "in" because it's a heavy color. Lighten this heaviness with a soft red, maybe introduce gold.
- Move from orange reds to bluish red and velvety red.
- Some examples: fuchsia great in a mardi gras. For a Casablanca theme, go for orangey red for the warmth.

Orange

- Most popular colors in the orange range are warm, soft tonalities—apricot, salmon, peach, clay, coral.
- Blends well with a range of oranges and yellows.

Yellow

- The warmth and brightness of yellow is always popular; yellow-greens are a good choice.
- Use in conjunction with a yellow/orange palette

Green

- When using with blues, choose complementary shades of green: aqua, teal
- Green is safe to use anywhere because it is one of nature's own colors. Lots of ballrooms have fresh foliage, and the green in sets can complement that.

Blue

- Blue is a receding color. Be careful if you do a whole ballroom in blue. It can be rather cool. If you use nothing else but blue, make sure that you've got the right type of lighting.
- Gives the feeling of space.

Violet

- Tones of violet can be lovely, tranquil, and relaxing. Use tonalities from grape purples to periwinkles to lilacs and mauves.
- Works very well with yellow.

Gray

- Gorgeous to use and very safe, because it's a neutral. Can be either warm or cool.
- Good to use if you're inexperienced because it is failsafe.
- See Color Plate 10. The ceiling is completely swagged to complement the flowers featured in the wedding reception ballroom—the neutral tones of gray act in harmony with all surrounding colors.

Brown

- Useful for a natural, neutral influence; especially the warmer browns moving toward red.
- Works well with earthy, natural themes.

White

- White is a pivotal neutral and a very important key color.

Theme	Harmonies	Combination
Australiana	Split complement	Apricot, red, brick, tan
Riot in Rio	Analogous	⅓ of wheel, primary yellow
Starlight Night	Monochromatic	Pale, mid, dark blue
Alcatraz	Neutral	Gray white, blacks
Casablanca	Monochromatic	Deepest tone of orange to red, orange, tans
Tropical Fiesta	Analogous	Blue green, lime green
A Gala Affair	Direct complementary	Gold and silver blended
Rock'n'roll 50s and 60s	Split complementary	Blue with red-orange and yellow-orange. Red with yellow-green and green.
Egyptian	Opposite complement	Blues and orange
New Orleans	Analogous	Green, blue, violet

Figure 4.1. Overview of party colors. This is a guide for working with colors. Expand on it when creating your own themes.

Study some of the color plates and review the effect colors provide for the following themed evenings. The Night in the Orient (see Color Plate 6) is a corporate dinner where the primary color used was red. This Eastern theme certainly calls for the use of this intense color. Notice the red sequined dragon on the black velvet wall. This 16-ft decorative unit with scaling in gold makes a statement and this concept is carried through to the stage and entrance, table linens, and tabletops.

The bright table linens are in red cotton with matching napkins, trimmed in red satin ribbon and gold cording. The detailing of these small accessories adds a high quality finish to the look. The 6-ft centerpiece shown in Color Plate 11 is made from three red lacquered pieces of bamboo strapped together to form a tripod. Fabric and florals tip the top. Oriental influence carries through to the use of umbrellas, fans with gold foiled fabric, red silk, and cheesecloth fabric for draping and swagging.

To complement the powerful influence of this color, waiting staff were dressed in authentic Chinese/Eastern dress such as the traditional happy coats and tasselled hats.

The bars and serving areas would also represent the merchant influence of the Orient and would be dressed in Oriental style. Refer to the conceptual art of Freddrik Campioni Garcia—Creative Art Director of Theme Travelers, San Antonio, Texas—in Chapter 6 (Figures 6.1 and 6.2).

The lighting and sound reinforce the Oriental theme as a fortune teller and Eastern dancers arrive to entertain the guests in this marketplace atmosphere.

Alcatraz—Escape is Impossible!

This event shows color contrasts in grays, black, white, and brown. An event with a difference!

The guests (or new inmates) arrive in prison buses, and have cocktails on the grounds of the venue (a museum is a good choice) to the accompaniment of a musical trio.

The scene changes when the prison doors are opened by the entrance guard, Constable Hefty, to admit the new prisoners. As they pass through security, Sergeant Thumbs takes fingerprints, Constable Snap takes the mug shot, and Constable Cuffs distributes the prison numbers.

As guests move inside, doors clang, sirens wail, and fog swirls around them. Blue spotlights circle the interior as the inmates are seated for dinner behind bars. The band plays Jailhouse Rock while the dancers imitate the lyrics.

The bench-style tables are clothed in charcoal gray and white stripe. (Figure 4.2). The tabletop features prison bars graduating in 3-ft to 5-ft heights, centered between two tables. The centerpiece, a great source of amusement, consists of buns and loaves of bread of all sizes which conceal chains, cardboard cut-out escape tools, mini stacks of potatoes with peeler, chains, wire, handcuffs, candles, and ball and chain. The individual laminated placemats (which the guests take as souvenirs) are in the form of a newspaper's front page featuring prison and company news. (Figure 4.3). A mock entree of a small can of baked beans with a slice of dry bread and a plastic spoon preceeds a lavish four-course dinner served by waiters in prison garb, coat, and cap.

Warden Grimly and his security guards occasionally throw a misbehaving prisoner or would-be escapee into "the hole", the electric chair, or the stocks. The ever-ready photographer snaps these mug shots on film for the record and for guests' enjoyment.

After the main course, the prison concert showcases the talents of some top performers and dancers, backed by a big band. Throughout the evening the

Figure 4.2. (above) *Escape is impossible.* A tabletop with a difference. Potatoes, onions, potato peelers, ferns, bread, cutout tools, rope, chains, gangster cutouts. The timber prison bars painted gray are securely centered on two six-foot trestles. The arrangement is long, low, and narrow, thus providing appropriate space for dinnerware and glasses.

Figure 4.3. (left) *The total look, even for Alcatraz.* The placemat is in keeping with the event theme so note the lettering—the key wording being Birdman.

The background of the photo shows tinned food with a blackened tin which holds a candle, rope, and potatoes hot glued together. The tin of beans, dried bread, and tin cup are a mock first course. Don't be alarmed. They are whisked away after two minutes and replaced with the delicious appetizers and a glass of wine.

large movie screen shows old gangster and prison movies, together with an intermittent focus on the prison guests.

The stage was set between two huge floor-to-ceiling scaffolding watchtowers (Figure 4.4). The Heathcatraz sign incorporates the company name (C.E. Heath) at the time this staff Christmas party was held. The company name has since changed to HIH Winterthur. Figure 4.5 shows the overall design format of an unforgettable corporate staff party.

The Italian Affair—An Evening In a Winery

See Color Plates 12, 13, and 14. This event was held in an isolated but divine location in the Victorian Vineyards in Australia. The old homestead and grounds proved to be a wonderful venue. The color scheme used was red and green in opposite complements.

Casablanca

See Color Plates 15 and 16. New themes and concepts always head the list as every event planner wants something new, different, and original. There is always new product but event planners can also draw on what has been done in the past by revising, revamping and re-presenting the change in a different format. For example, this Casablanca scheme is the result of hours of research.

The Casablanca concept, done in a monochromatic scheme, entailed quite a lot of research on the country, people, and the well-known Rick's Café. Predominantly, the streets are filled with beggars, thieves, and pickpockets in a market-style environment. This becomes the base for developing the pre-drinks area. Other elements included palms, windows, arches, terracotta and earth coloring, lamps, and bells.

The decor of the ballroom involved wall covering, so instead of hanging black velvet which is the usual procedure, canvasses are made to measure. In this case three cloths 40 ft in length with an 18-ft drop were used on the stage and left and right walls, interspersed with the black velvets. The full cover in monochromatic tones of buttercup, orange, and brick into tans was an outstanding effect.

The background of this photograph shows the style of scenic art that was created. The arches and shadowing bring dimension into the total look. To create canvasses of this size, space must be available. Some artists prefer to hang the canvas, pull it taut, and paint from there. In this case, however, appropriate short-term space was rented, the floor area was lined with inexpensive plywood sheeting 8 ft × 4 ft and the sheets were taped together with gaffer tape as

Figure 4.4. Scaffolding as décor. This themed party is ideal for using the scaffolding that is normally used for staging as part of the decor. The exposure of the beams is quite fitting for an Alcatraz party due to its prison environment. A wooden frame, covered with canvas and lettered, serves as the sign.

well as securing this base to the floor with gaffer. The next step was to lay down the canvas and secure it the same way. The sketching with artist's chalk begins. A canvas like this can take up to five days to complete because of the exacting detail and size.

Table linens complement the scheme by the use of color. The terracotta full length cloths and chair covers are used with a patterned overlay in terracotta and royal blue print. The timber candlesticks are a perfect accessory to complete the tabletop look.

An additional point of interest came with the waiters wearing a contrasting apron color of soft red stripe with Moroccan bells pinned at the knee level. As they walked, the ringing carried through the air.

Figure 4.5. The prison event—overall room. This venue seats 800 guests.

For this style of event, walkways between the table aisles are created for staff servicing. Notice the screens on either side of the stage and the heavy use of scaffolding that becomes part of the props. This, of course, is planned and designed to give this effect.

The background behind the stage is painted in gray, white/black, and splashes of tan. The timber chair also tied in with the look.

Chapter 5

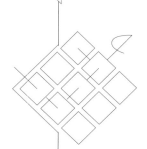

Innovative Design and Decor

Good parties become great parties if imagination can run free and create a theme. The party becomes so much more: a truly special event that will seize and hold the imagination of everyone invited.

Any event that is planned can evoke a sense of wonder and joy in the lucky guests. By spending some time brainstorming, a really memorable idea can emerge. By being creative, design elements can be selected that won't be too expensive. Color, discussed in Chapter 4, is one design element that can make a huge difference for little cost. Once it's time to decide on a theme, discard all those ideas that are too hard, too expensive, or inappropriate. Then take another look and whittle it down to one very possible, very achievable event.

Remember, when a party is created, *fun* is packaged. Themed parties are broad in concept: lighting technicians, stage builders, event designers and caterers are only a few of the people who work together to create an event.

A special event may be anything from a small family gathering to a large corporate event. A themed party could be staged for a fund-raiser, a charity ball, a gala launch, or just for the sheer fun of it!

Every event designer likes to imagine that guests will stand and stare in delight when they first see what has been created for them. After all, a lot of time, energy, and money goes into putting together that final effect. It's worth spending a little *extra* time to make sure that every element of that design faithfully reflects the vision.

In Chapter 1, the basic elements of art and design were examined. Those elements of design will be reviewed here and can be applied to create the overall look. The handy reference grid provided in Chapter 6 shows how to achieve an integrated design for a themed party, function, or event.

At all times, think **creativity**. One simple creative technique for exposing ideas that are both marketable and functional is called **"The Three R's of Event Planning."**

This technique is built around people's love of reliving the past. Most people enjoy being given the chance to visit a fantasy world for a few hours; perhaps a time when life seemed simpler or more carefree. Of course, this probably wasn't really the case, but escapism is what it is all about!

The three R's (**R**evise, **R**evamp, and **R**epresent) mean that we look at alternative ways to make what is old, *new* again by adding contemporary touches that give just the right impression. This technique simply turns back the clock to **revise** the event *styles* of yesteryear. **Revamp** the look and then **represent** the decor to transform the venue. At the same time be cost-conscious, creative, and chic.

Up to the Challenge?

When designing a theme, block out any negativity and stay positive, accepting the challenge of any approach that leads to creative thinking. Figure 5.1 shows a creative chart that meets the challenge, along with the chart for the 10-Point Plan in the Creative Process (Figure 5.2).

Mental Blockers and How to Fight Them

There's always a certain amount of fear connected with coming up with a workable theme. Accept it and

Curiosity. Question everything you do in design by asking **how, when,** and **why.** Start and end with a question because that assists with personal development.

Hunt. Hunt for new ways; strive for a fresh approach with the same or similar methods. Think "obvious," but be prepared to try the *un*obvious in design.

Application. Applying your skills to new thoughts in this *un*obvious way means you have to stretch like a piece of elastic, so be conscious of the change that it may bring.

Listen. Listen to your peers in the hope that they will inspire. Accept their point of view regarding design and creativity.

Learn. Learn to use the knowledge they have shared as a springboard for self-extension and development.

Expose. Expose yourself to other art mediums that tie in with art—e.g. pottery, painting, sculpture, and event planners.

Note. Note your likes and dislikes in design, then endeavor to get the dislikes working *for* you, not *against* you.

Grow. Grow by allowing the creative thinking process to be a daily exercise. Accept the fact that it will take time: anything worthwhile is never gained in a hurry. Allow time for growth.

Evaluate. Evaluate your thoughts by critiquing your work, learning to analyze, evaluate, and judge honestly. Avoid the mental block called "ego."

Figure 5.1 The challenge chart. This one word does what it says: it *challenges* you to grow both personally and professionally.

The 10-Point Plan in the Creative Process

1. **Offset.** Eliminate any negative thinking. Putting up mental barriers such as *"The client won't like it." "The color is wrong." "It will never work."* are restrictions from the outset.
2. **Reflect.** The process for developing something new often comes from looking back on what has already been done either by the individual or peers. *Look back* actually means refer back to an earlier job position. Once the delayed shock is worn off, *reflect* on the materials and method utilized. Years later the material can be used but the method will surely show dramatic change. The skill of designing comes from having the ability to use materials in many different ways. It is what we create with what we have.
3. **Isolate.** When creating a new theme, gala evening, corporate picnic, or company anniversary dinner, it is necessary to block out time to actually think about every detail that will ultimately make up the whole event. Now *isolate* and make time to be free of disturbances, i.e., no phones or people dropping in. Cut off from everything and everybody. Accept the time and take the time to think.
4. **Grasp.** Researching materials is of the utmost importance with the creative process. Refer to books and magazines, if resources are available at home, in the office or studio. Alternatively, the library is the other source of information. Over the years an enormous range of books, people, children's books, color, periods design, etc. can be built up as well as industry magazines. It doesn't matter if they are outdated. Resist discarding them. Without a doubt there will be one thought, or prop that can be worked to *identify* a theme. Disney books are quite inspirational, along with books on theater and classic movies.
5. **Navigate.** From all this browsing/research jot down every possible and impossible idea that appears. It is necessary to build the mental bank with every idea that suffices. Avoid tossing anything aside in this initial building of a theme. At this point, hold a brainstorming session with a team of people. Sit everyone down with pen and paper with the topic written at the top of the page. Allow 10 minutes without speaking and in point form only, jot down the thoughts that arise. Next step is to allow each person to tell the others. Thirty or forty points may be written on paper now, and it is time to sit and apply the D & E Formula (the discard and embrace method). Discard ideas that are not workable or unusable and embrace the three or four parts that will work and build a full concept from a base of ideas that can be worked and used. *Navigate* through this approach and practice to fine tune judgment. The mental exercise also keeps the mind open and not so ready to reject concepts that may work.
6. **Appraise.** The site becomes the next critical point and this must be sighted regardless of the size of the job. Remember, good things happen when they are planned. Discordant things happen on their own. So take the time to do it right. Knowing the advantages and disadvantages of the venue is a must before going into the job. Refer to the site inspection chart and use it as a reference. It points out three elements to record: length and width of the venue, ceiling height, as well as the lowest ceiling point. Check on power as well as entrances, exits, ramps, and parking access and facilities. Check also for kitchen and equipment. Also availability of tables and chairs. The necessity lies in *appraising* the venue and its components. Always view the venue. It will save you money.
7. **Levels.** The size of the room and height of the ceiling does determine the scale of the props and set decor that is to be used in the room. For example, if the ceiling is low, props must remain in scale with the room. Alternatively, the venue that is of considerable size requires props that are placed on different *levels* or rather outsized in construction.
8. **Impress.** Key features are needed to bring an impressive look to the room and it is equally important to know what to leave out, rather than what to put in. Key features indicate that one or two props are going to be heavily featured throughout the décor rather than have a mismatch of individual units.
9. **Tone.** Color and mood is one of the most important components of themed decor.
10. **Yardstick.** A measurable method to introduce is the contractors/team/client post-evaluation questionnaire.

Figure 5.2. This is a comprehensive working guide for creative development.

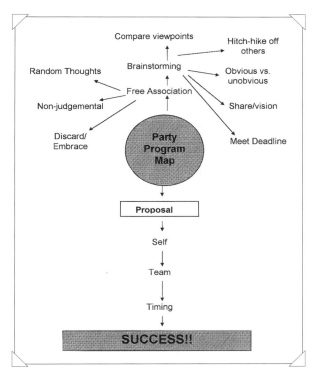

Figure 5.3. Lena's party program map. This is the flow chart I use to develop my client's events. It establishes clear lines of thought.

get past it. Don't allow blockers to start coming out. Blockers are negative thoughts like *It'll never work; It'll be too expensive; This is far too outrageous; The colors won't be right; I don't have enough time to pull it together; The client won't like it,* and *I'll get back to you.*

Avoid a negative approach to theme designing. Adopt a positive, active outlook. Head for a library or pull out reference books and look at what has been done in the past. Use the *Three R's* approach and then make a huge effort to stretch the mind and think about the *unobvious.*

Brainstorm by discussing ideas with a team or peers. Don't discount the possibility of bouncing ideas off someone in a related industry. For example, a good friend in the fashion industry may throw a concept in the ring and start the ball rolling. Try to think of how to utilize the idea.

Discard what's already been done and work through what hasn't. Jot down every thought without judging it. Free association works well. Remember, nobody can simply sit down and switch on the "idea factory."

Once you have accumulated ideas, start sifting through them. Discard whatever doesn't seem such a hot idea on second viewing; embrace what works well. Allow plenty of time for this process: don't leave it until the week before the event. Meet all deadlines with designers and suppliers. The old cliché "lead by example" is a must.

The party program map shown in Figure 5.3 is really the outcome of brainstorming with your team or peers. When a group of people sits around the room and creative thoughts are verbalized (with one person recording those thoughts on paper), all comments should be nonjudgmental because as many thoughts as possible must be gathered and collated. With a process like this the obvious may be stated but the unobvious may also surface and ultimately lead everyone to the final goal of sharing the vision.

A Dickens Christmas

For nearly two thousand years, Christmas has been a joyous religious festival and is celebrated as a happy family time worldwide. Goodwill is expressed in many different ways: the exchange of greeting cards, exchange of gifts either in person or across the miles, and of course, the family meal.

At this time of year, where do the new ideas and new looks come from? Each year in display houses, department stores, or floral studios, anything from a Christmas angel to a penguin; from a sequined bauble to a patterned bow is seen.

The question "Where does creativity start?" is best answered by learning to build mental muscles, because everyone has untapped talent waiting to be exposed and exercised.

The inexperienced designer tends to put too many ideas into one theme. For example, when thinking about decorating the home for the festive period, it would be inadvisable to have different colors and materials in every room. In fact, it is best to confine the decorative components to perhaps two or three varying forms and two colors.

Towering branches of willow sprayed in gold with decorative gold apples and pears with gold netting and cording would be ideally placed in a hotel foyer. Alternatively, the dining tables could display long, low arrangements with the decorative materials of apples, pears, cord, and net repeated. Take a concept and carry it through a room or function center.

Think about expanding the material into other decorative accessories. For example, the gilded apple becomes a candle votive or burner for the table, while the golden pear is decorated with leaves, berries, and bow to give to a guest.

The first thing to acquire from the venue or hotel is a floor plan of the room. This provides length, width, and ceiling height.

The tables are usually positioned around the dance floor, which is generally placed in front of the stage.

Color Plate 21 shows that the decorative trees are simply constructed from standard eight by four

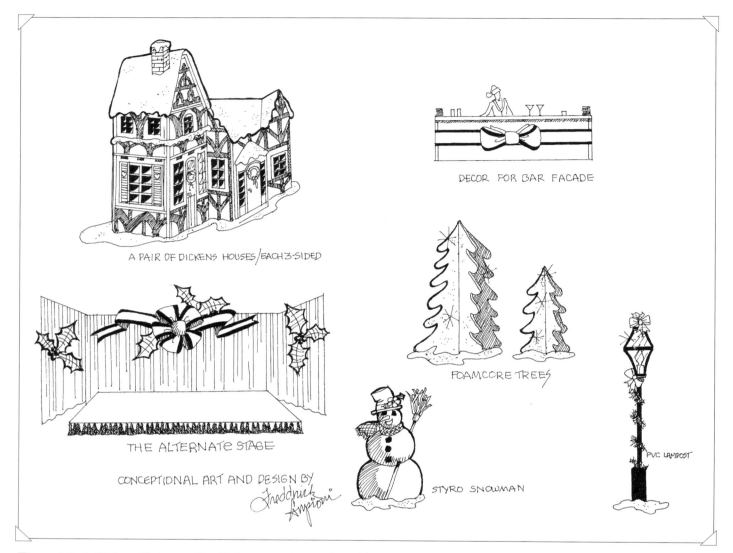

A PAIR OF DICKENS HOUSES/EACH 3-SIDED

DECOR FOR BAR FACADE

THE ALTERNATE STAGE

FOAMCORE TREES

CONCEPTIONAL ART AND DESIGN BY

STYRO SNOWMAN

PVC LAMPOST

Figure 5.4. A Dickens Christmas. Detailed conceptual art such as this is a winning element when presenting to your client.

sheets of plywood. The smaller trees require one sheet, while the larger ones require two to three sheets. It is important to remember that decorative units used for themed events must be life-size or larger. Once the plywood is cut into the tree shape, apply two coats of paint to give the appropriate finish, especially if the trees are sprinkled with diamond and dust glitter.

The trees are arranged around the four walls of the ballroom to surround the guests with fantasy and festive decor. As the color plate shows, the effect is quite beautiful as the lighting technicians soften the white by adding soft touches of pink lights. Lights are nestled at the base of the tree angled to reflect upward to the tree peak.

The rounded 6-ft tables are covered with white floor-length cloth with the fitted white cover that pulls over the chair. The centerpiece features Christmas decor and shows a festive collection of seasonal items.

The tree decor theme is repeated when incorporated into an urn placed in the foyer or reception area that leads into the party itself. Crisp white is used throughout the room from wall decor to white flowers on the tables, with accents of red and green satin bows on the back of the chairs. The concept is, of course, to take limited decor elements but work them to the limit. The conceptual art (Figure 5.4) of a Dickens' Christmas shows the stage set of Dickens' house, the festive bar, foam core trees, with the alternate stage design and flicker interest points of lamp and snowman.

Western Showdown

What is it about a good old western showdown that gets everybody involved? Maybe the whole atmosphere is so exciting that worries are left behind, or maybe everyone has common memories about the heroes in cowboy films, riding into town to fight the bad boys and save the townsfolk.

Whatever the reason, the tone is set for the evening when guests walk into the Wild West environment and are greeted by Chief Sitting Bull in full headdress. With toe-tapping music and energetic line-dancers on the dance floor, the energy level starts to rise.

Picture this scene. The guests have just walked into this Wild West fantasy. Chief Sitting Bull makes everyone feel welcome, and presents them with a fun token of the Wild West. The event will be even more memorable if the token is something actually wearable—a cowboy hat, an Indian headdress, a bandanna, or a squaw headdress!

The guests pass underneath a double-sided Wild West sign made of solid wood to enter into the town. Figure 5.5. shows the room decor. Throughout the room, positioned on the floor, five free-standing tepees help to set the scene. Each stands 8 feet to 10 feet high, with timber supports, a canvas cover painted with native stick figures, *and* a special smoke effect. Straw bales, trees, and wheels are also featured. (Figure 5.6)

The eye-catching stage features a canvas saloon backdrop which faithfully represents the period: bar, stools, pictures, lamps, stairway. Even the upright piano looks as though it belongs! The stage apron is covered and painted to tie in with the set and features more hay bales and wagon wheels.

The walls become a masterpiece of illusion. Painted on about 300 feet of wood panelling is scenic art showing banks, bakeries, saloons, the general store, livery and stables, and of course, Wells Fargo and the undertaker's office! These decorative wooden flats created from 8 ft × 4 ft sheets of plywood are specially tailored to fit the height of walls to give a perfect overall fit and sense of unity. (Figure 5.7).

Figure 5.5. Wild West—The total look. The overall look of the Western theme is shown with the township as a backdrop. Kegs, bales, dried grasses, Wild West painted cloths, and centerpieces are created to match the theme. Chair covers are tied with hessian sashes.

Figure 5.6. (above) The teepee concept can be displayed in the room with straw bales, wagon wheels, and trees as complements.

Authentic western decor is seen everywhere: hay bales, supply/grain bags, fiberglass cactus trees, Indian rugs, barrels, and wagon wheels. The tables are set behind corral fencing, painted in earth and terracotta tones. The table centerpieces will be one of three different heights, but at no time will the view of the entertainers be obscured. Who would want to miss the Dolly Parton lookalike, or the actors playing John Wayne or Chief Sitting Bull?

The stunning centerpieces are so authentic that they could be taken home. Created in frontier style, they feature grasses, bark, felt, leather, beads, weeds, cordifolia, blades of ginger, pumpkins, onions, vines, and moss. The decorative cutouts of cowboy hats, boots, and a mini-cactus add to the mood. A final touch is the votive candles inserted into hollowed-out miniature pumpkins. Figure 5.8 features table centerpieces and the large canvas backdrop. Notice the irregularity of the canvas hanging. A royal blue background brings color to the room and allows the church steeple, trees, and teepees to stand out.

The glass wall of this venue is covered with black velvet draping, and at a set time is drawn back to reveal the Indians and buffalo just outside. As the evening progresses, a top female country and western singer and actors play the parts of the Saloon Madam, cowboys, Indians, and various town personalities. There's also the western support band and a feature dance band. Everyone will go home plumb tuckered out, but ready to talk for weeks about their night in the Wild West!

Wild West conceptual art is shown in Figure 5.9 while buffet and bar booths are featured in Figure 5.10.

1945 Victory Party

For those born in 1945, these decorations will celebrate the Victory years, as well as their birthdays. This is also an excellent theme for a corporate dinner. The basic colors will be—of course!—red, white, and blue, and swathes of these colors are draped over the walls, creating a gala look.

A cutout of Betty Grable (made of foam core and painted), the most famous pin-up girl of the twentieth century, shows some leg and looks over her shoulder at the entrance. Flags everywhere help to sustain that Victory mood! (Figure 5.11).

On the walls, black material is draped from ceiling to floor, giving that authentic "blacked-out" feeling of the war years. All around the walls of the room are decorative cutouts of planes, guns, and tanks of World War II vintage, and the ceilings are

Figure 5.8. The overall effect of the Wild West. The tables are in place against the background of the Wild West theme party. Floor length black cloths are used with an overlay in Western print. Black chair covers complement the look with chair sashes in colorful hessian. The tripod centerpieces make a statement with the tall grasses and pumpkins, candles, and weeds complete the look.

festooned with camouflage nets. Large blown-up photographs of famous land and sea battles make guests feel that they are in that era.

The tables, alternately covered in red, white, and blue, catch the eye and really stand out against the gray, black, army green, khaki, and browns of the room. An alternative would be to do the linens in army khaki. This depends entirely on the look you want for the room. The khaki is subdued and blends in with the sets and props while the red, white, and blue combination tends to make a statement and adds

Figure 5.7. (opposite) Wild West decor. The plywood paneling, which is free standing against the interior walls of the venue, is painted in detail to depict the Wild West years. The stores of this Western era show the saloon, the undertaker, followed by the Wells Fargo Bank, and stables. The coloring is muted and a combination of gray, washed beige, tan, white, light blue, and old gold is featured in this theme party décor.

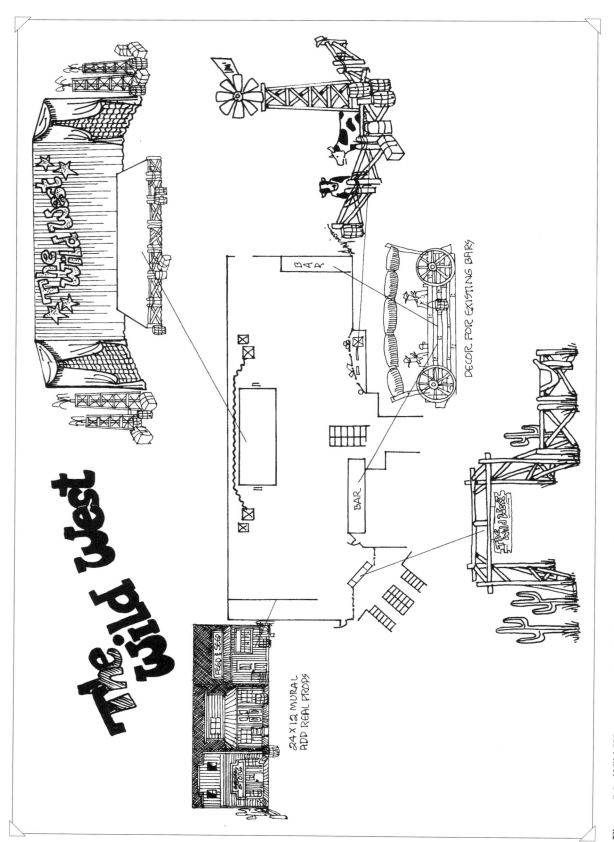

Figure 5.9. Wild West conceptual art helps capture your client.

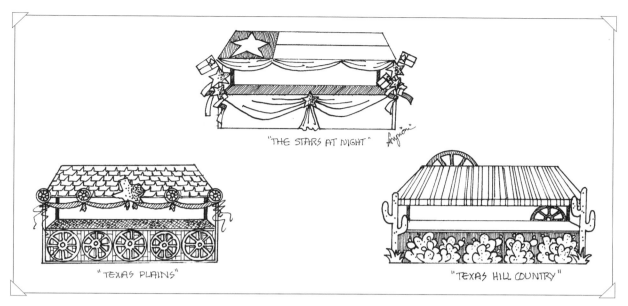

"THE STARS AT NIGHT"

"TEXAS PLAINS"

"TEXAS HILL COUNTRY"

Figure 5.10. Conceptual art of these Wild West buffets shows variation for food service stations.

Figure 5.11. Betty shows a leg. The entrance to a hotel venue shows a display of flags, huge palms, and red, white, and blue fabric door swagging with the decorative stars and the curving cutout of Betty Grable. The effect of the fabric used shows good coverage at the double doorways.

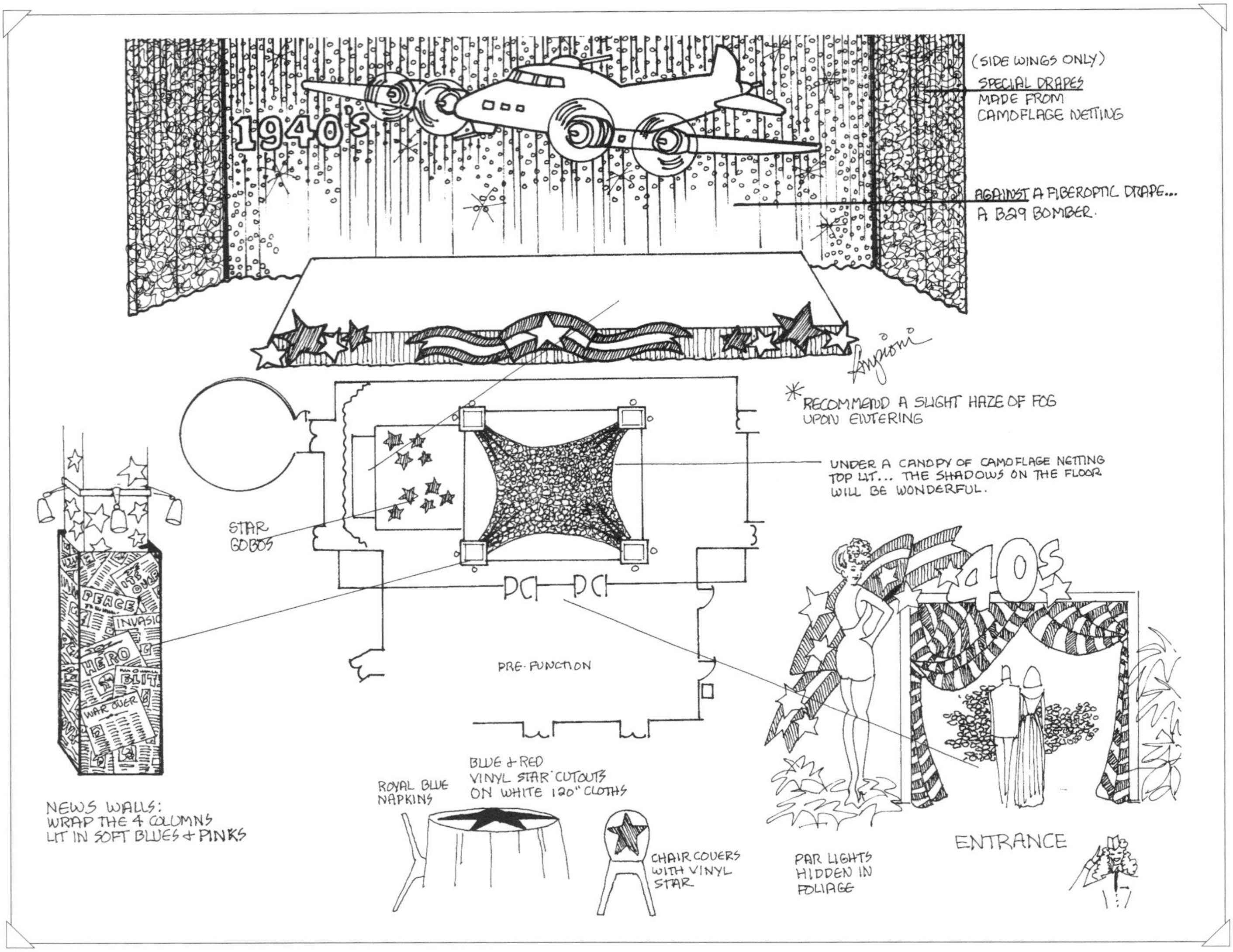

Figure 5.12. 1940s Victory Party conceptual art. No detail is left to chance. The room columns are dressed to herald the news.

color and lift to the room. See Color Plates 17, 18, and 19 showing three photos of the 1945 Victory party.

The table centerpieces draw admiring comments and curious looks. They're all based on genuine 1940s army paraphernalia sourced and purchased from army disposal stores: machine gun bullet boxes, field telephones, drink mugs, cups and cooking utensils, bayonets, and oil lamps; decorated with flags, wire netting, barbed wire, and masses of red carnations. The napkin rings are decorated with mini flags and matching ribbons.

The stage and ceiling add the final realistic effects: a large model 1940s plane painted and suspended from the ceiling brings home the reality of the war years.

With singers crooning, and character actors dressed in authentic army gear and forties dresses, guests dined, joined in the Victory celebrations, and kept celebrating until the wee small hours! (See Figure 5.12 for the Conceptual Artwork and Diagrams of Props.).

Roaring Twenties

During the period of Prohibition in the 1920s, drinking was illegal in the United States. So naturally people went underground to the so-called speakeasies, illegal drinking clubs. The most famous of these was Chicago's Cotton Club and to get in, you needed a password.

Guests will have an evening of fun and surprises if the Cotton Club is used as a theme for the event. First, guests are offered cocktails outside the ballroom, then ushered in through the funeral parlor which forms the "front" for the club. As patrons dressed in black and white (as instructed on the invitations) are guided past the caskets, candles, and floral arrangements, they'll be frisked by Al Capone and his hoods before being admitted to the ballroom, decorated to represent the Cotton Club.

Inside, ongoing entertainment is provided by gangsters, showgirls, and a big band. The crowd will dance the Charleston until around 11:45 or so, when the police will raid the joint and herd everyone together, ready to haul them off to jail.

Gaiety, glamour and gangsters make this a popular evening for all. The authentic 1920s decor will include full black interior, 1920s screens and pedestals with ferns and feathers, a stage setting from the 1920s, and table covers in black and white. The stunning tabletops feature perspex arrangements with white ostrich feathers, roses, gangster hats, cards, cap guns, and novelties. See the Cotton Club stage (Figure 5.13) and one centerpiece shown in Figure 5.14.

highly stylized dragon backdrop with exquisite oriental umbrellas to the forefront. The band has an oriental influence, and the serving staff are all dressed in authentic Chinese/Eastern dress such as happy coats or full regalia.

The bright table covers feature bamboo and silks, and the 6-ft high centerpieces with their silk, umbrellas, fans, exotic blooms, peacock feathers, and candles catch the eye of every guest.

Everywhere, the decor suggests images of the East with fans and rickshaws. The bars and serving areas are designed to represent the merchant influence of the orient. Even the ceiling features silk and cheesecloth swagging.

The lighting and sound reinforce the Oriental theme as a fortune teller and Eastern dancers arrive to entertain the guests. Everyone is delighted with their miniature giveaways of Eastern ornaments and an Asian good luck scroll.

Night in the Orient

Ah, the mystery of the East, a favorite with corporate clients. See Color Plate 11; the stage features a

An Evening In Paris

This event recreates the atmosphere of the Moulin Rouge.

Figure 5.13. The Cotton Club stage. The Roaring Twenties is always a popular theme with the corporate client and appealing to the guest. Black and white is strongly featured in signage and screens made from sheets of white foam core. White ostrich feather trees complement this look while black and white chair covers create the necessary strength required with masses of red roses on the stage apron. This period is known by the red rose and carnation.

Figure 5.14. Cotton Club centerpiece. The gangster hat acts as a base for this themed centerpiece. A hole is cut in the top of the hat and the bowl and foam is hidden under it to hold the feather, gun, and orchid firmly in position.

As the guests enter, they'll find the walls blacked out with draping to provide the optimum contrast for the flamboyant Parisian can-can dancers, cut from foam board and jazzed up for the occasion with theatrical paint, glitter, and net frills. Theatrical paint is used because of the strength of the color and the intensity of the paint.

The stage displays the impressive Eiffel Tower, and the Moulin Rouge club sign, suspended over the heads of the musicians, provides a dramatic focal point (See Color Plate 20.). Masses of plotted plants and florals are used to decorate the apron of the stage. The pink, purple, and blue ostrich feathers in huge urns around the room add to the decadent effect that guests will enjoy.

The tables are dressed in black lamé cloths with silver overlays and boast a tabletop mirror to reflect the 2–4 ft high Eiffel Towers placed in the center of each table. Because the tabletop Eiffel Towers are beautifully detailed and so close to the guests, they tend to become the conversation piece of the evening. Surrounding the towers are crisp pink roses and assorted ferns, coupled with candles that give a wonderful glow. Napkins are trimmed with a bow and feathers to complete the setting.

The lighting is subdued, but versatile enough to create dramatic effects during the cabaret showtime.

Chapter 6

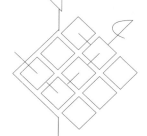

Theme Creations

To achieve a totally memorable and successful evening, theme creators need to experience a special kind of energy. They need not only to conceive of an illusion, but to plan, design, and organize it in such a way that they bring that illusion to reality for their guests.

Selecting the actual theme is not the easiest task. It helps to ask questions based on the 4 W's:

What is the event for?
When will it be held?
Who are the guests?
Where is it to be staged?

Once you have the answer to these questions, look at the theme party menu and choose . . .

Some Theme Party Ideas

Riot in Rio . . .

A hot and spicy evening surrounded by the lushness of the tropics. Picture parrots, splashes of vibrant color and reggae bands to give guests that holiday feeling. Think warm Latin nights. See Figure 6.1—imagine royal blues, orange signage for the words "Rio" and "Carnivale," a yellow pineapple, a rose pink watermelon, a multi-color parrot, and green pear—this stage spells *impact*. A Riot in Rio theme sets the mood for this Latin American evening. The theatrical lights on the back lighting rig also show rays of light that complement the decor. The decorative units are made of foam core and are ideal for transporting because of their light weight.

The trees in Figure 6.2 make a wonderful prop for a number of parties. Certainly Rio Carnivale . . . and extend the thinking and take it beach side. The decor fruits add the feature and finish.

Figure 6.1. Rio stage set.

Figure 6.2. A collection of green glittered trees for Rio.

Champagne and the Gala . . .

Guests gaze around wide-eyed at a room full of champagne bubbles, spectacular flowers, and twinkling fairy lights—a popular event staged with glitter, glamour, and sophistication. A gala skyline on the elevated stage shown in Figure 6.3 displays good use of straight and askewed lines which are the basis of a good design. The fairy lights silhouette the outline which shows a series of shapes. Colored in gold, silver, and black, this trio of color creates a dramatic look. The centerpiece of gilded palms is elevated well above the heads of guests providing good sight lines to the stage.

Figure 6.3. (below) Gala skyline.

Plate 1.
Foliage Backdrop.
A foliage measuring 50 ft x 16 ft is massed with leaves and flowers and then threaded with lights—chicken wire is the base. All the foliage is secured with wire. The backdrop is made in panels to ensure easier handling.

Plate 2.
Floor Lighting with Stage Columns.
Dance floors lit in this fashion create an exciting look for guests entering the room—especially if the scrolls of light move slowly. Various patterns and moves will be designed by the technical producer; however, always experiment with this at sound check time to ensure that the look is fitting with the total concept. Notice the wall of five pedestals that back the stage—this is a stunning effect.

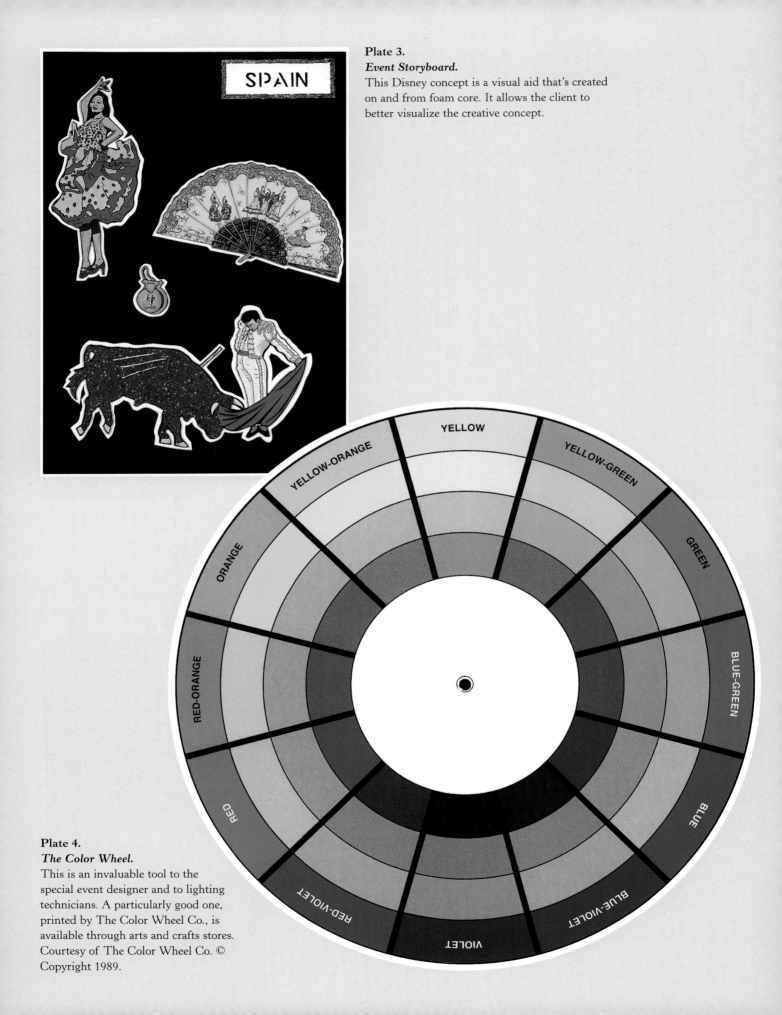

Plate 3.
Event Storyboard.
This Disney concept is a visual aid that's created on and from foam core. It allows the client to better visualize the creative concept.

SPAIN

YELLOW
YELLOW-ORANGE
YELLOW-GREEN
ORANGE
GREEN
RED-ORANGE
BLUE-GREEN
RED
BLUE
RED-VIOLET
BLUE-VIOLET
VIOLET

Plate 4.
The Color Wheel.
This is an invaluable tool to the special event designer and to lighting technicians. A particularly good one, printed by The Color Wheel Co., is available through arts and crafts stores. Courtesy of The Color Wheel Co. © Copyright 1989.

Plate 5

Plates 5 and 6.
A Halloween Story.
This highly decorative corporate event displays a total look concept of Halloween. The walls are canvassed out from floor to ceiling, and scenic artwork creates a spectacular event. The theatrical use of color was employed here with oranges, reds, and purple dramatically featured throughout the room. Skeletons, ghosts, black cats, and witches all attended the party.

Plate 6

Plate 9

Plate 7

Plate 8

Plates 7, 8, and 9.
A Casino Opening.
This hokka was one of the largest brought into Australia for the Cairns Casino opening in Queensland. Refer to the discussion of the event in Chapter 11. Venables Catering Entertainment of Sydney contracted me to design the gala for them. In keeping with the environment, blues, greens, and mauves were featured, and masses of shells, perspex, candles, orchids, and fabrics were utilized throughout. The fairy lights from the ceiling were cradled in blue and green cellophane to reflect a colored glow. This was a massive project that took 10 days to set up and involved the work of myself and 11 florists.

Plate 10.
The Wedding Reception.
Soft grays and pinks were used
throughout this room—even
extending to the ceiling, where over
1,500 yards of silver foil and gray
silk fabric, plus 1,200 yards of fairy
lights, were applied. Tables displayed
a gray satin floor-length cloth with a
silk brocade padded edge overlay.
Gray napkins coordinated in
trimming.

Plate 11.
A Night in the Orient—A Chinese Marketplace Experience.
On entering the banquet hall at the convention center in Hong Kong, the 1,700 delegates walk under
two suspended 16-ft dragons, and their senses are heightened by a wide variety of visual areas. First,
they take in the vista of the ceiling, decorated with silks and fan lantern mobiles in Oriental colors.
Adding to the atmosphere, a low fog cover on the floor and stage gives the effect of the Asian mist.
Around the room, further sights and sounds are experienced as the delegates explore and participate
with the fortune teller, noodle maker, grass weaver, joss stick maker, and a calligrapher who stylizes
their names.

Entertainment included the Chinese orchestra, dragon and lion dancers, aerobatics, and Kung Fu
displays. The backdrop for these presentations was a 40-ft x 20-ft scenic dragon stage backing in black,
red, and yellow. Fans and fabric dressed the front of the stage. The 80 tables featured designs that were
both high and low bamboo tripods, and were made and dressed with alternating dragons, ferns, and
Asian orchids. The food stalls were dressed in marketplace style for an overall effect.

The Oriental spectacle was completed by soft pink lighting effects filtering through the decorations.

Plate 12

Plate 13

Plate 14

Plates 12, 13, and 14.
An Italian Affair—A Decorated Marquee in a Winery.
The overall look shows a stage dressed with arches
depicting an Italian environment. The scenic background
is a canvas painted with areas of Italy. The tables are
dressed in green linens with red checkered silk cloth. A
glass lantern, bread rolls, and blooms are featured. Empty
single wine bottles are used as an accessory to hold the
candles.

The trees are the focal backdrop—when darkness
descends, the lighting in the grounds will surprise the
guests. As the technician throws the switch, wonderful
primary colors are exposed.

Plates 15 and 16.
A Night in Casablanca.
A most beautiful look was achieved when the
interior walls of the Regent of Sydney ballroom
were covered with scenic art canvasses of Rick's
Café in the movie *Casablanca*. The color scheme
was based on monochromatic harmony ranging
from the lightest apricot to the deepest terra-cotta.
Shadows and shadings provided an outstanding
look to a room that was dressed for this occasion.

Plate 16

Plate 15

Plates 17, 18, and 19.
1945 Victory Party.
These three photographs show a 1940s theme party for a seated dinner for 200 guests. The centerpiece arrangement is styled with authentic World War II accessories, along with the 1940s red carnation flower. A red and white silk parachute is reversed and hung from the ceiling with camouflage nets, while flickering interest points are created with decorative tank, gun, and parachute cutouts.

Plate 17

Plate 18

Plate 19

Plate 20.
Evening at the Moulin Rouge.
The Eiffel Tower is featured on the stage of this Parisian night. Silver tableware and linens, can can cutouts, feathers, fabrics, and masses of potted plants were used to create the atmosphere.

Plates 21 and 22.
A White Christmas.
A fantasy look of a white Christmas—or a Christmas from Dickens. White linens and chair covers with accent colors of red and green complete the tables. The walls are decorated with trees ranging from 12 ft to a miniature 4 ft—painted, glittered, and dusted with diamond dust. Lights silhouette the shapes, giving a wonderful look to the room.

Plate 22

Plate 21

Plate 23

Plates 23 and 24.
Golden Gala.
A golden and gala event with tables dressed in gold lamé and matching chair covers with bronze and silver sashes. The skyline panels tower from floor to ceiling and are shaded in gold, bronze, and splashes of silver.

Plate 24

Plate 25.
The Race Is On for a Glamorous Evening.
An evening at Ascot is the perfect event for black and white decor to be used. This photo shows the use of black and white striped silk cloth with an elevated centerpiece of quality white roses suspended from a plexiglass rod. The base is massed with white roses and ferns, giving a completed look to the whole design.

The table at the back left shows another table arrangement where a sequined hat, with a black and white bow, holds a succession of drops of white roses. In designing a quantity of tabletops for an event, use the same type of florals, but show three different styles.

Plate 26.
The Ascot Storyboard.

Plate 25

Plate 26

Plate 27

Plates 27 and 28.
A Formal Setting in Cream.
These tables are dressed in cream
brocade floor-length cloth (130" in
diameter) with a matching overlay
that measures 90" square and chair
covers in matching fabrics. This
linen was supplied to me by Something Different of New Jersey. The
wall features were designed with
the column and fabric look, as
shown on the wall behind the
tables.

Plate 28

Plate 29.
The Wedding Church.
A most beautiful and sensational effect was created within the church by this abundant, but arranged, look for the pews. It was estimated that 1000 hours were spent on floral work alone for this wedding. It was dressed in detail!

Plate 30.
Wedding Blues.
The ballroom of the Intercontinental Hotel, Sydney, is dressed for the occasion of this sophisticated wedding. The blue satin tablecloths and matching chair covers provide a strong look for the room where the tabletops stand 48" high and phalaenopsis orchids and white tulips dominate the look. Huge white silk bows give accent to this formal occasion.

Plate 31

Plate 32

Plates 31, 32, 33, 34, 35, and 36.
The Fabulous Fifties.
The theme of this 1997 event at the Sydney
Convention and Exhibition Center was kept secret
until the doors opened to the surprise. And there it
was—fun, fantasy, and the '50s. The key features are
guitars, ice cream cones, and flamingos, finished to
perfection with fabric and trim. The dance floor
and tabletops are covered in black vinyl and colored
polka dots—a stunning effect. Balloons are an
integral part of the look. The table centers show
ice cream cones, hoops, flamingos, and guitars.
The 750 guests, who are dedicated staff members of
HIH Winterthur, received stylish micro laser glasses
and electronic yo-yos and hula hoops. There was
much twirling, turning, and twisting. Strong colors
in royal blue, hot pink, kelly green, soft apricot, and
mauve make the statement. Over 70 limousines and
minibuses were there at midnight to take the guests
home. The generosity of HIH Winterthur toward
their employees is certainly evident with this yearly
event. Often, when I walk into the offices, staff
will ask "What are you doing this year, Lena?"

Plate 33

Plate 34

Plate 35

Plate 36

Plate 37.
Broadway Nights.
A black and gold theme depicts the Broadway scene with Fred, Ginger, top hat and tails, piano cutouts, and gold fabrics.

Plates 38 and 39.
A Brazilian Carnivale.
A night of color, special effects, dance, and decor. Another HIH Winterthur Christmas party for their 750 employees, this stunner was staged at The Australian Jockey Club in Randwick, Sydney, Australia, in the Shannon Room under the managerial direction of Mr. John Rohanna. Huge 16-ft cutouts of Brazilian dancers, hibiscus, fruits, and leaves painted in scenic style decorate the room.

Plate 38

Plate 39

Aladdin and the Arabian Nights . . .

Step into the king's treasury! An exotic world of gilded palms and jewelled treasure chests surrounds guests as they are welcomed by staff clad in rich fabrics and turbans.

Strictly Christmas . . .

Garlands and glamour in the traditional style from red and green to silver and white . . . or your own corporate colors. Use Christmas trees or creative floral art, Santa Claus or jesters, reindeers or fantasy creatures straight from a Christmas fairy tale . . . let your imagination run riot. See Color Plate 21 for glittery Christmas trees. Color Plate 22 shows a Christmas tabletop design featuring presents.

An Australian Vignette . . .

No flies or dingoes, but plenty of cool ale and hearty food at the Goolagong Hotel. A typical Aussie outback get-together featuring snippets of Australiana. Picture the rough-hewn outback pub, the mateship, and the wildlife peeping from behind gumleaves and scrub.

An Invitation to the Moulin Rouge . . .

Excitement in the rich tradition of the Can-Can era. Lots of lace and legs with the typical Parisienne flair; wild music to fire your blood, decorative dancers, feathers, and roses. This is a party with vivacity and verve—a trip into the past that's both naughty and nostalgic. See Color Plate 20.

Viva Las Vegas . . .

Glamour and glitz, feathers and fantails take you into this sensational world of high rollers and lucky chances. Glamorous signage, dice, and freestanding royal blue dollars say it all and could lead us into the croupier's room where the guests are ready to roll. This room would be dressed with special signage to support the theme.

Figure 6.4 shows clever use of space, as the ballroom allowed for comfortable seating for 150

Figure 6.4. Viva Las Vegas.

yet 180 guests attended. Round banquet tables were substituted for long narrow trestles, suitable to the Las Vegas theme.

The felt gambling cloths were utilized as overlays but all the decor was hung on the scaffolding and did not protrude onto the floor area in any way. The tall palm trees are indicative of this area and signage displaying Las Vegas night spots is featured on the black velvet that covered the walls.

Alcatraz—Escape is impossible!

This is the ultimate Jailhouse Rock party. Sidle past stern jailkeepers to have your mug shot taken; then you'll eat behind bars and meet the Birdman. Fabulous entertainment and authentic decor.

A Night in Vienna . . .

A classical evening formally decorated in a traditional manner for a grand VIP event. The orchestra plays on a stage dressed with urns of roses. Think waltzes; think lilting loveliness; think quiet sophistication. Ah, for a night in Vienna!

The Grand Hyatt Ballroom in the Grand Hyatt Hotel in Melbourne is certainly a grand venue for a corporate dinner, themed around a Viennese concept. This ballroom has the seating capacity for 800 people, usually arranged in tables of 10. An interesting aspect of this ballroom is that it offers a two-tiered seating arrangement with beautiful pillars and columns of lighting surrounding the interior.

The decorative props shown in Figure 6.5 are fashioned on the style of Viennese window framework. These free standing panels, made of plywood, stand 12 ft × 4 ft and are shaded in cream with washes of gold foil paint. The backing to these windows is made of architectural tracing paper. This paper offers a quality and texture that

Figure 6.5. A Night in Vienna.

is exceedingly complementary to the lighting effects placed behind the panels.

For an evening filled with classical music and dance, the table linens and chair covers complement the theme with a deep red plush velvet. The floor length cloth in black measures 130 inches in diameter and acts as an undercloth under the table. The overlay is in plush velvet and measures 90 inches square. The chair covers are also plush velvet.

The candelabra, made of steel and holding nine candles, is covered in gold fabric and trimmed with gold beads attached from arm to arm. The floral arrangement at the base of this candelabra consists of deep red roses, asparagus fern, and camellia. The napkin is trimmed with matching ribbons and gold cording, while the menu, positioned standing on the table, follows through in cream with touches of gold.

On Safari . . .

See the jungle come alive at night! Shiver at the glitter of amber eyes through foliage; listen to the throb of jungle drums and the sounds of predators. Eat under a canopy of tall trees overhung with vines, and watch out for the wildlife—giraffes, elephants, and monkeys swinging overhead.

VIP guests hold their breath as they enter an On Safari theme party. This corporate occasion was a thank-you dinner to clients. The entrance featured screens made from brush which held the huge three-dimensional molded tiger's face. The walls were filled with elephants, rhinoceros, giraffes, gorillas, and monkeys together with masses of trees, branches, driftwood, mosses, and grasses to create the look (see Figure 6.6). The tables were covered with floor length black cloth complemented with leopard print overlays and matching chair covers. The 8-ft high table centerpieces were designed with brush and leaping tigers.

Figure 6.6. On safari.

The Cotton Club . . .

Enjoy the funeral parlor entrance to this prohibited nightclub, as you're checked out by watchful door-keepers. Sit near gangsters and their ladies to enjoy the entertainment in the age of Prohibition, brought to life with a startling and effective black-and-white feathered decor.

Night in the Orient

Walk through the dragon's mouth into a complete Asian experience. Chinese marketplaces, hanging lanterns, and bamboo designs create the atmosphere for a small or large affair. Conceptual art (Figure 6.7) shows the diagram for a stunning centerpiece displaying foam core dragons, peacock feathers, and orchids. Figure 6.8 shows the dragon resting on the buffet table.

Figure 6.7. (right) A hand-painted centerpiece design for guest tables.

Figure 6.8. (below) An elegant dragon buffet centerpiece with built-in smoke machine.

New York, New York . . .

Experience the glamour and excitement of opening night on Broadway with the New York skyline as your backdrop. Excitement sizzles in a night which becomes a Broadway production in itself.

Figure 6.9 shows how clean cut panels of plywood placed on an elevated platform make an impressive skyline backdrop for a New York theme party. The panels are freestanding and a series of openings is cut and lined at the back with architectural drafting paper. The panels are then lit from behind in a color of choice. They range in height from 8 to 12 ft high. The fantasy tree on the right stands 12 ft high colored in soft black and massed with fairy lights around the outline.

Figure 6.9. The New York skyline as backdrop.

Wharfside Party . . .

Imagine your meal served on a moored vessel with spectacular views of the city. Sip wine and drum your fingers to the beat of music while watching the talented sight performers. Then eat your fill, while on the wharf, food stall vendors create a busy, colorful marketplace.

A Night of "Honky Tonk" . . .

Let a theme park be a playground for guests as they return to childhood and enjoy the rides and eat popcorn and cotton candy. Be entertained in the side show alley, laugh at the clowns, marvel at the magicians, and duck the stilt-walkers.

Calypso Capers . . .

Palm trees and flamboyant dancers tower over the magic of toe-tapping, hip-swaying calypso bands. This warm and sultry atmosphere encourages your guests to unwind and ease into an evening of total fun and relaxation.

Researching periods or countries provides creative inspiration for highly decorative props such as the Brazilian dancer shown in Figure 6.10. The material used is plywood and the shading passes from the palest to the hottest pink. The soft tan used on the body makes it an almost three-dimensional event prop. Feathers tower from the headpiece giving an overall height of 16 ft to this floor piece. The huge hibiscus on the left is shaded in tones of rose pink and soft apricot. The table displays large paper flowers in coordinating colors with clusters of fresh fruit and candles.

Figure 6.10. (right) A Brazilian dancer.

Cartoon Capers . . .

Bring cartoon characters to life as they entertain your guests in a ballroom transformed into a playground. Laugh with the larger-than-life cartoon characters who mingle with the guests. Blue, pink, and green cocktails are offered, while a huge screen shows animated cartoons. Guests come dressed as their favorite characters.

Western Showdown . . .

This Wild West atmosphere brings the line dancers, the madam, the sheriff, and undertaker out to entertain the township of guests. Then it's poker time: the stakes rise as gold nuggets and dollars cascade onto the table.

The Beach Party . . .

In a torch-lit area under a mass of colorful umbrellas, tables are laden with tempting buffets and tropical cocktails. Bongo music introduces the limbo dance and interactive games on the beach—carefree and fun for all! Figure 6.11 shows the beach party centerpiece. "More skill, fewer flow-ers" is the idea featured in this decorative tabletop, designed by Sharon Malouf. It is viewed from both sides so both sides are painted for overall viewing. The board, umbrella, shells, and weeds get us ready for the beach.

Figure 6.11. Beach party centerpiece.

Night in Hollywood . . .

Costumed producers and directors meet, greet, and seat the guests in a ballroom transformed into a glitzy film set: black, white, and silver decor carries the theme while movie-star lookalikes mingle with the guests throughout the evening. See the conceptual art in Figure 6.12.

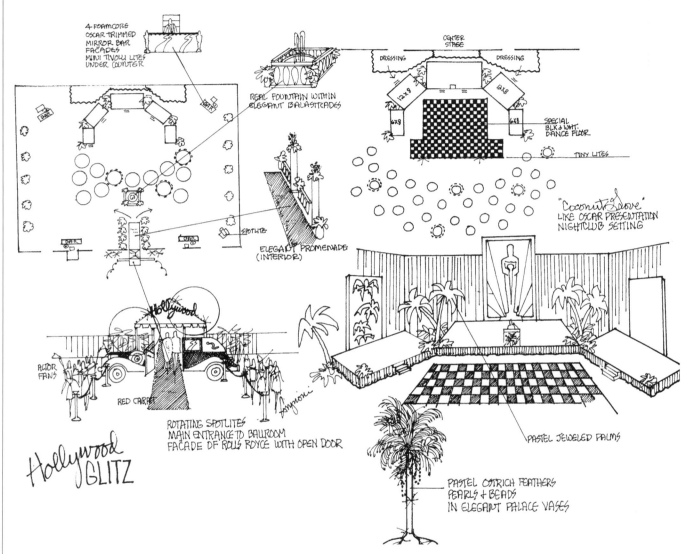

Figure 6.12. Night in Hollywood conceptual art. This type of detail is required when you are presenting for a major function. It is also excellent future reference to keep on file for future work.

1945 Victory Celebration . . .

Victory! Dancing in the streets—joy—a gala event. Everything's red, white, and blue, and there's an ominous-looking giant model plane suspended from the ceiling. You'll see walls festooned with camouflage nets, and huge blown-up renditions of land, sea, and air battles. See Color Plates 17, 18, and 19—notice the scenic panels, camouflage ceiling nets, and themed tabletops.

Water Luncheon . . .

Take an exhilarating coastal trip by seaplane, enjoying the bird's-eye view of exotic beaches, where the ocean laps against the sand. As you observe stunning vistas, you arrive at an out-of-the way restaurant where you can relax in a setting inspired by nature. Over a sumptuous lunch, you are treated to a spectacular aerial display, with the finale of sky-divers jumping from planes trailing your company banner.

Australiana Bush Party . . .

Then of course there's always the opportunity to bring the country to you! Imagine your reaction when you enter your five-star ballroom to find it transformed into an Australian bush party with a difference—amongst gum trees and billabongs, you can watch sheep being shorn, pat kangaroos and koalas, or get acquainted with Australian reptiles. There are bush poets to listen to, a bush band to dance to, and bush fare of damper (campfire bread), barbecued meat and vegetables, and a pavlova (meringue cake) to tempt the tastebuds. Figure 6.13 shows the entrance design that sets the theme for things to come! A pair of arrangements is designed specifically with all-Australian natives. When placed on either side of the doorways they create an impressive entrance.

Figure 6.13. Entrance pedestals.

Galactic Gala Theme Party . . .

Ask your guests to dress in black or white only and watch them gasp in delight as they enter the party room featuring starred white vinyl tabletops and matching white vinyl dancefloor. Special accessories embellish the room crossing light years of space—this is a galactic experience like none you've ever had before.

King's Treasury . . .

Glittering treasures and stolen crown jewels spill from chests. Gold pedestals are topped with waterfalls of gilded ferns and ivy. Gold lamé and crushed velvet cover the ceiling with banners; draped columns and jewelled urns add to the illusion.

Medieval Madness . . .

An evening filled with surprises. Minstrels roam and jesters perform in a make-believe castle setting. The tables groan under the weight of candelabras, candles, trenchers of ale, and a sumptuous medieval feast.

Menu for Theming Accessories

Figure 6.14, a menu for accessory theming, will serve as a quick point of reference for the type of theme you wish to create, the color appropriate to that theme, and ideas for the invitation, carrying through to valuable points on the props and cutouts to be used, which in turn would suggest the accompanying florals and accessories.

Theme	Color	Invitation: Write on Card and/or Tag On To:	Décor—Props and/or Cutouts	Flowers and Accessories
Rock & Roll	Yellow, Hot Pink, Black, White	• Sheet music • Label on old record • CD cover • Invitation inside sock • Large note	• 5 ft. records • Swags of music • Large guitar • Juke boxes • Pink flamingo	• Music notes • Braids, ribbon • Hot pink and yellow socks • Toy guitars painted
New Orleans	Purple, Green, Hot Pink	• Tag with 4-inch feather • Invitation with envelope and glitter • Mask and tag	• Jazz players • Wrought iron balcony • Terrace house shapes • Street signage • Huge masks	• Purple and pink beads • Ostrich feather • Candles
Rio Riot	Greens, Orange, Yellow	• Square of colored board • Paper mache fruit	• Palm trees • Fruits • Tropical birds	• Tropical flowers • Candles in rockmelon • Watermelon slices • Fresh fruits • Interesting leaves • Balloon option
Aladdin	Fuchsia pinks, purples, or multi	• Bag of pearls • String of beads • Silk bag	• Huge pots • Huge baskets • Seven thieves • Slave girl • Lamps and lantern • Pillars	• Brass vases • Gold bricks • Beads • Sacks of potpourri
Australian Vignette	Earth tones	• Boomerang • Piece of leather • Large gum leaf • Small plywood box	• Outback pub • Telegraph poles • Cockatoos • Koala bears • Water tanks • Saddle/fence	• Camp fires • Australian blooms • Sheets of bark • Lanterns

Figure 6.14. Menu for theming accessories. This comprehensive guide is an excellent reference for the special event designer and offers a fabulous choice from the client's perspective.

Theme	Color	Invitation: Write on Card and/or Tag On To:	Décor—Props and/or Cutouts	Flowers and Accessories
A Dickens Christmas	Red/green Silver/gold Bronze Your option	• Christmas card • Cardboard holly leaf • Bon bon • Cone and bow • Envelope with glitter	• Fresh trees • Artificial trees • Huge bon bons • Covered boxes • Pots of poinsettia	• Florals and candles • Branches and bows • Cones and parcels • Ornaments • Bells
Moulin Rouge	Pink/purple, or Deep green and maroon	• Ostrich feather • Eiffel Tower • Perfume • Silk stocking • Champagne glass • Garter in lace	• Can can girls • Pots of blooms • Lengths of flowers • Panels of mirrors • Pedestals of flowers	• Silver candelabra • Glass ornaments • Champagne bottle and champagne glass
Viva Las Vegas	Black and one color, or Multi-colored	• Paper money • Invitation with chips enclosed • Glittered bow • Scroll and cord	• Hotel signage • Las Vegas cowboy • Las Vegas cowgirl • Large dollar signs • Gambling chips • Roulette wheel • Huge playing cards	• Roulette wheels • Packs of cards • Dice and dollars
Alcatraz	Gray, white, black	• Summons • Tin of baked beans • Toy gangster gun • Handcuffs • Fingerprint paper • Cell number	• Window bars • Scenic art on canvas • Mug shot board • Wanted board • Signage • Wanted posters	• Bread buns • Chains • Weeds • Cardboard tools • Press clippings • Potatoes/onions • Peelers
A Night in Vienna	Burgundy and gold	Top hat • Gold box • Scroll and velvet tie	• Opera windows • Huge pedestals • Leaf motifs—golden	• Candelabras • Glass lanterns • Potted blooms
On Safari	Animal prints in earth tones and black, or All deep green	• Scroll and leather tie • Leather bag	• Safari animals • Vines • Screens of branches • Ropes • Safari nets • Huge trees • Dried palms	• Toy elephants • Variety of leaves • Lanterns • Bulrushes
Cotton Club	Black, white, and red	• Toy gun • Handcuff • Tin cup • Red carnation	• Gangsters • White feathers • Signage • Feather boas • Gangster hat	• Red carnations • Candelabras • Dollars and dice • Tin cups • Wine bottles/No labels
Night on the Orient	Red and gold	• Fan • Basketweave mat • Passport	• Dragons—glittered • Chinese umbrella • Gold fabrics • Lanterns • Rising sun—glittered	• Oriental fan or hat • Seaweed squares • Chopsticks (painted) • Gold candles • Mirrors
New York Affair	Black and white and silver	• Top hat	• Huge street lamps • Top hats & canes • Signage • Street signs • Building silhouette	• Silver chalice • Glass balls • Silver cording • Mirrors

Figure 6.14. (cont.)

Theme	Color	Invitation: Write on Card and/or Tag On To:	Décor—Props and/or Cutouts	Flowers and Accessories
Calypso Capers	Chartreuse Blue Orange Apricot	• Foam stars • Single bloom	• Huge paper florals • Glittered stars • Glittered moons • Huge net flowers • Multicolored napkins	• Multicolored flowers • Multicolored boxes • Multicolored ribbons • Pots of flowers • Colorful cording
Wharfside Party	All colors incorporated	• Toy vessel • Ship cutout • Bottle of sand	• Lots of signage • Nets • Rope • Calico sails • Lamps	• Beach accessories • Sand bucket • Outsize sunglasses • Ice cream cones • Beach basket
Night in the Bronx	Browns, gray, and blacks	• Rolled newspaper • Toy garbage bin • Black flag or gang banner • Wire netting square	• Graffiti panels • Wire fences • Street lamps • Street signs • Brooms and buckets • Painted tins and bins	• Rolls of newspaper • Newspaper flowers • Toy guns • Plastic cups painted • Eye patches • Washable tattoos
Beach Party	Cream to yellows	• Box of sand • Sole of new thong • Tag and rope	• Huge beach balls • Canoe • Scenic art backdrops • Huge buckets	• Sand castles • Foliage sprayed blue • Pail and shovel • Sunglasses
Hollywood	Black, white, and bronze	• Contract • Top hat • Roll of silk • Oscar shape • Glitter on tags • Glitter in envelope	• Building shapes • Fred and Ginger • Oscars • Film posters • Film clip • Cameras • Directors chairs • Signage • Hollywood stars • Street lamps	• Music notes • Stars glittered • Scrolls of music • White feathers • Strings of pearl • Strings of diamantes
Western Hoedown	Earth tones	• Leather square • Mini cowboy hat • Hessian sack • Parchment paper • Indian print scroll	• Bar and piano • Tepees • Bags of grain • Wire fences • Water trough • Cowboys and Indians • Saddles • Wheels	• Weeds & grasses • Stemless blooms • Pumpkins • Lanterns • Leather and beads
Evening in Space	White and silver	• Square of mirror • White silk • White rice paper • Glittered stars	• Global shapes • Sizes of stars • Space ships • Clouds of balloons • Martians and UFOs	• Clouds of baby's breath • Candles galore • Masses of stars • Huge sequins
Medieval Madness	Black and red	• Beige scroll • Chalice • Velvet bag • Small banner	• Vultures • Axes • Swords • Ropes • Painted dungeons • Medieval scroll • Long fabric banners	• Loaves of bread • Cardboard axes • Thick candles • Rope • Vines • Bird and nest

Figure 6.14. (cont.)

Theme	Color	Invitation: Write on Card and/or Tag On To:	Décor—Props and/or Cutouts	Flowers and Accessories
Circus Carnivale	Multicolor	• Sample bag of candy • Flag	• Yards of fabric • Clown faces • Streamers • Colorful wagons • Colorful food stalls • Banners and flags • Trees and lights • Drums and trumpets	• Balloons • Streamers • Lollipops • Candy sticks • Fruits
Hawaiian Hullabaloo	Greens	• Leaf and tag • Basket of fruit and tag • Lei and tag	• Napkin rolled inside leaf • Sheet music • Leis of tropicals • Fruits	• Palm leaves • Rockmelon • Papaya • Mangoes • Strings of orchids
Evening in the Pink	All pinks	• Pink flower • Pink face mask • Pink doll • Pink elephant	• Pink butterflies • Pink fabrics • Pink pedestals	• Flowers and accessories • Pink exotics • Pink seasonals • Pink tropicals • Mini butterflies • Pink candles
24-Carat Gala	All gold	• Masks • Gold lamé bag and potpourri • Gold disc • Flower and tag • String of gold beads	• Huge gold mask • Glittered stars • Opera window • Floor size candelabra	• Chandeliers • Gold beads • Gold stars • Gold lamé roses
Kentucky Derby Evening	Black and white	• Race book • Flowers	• Life-size horses • Gold chalice • Swags of fabric • Raceday flags • Jockey shirts	• Straw hats • Silk squares • Race books • Tickets • Whips
Heavenly Disco	Full white Touches of silver	• Mini white balloon and tag • Rope of pearls • White stole	• Huge clouds • Huge stars • Pearly gates • Life size angels • Man in the moon	• Clouds of baby's breath • White balloons • White silk squares
Water Luncheon	Colors of nature	• Attractive shells • Foam fish cutout • Beach postcard • Model plane	*(At Luncheon Site)* • Huge shells • Cutout King Neptune • Seaweed mobiles • Cascading ferns sprayed blue • Beachballs	• Mini beach balls • Sandcastles in tray • Sunglasses • Shells
Australian Bush Party	Ochres, natural colors	• Toy koalas or other stuffed animals • Native flower • Tag on billycan • Tin cup	• Huge gum trees • Specially created billabongs • Backdrop of country scenes • Fencing • Sheds	• Toy koalas • Australian native plants • BBQ logs and bricks • Lanterns

Figure 6.14. (cont.)

The A to Z of Creative Change

Within the creative field change is inevitable and it should only be viewed as wanting to do things better and improving on past performances. A lot of this has to do with the attitude you extend towards the people around you and the profession you are in. The A-Z Creative Change Chart (Figure 6.15) is meant to serve as a springboard for your own creative development.

A. **Alternative ways: look for another way of doing it.** It makes sense to search for alternative ways with events—standard methods are unlikely to give that distinctive, innovative look.

B. **Benefits must be evident, otherwise ideas have no value.** Ideas are of no use unless they can be worked into a plan that fits the client's budget.

C. **Concept is thought—but specifics bring Reality.** Random thoughts should be jotted down from any brainstorming sessions. Don't discard ideas but quickly explore the value of the thought giving merit to every possible and probable concept.

D. **Dress a basic form in various ways.** Revise what has been done in the past and ascertain what sets and props you have access to. Revamp them by change of color, fabric, or other surface finish. Represent it into a completely renewed look.

E. **Energy and emotion enhance positive ideas by removing distractions.** A sift-and-sort processing of ideas is what provides the foundation of a scheme. Avoid a mish-mash of thoughts. Select two or three features and strongly implement those features throughout the room.

F. **Find a connection point for ideas.** Brainstorm associated words for theme-building and discard unrelated components. Make a connection point with the most associated thoughts and utilize to its fullest capacity for an event.

G. **Generate a list—offer benefits and advantages.** Research the theme topic through the use of the library or industry magazines. It is also possible to shirttail on the experience of your peers, so approach them for ideas that may assist you.

H. **Harvest as many probable and improbable ideas as possible.** Harvest a bank of ideas drawn on past events and experiences. List those that seem beyond the realm of reality balanced by those that are achievable and actually fit within the given budget of the client.

I. **Isolation allows thinking time.** Take time away from the office, studio, or work environment. Be surrounded by quietness, free of phones and faxes. Focus on nothing but developing something new. Creating head space is essential.

J. **Judgment is fine-tuned to recognize potential.** Judgment is concerned with *"yes, this is useful, embrace it"* or *"no, this is not useful, discard it."* It is about comparisons and running with ideas that work rather than laboring over fantasy concepts.

K. **Knowledge is only useful when applied.** The thirst for more knowledge is what continues to give personal growth. It brings consistent performance, higher skills, and better managerial knowledge. A higher competency level is the aim.

L. **Look into things that others pass by.** Sources of inspiration are everywhere. Clusters of trees from parklands can be used to decorate a ballroom. City skylines can be interpreted as wall silhouettes and water environment can inspire.

M. **Motivation—Spend eight hours on *"New"*.** Motivation gives you a chance to excel providing you stay focused. Employers can provide motivation for their employees by using a few simple words—"thank you for a job well done!".

N. **New information must be integrated with old.** By increasing product knowledge a higher level of competence is reached. If someone asks a question and the answer isn't known, file it in your memory bank. Find the answer to build product knowledge.

O. **One direction stunts creative growth.** Tunnel thinking restricts personal development.

Figure 6.15. The A to Z of creative change—A different style of alphabet to keep you on the upward curve. It offers solid solutions, good alternatives, and positive thoughts.

One way, one method of application, and one approach displays lack of intelligence and places restriction on every aspect of the event.

P. Peer and team networking groups can act as creative springboards. Roundtable sessions with staff or a peer group could expose ideas that would otherwise have been missed. Pooling of ideas expands the possibility of theme building.

Q. Questions to start—Questions to finish. Curiosity is the start for the questioning process to begin. This process acts as the mover that brings ecstatic thought into an act of reality. Post event questions allows us to improve performance.

R. Read and re-read for resource inspiration. Quality slips unless the event planner is completely conscious of updating and lifting performance on the job. Continually researching industry information keeps you ahead.

S. Strive for creative differences rather than rest on your laurels. Stop, stare, and style. If it has been done before, that of course is the obvious way to repeat it. Take the alternate path, avoid repetition, and search for concepts and methods that are unobvious.

T. Transfer décor from walls to ceiling. In all venues there are four walls—ceiling, floor, entrances, and exits. The total look has to be the ultimate aim linking up those components within the venue. Search for a common link in theming.

U. Unworkable ideas need to be discarded. Don't labor over elements that are unrealistic, out of budget, impossible to procure, or beyond the team's capability. Know the strengths of each person and recognize and duly respect any weaknesses.

V. "Vision-Intelligence" views the total concept. Vision gives deeper insights into the bigger picture concept and by reversing thoughts or turning them inside out, you develop perspective. Vision means thinking beyond present time.

W. Work Towards fewer key features. When budget is restricted avoid placing a prop here, a prop there, and shot-gunning the decoy units. Encourage the client to have the stage as a feature with beautiful table tops and linens for impact.

X. Photocopy and file, print ideas and pictures from researching. Researching the topics is essential for creative development. Books on theatre, art, movies, plays, and videos can always offer inspiration. Store new information with old and let it accumulate.

Y. Yardstick measurement brings success. Test a concept before you reject it but more importantly if it is put to use, endeavor to measure the acceptance or success of what has been done through post evaluation questionnaires.

Z. Zigzag through a bank of ideas, then aim and fire. To zigzag through the ideas bank where twenty or thirty thoughts may have been expended. Aim at two or three features that you prefer to utilize and then fire to bring the theme into a creation.

Figure 6.15. (cont.)

Chapter 7

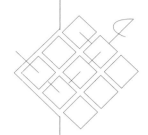

Understanding
Design Principles
and Elements of Art

A basic understanding of the principles and elements of art is of great value to the event planner and producer, but especially to the designer. These principles need to be considered for every event where décor and flowers are involved. Whether the designer is looking at a stage set, a decorative panel, sculptured foam, a painted backdrop canvas, or a flower arrangement, the starting point is always a simple blueprint. Design entails the following:

Principles of Design: Line, form, color, texture, pattern

Elements of Art: Space, dominance, scale, rhythm, harmony

The above summary can be expanded to give a useful guide for both floral design and event props.

Principles of Design

Line

Floral Design

Straight lines give strength to any arrangement especially when the line is used in repetition. A rectangle frame and vertical style is commonly used for buffet table designs where elevations are featured. Ideal materials are gladioli, delphinium, flax, black-boy grass, or larkspur. Straight lines give the feeling of strength and, in the floral world, known as "The Line of Aspiration" because it is a suggestion of strong growth. It is also an excellent line to use since a minimum of blooms need be used. The study of Ikebana teaches us to utilize nature's growth as it is, so we try to select plants with the required stem form. Don't try to bend or force a curved stem into a straight line.

Refer to Figure 9.3 in Chapter 9 to see how this buffet layout is designed. The table is completely covered and skirted. Blocks and crates can also be covered in matching fabric to elevate the food platters and a series of verticals are styled to suit a buffet featuring the series of fresh florals on the table.

Decorative Prop

Straight lines for sets and props can be quite a statement when lines are repeated in varying heights. Straight lines in décor can be used through a series of straight-sided columns or through stage trussing. An example of this is Figure 4.5 in Chapter 4. The steel tubing becomes part of the vertical pattern clearly defined in the Alcatraz theme party photographs. Certainly straight lines for props that are vertically placed show uniformity and strength of design. The repetition of the line gives strength to the look as well. Straight lines in set décor are far easier to work with than trying to create a series of curves.

See Color Plates 23 and 24, which show the golden gala themed evening. A series of panels varying in height, but not width, decorate the blackened wall of a ballroom. Straight lines in repetition surround the guests with a pleasing effect as it is softened in gold. Even the decorative windows in the panels repeat the straightness of the line. This is seen as a design feature.

Form

Floral Design

Form refers to shapes; for example, round, oval, straight, or curved. Therefore, each shape needs to show its importance in a design. To achieve this, avoid massing or crowding flow-

Decorative Prop

Form or shape is much clearer to the eye when brought into play with set décor and state props. When the theme is researched, usually a list is compiled of the components that make

ers and leaves. Some floral designs show only one kind of flowers, for instance a bowl of roses or tulips. One kind of flower shows repeating form while contrasting form would display the same bowl of roses combined with flax leaves. The sharpness of the tall spiked flax teams with the rounded form of the roses. The combination of shapes is an important aspect of the design process. The art of the mix and match theory is one to develop.

Refer to the "Lush and Lovely Look" Figure 7.1. Three types of foliages (camellia, fern, and magnolia) are usually used. This style will always be appealing and timeless in presentation. All guests love to see an abundance of flowers. Another reference which clearly shows form is Figure 8.2 in Chapter 8.

up the prop side of the job. In the selection of any decorative props, balance one shape against another. A good rule of thumb here is to select 70 percent of one shape and 30 percent of the other. This approach outweighs a random number of equal quantities of both. A perfect example of form for decorative props is shown on the stage set designed for the Australian Gaslight Company in Australia (Figure 6.3). Note the series of shapes outlined by fairy lights.

A Wild West night shows how the western accessories display a variety of shapes. Refer to Figure 5.6 in Chapter 5 which shows boxes and bales in different shapes, for example, the pattern of the hessian-covered box with the rounded hessian-covered bag of oats. Conscious selection of the props for an event provide a look unlike any other because it shows that the event planner has done his or her homework.

Figure 7.1. The lush and lovely look. A timeless floral design that is massed for effect using larkspur, roses, lizzianthus, tiger lilies, and the large aratum bloom. Soft tones of dusty pink are featured on the rosewood table which takes pride of place in the prefunction area of a hotel. Large traditional bowls of blooms with bow accent can offer appeal in this area as guests gather for cocktails.

Color

Floral Design

The various color contrasts bring harmony and appeal to the total look. Strive to allow colors to blend rather than having the florals jump out and say "Here I am—look at me!". It is far better to hear a guest acknowledge the artistry of this medium with an overall appreciation of the total look. See Color Plate 34—there is unity and harmony between florals and all other surrounding elements. This themed event is shown in this center spread. In today's designing the florals must be selected as first quality blooms but importantly subtle in color. The preference in floral event designing is to blend and fit the color of the flowers and foliage needed for the tabletop.

See Color Plates 12 and 13 of the Italian affair, with its opposite complementary colors of red and green. The cascading water form of foliage behind the table is a most impressive piece, standing 9 ft high and massed with ivy, ferns, leaves, vines, and willow. A variety of greens is incorporated which brings shading through the design. Red roses and carnations fall slowly through it.

Decorative Prop

The decorative prop is critical in the correlation of design units for an event. Color can make or break the mood of an evening, because different colors have different effects on the moods of the guests. Reread Chapter 4 on The Power of Color until that information is absorbed. The office workroom or studio should have a color wheel because the effects created in a ballroom with lighting alone can be used as a cross reference when discussing color effects and moods. The color wheel is exceptionally useful when clients are sitting in on meetings. It assists them in visualizing the overall look. Never underestimate the importance of this aspect.

Interesting projects can be lifted to the sensational level through this one principle of art. See Color Plate 14, which shows the use of clever coloring achieved on the trees in a winery. Reds, greens, and yellow create an outstanding effect as light and color silhouette the outside area. This acts as a reveal filled with surprise for the guests when the switch is thrown after dark.

Texture

Floral Design

Texture with the use of florals is achievable with fresh materials: rough, smooth, shiny, dull, coarse, and fine may all be applied with leaf or flower variation, which brings interest and accent. This textural compatibility is a subtle effect on a floral design but one that should not be missed. Mixing texture creates interest throughout any design and combining the shiny texture of camellia with a dull surface quality of the eucalyptus adds to the completed piece. All designers or artists are conscious of the surface finish. This applies to fashion designers, weavers, potters, painters, and interior designers. Texture appeals to the sense of touch as well as the sense of sight.

Refer to Figure 7.2 which shows the free-standing butterfly that stands 16 ft high × 8 ft wide giving lots of dimensional to a arrangement that displays textural compatibility with all the components that are utilized.

Decorative Prop

Textural surfaces and their compatibility to the surroundings can be emphasized with sets and props. As a general guide, if a smooth surface is used, a rough finish would make a good contrast. Alternatively, the textural opposites of shiny and dull marry together well. Whether it's wood, board, or foam core this texture through various paint surfaces adds to the prop's look and finish. The paints today can be worked to create a variance in look by adding sand or sawdust on wet paint. Leave it to dry and recoat it as a final finish. Papers and materials can be selected and used with sets and props to give a look of interest.

An example of texture is shown in the Las Vegas theme in Figure 6.4. The surface qualities are essential to the finish. Undoubtedly, the paint and paper finishes available today offer a range of applications suited to display work in event theming. The signage for this themed event shows textural compatibility. By using flat and now shiny paint with accents given with Design Master high shine glitter, the effect is quite distinctive.

Figure 7.2. 12-ft high butterfly design. To tie in with the foyer design of the butterfly, this matching piece is arranged on the steel pedestal for a total height of sixteen feet.

This is an impressive floral for corners of a ballroom. It can be featured as a series of columns for walkways and/or stage providing background to the band or performer. Notice the effect the lighting has on the design which truly expresses the power of the globe.

Pattern

Floral Design

The pattern of any arrangement is made up of solid form and is based on a framework of geometric forming: the triangle, circle, rectangle, and diagonal. This becomes the blueprint on which to build. The best way to approach this is to inspect the venue and list the areas in which flowers are to be displayed. The next step is to decide on the pattern. For example, the oval, circle, or horizontal pattern ties in with the dining table. The symmetric triangle is the obvious choice for a foyer because of its equal balance. Alternatively the asymmetrical pattern with its unequal balance is ideally located when arranged as a pair on either side of the stage as floral decorative units. Decide which pattern fits best in each area: there are many uses.

The patterns used today are the same as those used in the past—the triangle, asymmetric triangle, diagonal, rectangle, circle, and horizontal. It includes the space and the mass that has been created within any of the above framework. Review the patterns in Figure 7.3 because these are all constructed within the framework of a pattern.

Decorative Prop

The pattern for sets or props depends entirely upon the area for which they are intended. Sets are usually three-dimensional: however, they can be constructed on a flatter plane depending upon budget. Patterns for décor begin with the event artist's impression, otherwise known as conceptual art for presentation visuals. This develops into the blueprint for the overall design and is the artist's impression that sets the pattern in motion. Conceptual art is featured throughout this book and Freddrik Campioni Garcia of Theme Travelers in San Antonio is the *"Master with the Pen."* Most importantly, he is also an events man and aware of the needs of the planner. This is a major plus in presentations, as the client can visualize the look, understand the mood, and appreciate the knowledge and skill required to successfully produce the event.

The references on pattern are shown in Figure 7.4. Notice that the shapes are distinctive and bold. They are clearly defined and distinctive in look.

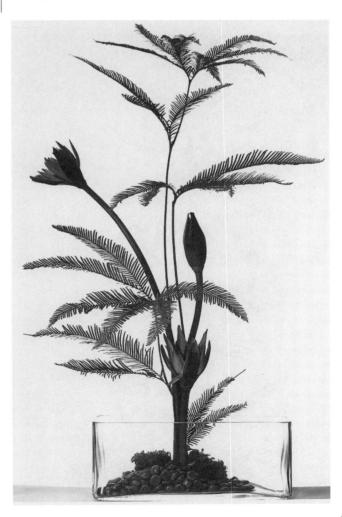

Figure 7.3. (above) An ornamental fruit. The pattern of the fruit is clearly defined. The fern, orchid, and leaves simplify the look.

Figure 7.4. (right) Pattern is a base. The pattern of this striking arrangement clearly shows the silhouette of leaf, bloom, bowl, and stone.

Elements of Art

Space

Floral Design

Knowing what to leave out is equally as important as knowing what to put in. There is a vast difference between the void in the design and space that beautifies. A void in a design is a cap, in contrast to areas or space that are left clean and crisp to the eye. If you always remember the basic principles of art and the elements of good design and use them in your floral arranging, your work will forge ahead. Today's trend is towards less conformity and greater simplicity. Good design therefore assumes a new importance and an understanding of these basic concepts is vital for success.

The element of space is clearly seen in Figure 7.5. The sporty arrangement with the foam core tennis racquet shows there is space on the sides and top while the base remains uncluttered.

Decorative Prop

Space costs nothing. It helps beautify and complement sets and props that are used on areas required for the show. When decorating a ballroom for an event where a load of props are required, the first thing to do is get the floor plan from the venue and position the stage with the props you wish to see on it. Then fill the corners with another or same type of decor. The wall areas are the next consideration. Review Figure 6.4, the Las Vegas theme party in Chapter 6. Notice the space created between the signage. Refer also to Figure 7.6, which shows airtubing and decorative cutouts.

Refer back to Figure 5.6, the Wild West photo in Chapter 5 and notice the placements of tepee, bales, hessian packs, and trees. Outside the barn doors, Wild West accessories are placed in clusters but with planned space within the confined design area. This allows guests to be involved as the props provide walkway interest. Guests tend to walk around props when space is created. Sets then become conversational.

Figure 7.5. A sporting centerpiece. This decorative arrangement can be utilized as an eye-catching centerpiece to the buffet table for the sports luncheon or dinner. The foam core racket stands five foot high and is double-sided thus giving an overall and pleasing look from all sides. The ferns and flowers are intermingled with tennis balls and long runs of flattened cane.

Figure 7.6. Airtube for theatre style. A very distinctive look is achieved for this corporate conference. The airtubing is available in a variety of colors but in this case the white and red worked to create a surprise element for participants. The tubing offers flexibility and function as the ceiling work shows. *Mr. Balloons* of Australia and *Doris Gazet* of the United States supply this unique product. The sporting figures cut from foam core are secured to the black velvet floor to ceiling drape with *Velcro*™, and can be angled in any desired position or location.

Dominance

Floral Design

Almost any component of the floral family can become a dominant point in the arrangement, providing it is strong in shape or color; for example, leafage of a distinctive shape, lilies that are full blown and gold, a beautifully tailored bow, or an accessory that ties in with the scheme. With event designing often another element can be added. A perfect example is the use of living statues within or near the designs. The dominance of this element created much talk as the statue-like bodies complemented the fresh florals.

Materials are emphasized if grouped rather than scattered and visual height is evident when groupings are weighted correctly. Leafage or choicest blooms play a more dominant role if selected and shown at their best. Dominant points are easily detected because of

Decorative Prop

Event props are often best displayed in groupings and not as a single unit placed at random. This way decorative cutouts, boxes, huge cutout fruits, or other accessories go well together if they are coordinated to fit like a jigsaw puzzle. Think of the dominant element as features and accents and repeat the decorative props.

This element is an important one as accents and interest points are spread throughout a room dressed for an occasion. See Figure 5.5 in Chapter 5 on the Wild West and note the dominant look gained on the table by the bark-covered tripods. These centerpieces are 6 ft high and trimmed with leather, felt, and beads with grasses exploding out of the top. Another excellent example is shown in the Christmas photograph in Color Plate 21. The decorative

this visual appearance. See the florals used in the Fab 50s theme, shown in Color Plates 31–33.

cutout trees range in height from 10 ft to 4 ft high × 4 ft wide. Another perfect example of dominance is the pathway of 14 ft high palm trees in Figure 7.7.

Figure 7.7. Pathway of trees. An impressive entrance to any venue, the plywood cutouts tower to 14 feet in height and are freestanding, supported by a wooden brace at the back of the tree. The coloring on the tree trunk is in soft bronze and tan. Glitter is added to the trunks. The tree tops are artistically painted in shades of green highlighted with splashes of white. This is a perfect example of repeating form.

Scale

Floral Design

A standard size centerpiece appears to be in scale when it is sitting on a coffee table in the room of a home. Put that same flower arrangement on a side table in a ballroom and it is way out of proportion. A pair of arrangements placed on either side of ballroom doors would need to tower to 7 or 8 ft in total height. Stage arrangements, for instance, could range from

Decorative Prop

Proportion of a set or prop is determined by the area to be filled. Sets and props can be high, wide, low, or narrow depending on the wall measurement, ceiling height, width, and depth. When visiting any site the ceiling measurement is most important and it is necessary to measure the height at its highest point and then of course, the lowest point in the room. High

5 to 10 ft to really make a statement in the ballroom. Review the size of the table prop in Color Plate 7 on the Casino opening. The room was generous in size and therefore tabletops of this size are quite appropriate due to the facility and ceiling height. This extended type of floral still allows vision to stage.

Another example of the element of size is shown in Figure 6.5 in Chapter 6. A candelabra made of metal and trimmed with bead trims is combined for a Viennese evening. This tall tabletop is 6 ft high with candles and fabric swathed up the stem. It is a variation of a design in a book called *Art of the Party*, by Renny Reynolds.

ceilings take outsized props while a standard 10 ft wall will only display units up to a 9 ft height. This element is as important as all others, if not more so. You need to develop the eye which comes from experience and certainly, training. Unless the set and props fill the areas to satisfaction, the value of the job will not be noticeable.

The scale is accurate in Figure 6.9 in Chapter 6 as a backdrop of New York City with its Statue of Liberty and 14 ft high fantasy tree. The Evening in Ascot party in Color Plates 25 and 26 shows lifesize horses in this themed party. The horses measure 7 ft to 8 ft high and long, and 40 were used in the room.

Rhythm

Floral Design

In contrast, rhythm in design begins at the tip of the tallest bloom and flows gently to the lowest point of the arrangement. Rhythm means movement. (Refer to the butterfly mobile in Figure 8.5.) Notes of music flow from left to right; in literature, too, words flow across the page. In floral design, by contrast, the rhythm or movement being at the tip of the tallest flower and finishes at the bottom of the lowest flower or leaf in a container. Rhythmic movement is created by flowers cut at varying lengths and arranged in space to begin the flow. Every stem is cut at a different length, perhaps only a small difference, but a difference nevertheless. The differences become noticeable when the picture is complete and the rhythm flows through the design. Work toward a smooth and steady flow of material and avoid unnecessary and unsightly gaps. Remember that while space can be a vital part of the pattern, a hole or great gap is unsightly. Space is gained by allowing every flower to have its breathing space.

Refer to Figure 7.8, which shows how the flow of the 8-ft-high tablepieces moves smoothly from top to base. The gilded and gorgeous tabletops start at the door, encircle the room, and return to the door. A lower style is featured in the central area of the room for guest sight lines.

Decorative Prop

Rhythmic movement in set and prop design is created with the placements of props, sets, and florals in offerings of varying height, size, color, and shades and arranged in the allocated space to create the visual flow. It is important to be aware of the flow of material and props to avoid unnecessary and unsightly gaps. Space is an essential to be involved as a vital part of the pattern. The rhythm in the room décor starts at the entrance, encompasses the walls, moves onto stage, and returns to the entrance doors. The differences of shape and size are only noticeable when the three-dimensional jigsaw puzzle picture is put together.

The golden gala in Color Plate 23 is another example of rhythm, movement, and animation combined. The skyline is created by designing, cutting, and reinforcing the 8 ft × 4 ft panels of plywood. The movement is created by the different heights and the variety of shapes at the top along with the variation of shading of the paint finish. The colors extend into gold, bronze, and touches of black.

Figure 7.8. Gilded palms. This impressive tabletop towers over the heads of the guests as it clearly shows the space between the top level designed with the gilded palms and the base of the arrangement which shows a collection of seasonal flowers, ferns, and votive candles. A black wrought iron stand is 4 ft in height, holds the palms and allows visibility across the table.

Harmony

Floral Design

To achieve harmony, be prepared to experiment. Rearrange colors, interchange decor panels and foliage, reverse a fabric to emphasize dullness rather than brightness. Develop a variety of shapes and surface finishes. Manipulate old and new; mix and match. Strive to create completeness and harmony in your design for therein lies the skill of the truly original designer.

The worst thing that can happen is to have planned, detailed, made, and worked the design, then to view it objectively and recognize that something has been missed. The words "if only" need to stay at home. Companies today have exceedingly high expec-

Decorative Prop

Harmony with sets and props virtually means working towards a total look without any discordant features. The key is to play up one idea and carry it through rather than have a barrage of varying props in shapes and colors that is not coordinated or planned to fit. Harmony is the relationship between the component parts selected for the event. An harmonious event design is a unified design. The units must gel together in color, texture, form, and style.

Refer to Color Plates 17, 18, and 19 to see how this is achieved in the 1945 Victory Party. The research gave us the 1940s pin-up girl (seen in Figure 5.11) in a surround door wrap

tations of their planner, producer, and designer, so the responsibilities lie in providing the best possible in all aspects of the job. Hours of work will give harmony and the overall total look expected. Refer to the Ascot photo in Color Plate 25. This shows a well-coordinated look for an evening at Ascot featuring black and white linens with white blooms and trim. Note the storyboard in Color Plate 26.

of the red, white, and blue fabric. This theme shows the harmonious effect created with florals and props to interpret the 1940s.

The Basic Elements of Design

The basic elements of design will give you general knowledge about the principles utilized by any designer. To differentiate the two words, the principles are line, form, color, texture, and pattern, while the elements display the use of space, dominance, scale, rhythm, and harmony. Below is a handy reference chart to understand the balance and requirements of true design.

The Basic Elements of Design

Line

Straight. The lines can be straight and give emotional quality to a design.
Curved. Lines can be curved for movement.
Combination. A good design combines both.

Form

Repeating. Foliage can be all the same shape—all ivy leaves or all roses, etc.
Contrasting. Leafage can be in contrast (i.e., camellia with blade of flax).
Function. Form holds its place in the design and strengthens the heart of it.

Color

Appeal. Instinctively this is the most important point to the viewer.
Harmonize. Color can be placed in harmony with setting (i.e., creams with yellows or pinks with burgundy).
Contrast. Contrasting color patterns create impact (i.e., yellows with violets).

Texture

Surface. The surface of the leaf, flower, or accessory is visually important.
Compatability. The textural surfaces must marry well.

Interest. The various finishes create interest, accent, and flicker points.

Pattern

Solid. The pattern is made up of solid forms, then areas of mass.
Voids. These become part of the pattern allowing the materials to show.
Dimension. The three-dimensional look must be noticeable otherwise the design will be flat and boring.

Space

Restraint. It is just as important to know what to leave out, as it is to put in with flowers and foliage.
Isolate. Space costs nothing. It helps to beautify.
Recognition. It shows the shape, style, and stability in the design.

Dominance

Groupings. Materials are emphasized if grouped rather than scattered.
Balance. Visual height is evident when groupings are weighted correctly.
Distinction. Leafage or choicest blooms play a more dominant role if selected and shown at their best.

Scale

Interior. Proportion of a design is determined by the area to be filled.
Ratio. Can be extended to at least six times the height and depth of the container.
Taste. Style can be low and compact, or high and spectacular.

Rhythm

Force. Gives movement of material without showing a monotonous effect.

Motion. Materials must arrive at a logical point in the design and then flow on.
Transition. Can create value with materials used and therefore the apparent flow becomes evident.

Harmony

Relationship. This exists when all parts do not conflict but rather form a concordant picture.
Impression. Creating completeness is the intention with materials and colors.
Attitude. Old and new can come together. With an open mind progress is inevitable.

Fourteen Workable Combinations

1. One kind of flower as a feature for instance all roses, all tulips, all gerberas: the one of a kind combination of blooms.
2. Three of a kind floral combination if 60 tables are required. Break the collection into 20 tables with roses, 20 with tulips, and the remaining with gerberas with soft asparagus fern.
3. An unusual look is achieved with bowls of green apples and green glasshouse chrysanthemums and miniature monsterio leaves. Alternatively, use large single ivy leaves.
4. Baby's breath massed in a posy style with glasshouse roses is a favorite of the past, but always appealing especially if the baby's breath is sprinkled with diamond dust, which gives it a glamorous sparkle.
5. A collection of fruit. For example, three oranges, two apples, two bananas, passionfruit, and rockmelons cut and seeded to hold a 2-inch candle and orange or yellow gerberas.
6. The daffodil posy with gray eucalyptus will combine well with a colorful cluster of balloons flying in the air.
7. Blue purple liathus with hot pink gerberas and soft purple misty coupled with miniature gray gum.
8. Striking strelitzia with its bright orange head teams with the exotic orange anthirriums.
9. White Singapore orchids with leather fern, sasanqua leafage, and white cymbidium orchids are quite stunning.
10. The English look of violets and lavender bunched into a big hand posy create positive comments.
11. A gold or silver theme could require larger leaves sprayed in the required color with a single stem of phalaenopsis and ming fern.
12. The not so popular sim carnation looks really attractive when a bunch of white carnations is arranged with huge strawberries and an occasional mushroom tooth-picked for interest.
13. For a wine launch, add a long stem rose to an empty wine bottle and use a collection of five or six in the center of the table.
14. For a press conference, use rolls of old film with old magazine covers incorporated with six or seven roses.

The art of floral combination is a special skill: mixing and matching to achieve just the right combination. Shapes and sizes generally do not pose a problem, because sense prevails when talking about what flowers to use in what position in the ballroom or event venue. The tables demand the most attention because guests are viewing the florals in close proximity. It's a mistake to try to be clever by selecting and requesting flowers that are difficult to come by, color that may be a problem, or types of blooms that are in short supply (or available at present, but difficult to procure at the time of the event).

As a general guide, advise the florist that the preference is to use not more than three types of foliage in the bowls, matched with one or two kinds of flower types. This is not a hard and fast rule, but it works if florists are experienced. Arrangers who have had years in the industry tend to experiment with concepts that have been read about or observed.

The Stages of Development for Floral Arrangements

The Background

The background must be boldly secure and clean in outline. If it is not well constructed and the pattern not clearly defined, the completed arrangement will not come together in function or appearance. This area is the silhouette of the design, made up of the solid forms of flowers, foliage, and the space.

For solid background formation, choose flowers or foliage with the tallest and strongest stems. The first step in designing an arrangement is to group the materials with which you are working. Buds, branches, and tall or spiked forms should be put aside to create the background.

Knowing the type of material that is suited to each specific area means that you're halfway there. Regardless of the shape or pattern being planned, gladioli, bulrushes, or blossoms will give a strong outline because they all have good length and solid stems.

The shape and pattern of geometric material will dictate the geometric pattern, whether it be triangular, rectangular, or circular. For instance, outlining a simple triangle with gladioli will ensure that the framework is held. The stems should not extend beyond the triangle frame. They must be (and appear to be) bold and secure. When the structural pattern of the design is evident, check that the height is proportional to the width.

In this part of the construction, be careful to avoid crossed lines. Do not allow branches, twigs, or foliage to cross or confuse pattern shape. This will cause visual conflict and detract from the overall design.

The Midground

This is the important transitional or filler area which links the background of the arrangement with the heart or focal point of the design. It provides the steady flow and gentle movement between the background area and stage three, the focal point. Usually the stems are of medium length and the flower heads and leaves are of smaller size.

This area can be troublesome if you don't understand just how little is really needed. Because it is known as the filler area, some arrangers tend to fill it up by packing in material. It's important to be conscious of space, so show restraint and use every

stem to advantage. Keep the area free of confusion and clutter. It is tempting to use too many stems, to pack them in simply to cover the flower foam, or to use up all the material on the table or bench. Remember, restraint is necessary to create crisp, clean lines.

Trimming the filler material is essential in the midground. Remove excess foliage or leaves from the bottom of the stem too, to prevent the flower foam from becoming compacted with unnecessary stems. Again, stems are different lengths to emphasize movement and create a stronger line.

The forms here differ from the previous list in that they are of medium length and smaller in size. Soft pines and ferns are also excellent fillers. Take care to give the flowers breathing space—allow them their own space to show off! Don't crowd them too closely together and be aware of the space you create, for this too will become part of the overall pattern.

The Focal Point

The focal point is the center of interest and the choicest blooms are usually held in reserve for this dominant part, or heart, or the arrangement. By this stage the lines of height and width have been established, and the filler has softened these lines so that they can converge without interruption to this point of dominance.

It is important to group and sort the flowers of distinction in readiness for this dominant area of the composition. These prominent blooms should be arranged in the container so they flow through and cascade over the container's edge. The eye must continue to flow, so each bloom is cut at a different level. The smallest blooms should be placed toward the top of the arrangement and the biggest and fullest blooms at the level of direct eye contact.

Understanding your material and its potential is vital not only to successful floral design, but to the design of the whole space in which the event is to take place. Avoid clutter, use space, don't allow scrappy bits and pieces to detract from the overall look. Dominant flowers should be worked so they flow to the focal point: dominant colors/cutouts/models should be used to point to the main attraction in the room.

When you're constructing a flower arrangement, one large flower or blob of color won't do justice to any design. It is this heart of the arrangement that first catches the viewer's eye and the flowers must flow smoothly from step to step without any obvious discordant gaps. Similarly, plan the flow of your entire room.

Chapter 8

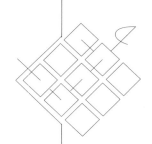

Special Flowers and
Special Events

Designers planning the floral art for a special event can find it easy to become intimidated not only by the choices available—bloom, type, texture, and color—but also by the different ways these florals can be approached.

It is important to keep in mind one vital fact: each style and method of decorating a venue with flowers is just as important and valid as the next. The savvy events person knows that quality of design outweighs quantity, regardless of size, location, and style. Take into account not only what is in vogue right now but what suits your theme. Just as fashion changes from season to season, year to year, so do trends in floral design. In fact, over the years, designs and styles have changed quite dramatically.

Floral designers continually search for new ways, new styles, with quicker production methods. Events can go from one extreme of style to the other. The secret is to maintain the consistency of quality control.

If the budget allows it, flowers do a wonderful job of highlighting the pre-dinner drinks or pre-function area of the venue. Doorways might be dressed with florals; wall areas might be featured. The stage could be dressed in florals while tabletops become conversation pieces.

The innovative event professional uses any creative source available. This, incidentally, applies not only to the floral designer, but to the person who blows a balloon, tosses a salad, throws a switch, creates a sound, or organizes the guests.

One invaluable resource to floral designers is the work done by past masters.

A knowledge of the basic principles of design will give you a variety of patterns and shapes that can be worked and reworked to give different looks. If you remain alert to other elements of design and staging, it becomes easier to create a more intriguing mood or tone. This will only happen if you keep researching with the aim of knowing more in order to give more. Looking back to see what has been done before is a positive, not regressive, step. Traditional styles act as a springboard for trendy design: the events producer, organizer, or artist needs that hook on which to hang their creative hat.

When it comes to florals, there are four basic categories: Traditional, Contemporary, Oriental, and European. Each influence has a primary feature and a primary use. Secondary terms such as Freestyle, Eastern, Abstract, and Modern are used, too, but it's easy to get confused if you rely too much on labels.

Borrow from the Masters

The Development of European Floral Design

While plant material has changed very little through the ages, the methods used to decorate with it certainly have. Following the so-called Dark Ages of the medieval period, there was a tremendous flowering of culture and release of creative energy during the Renaissance of the fifteenth and sixteenth centuries. The Baroque period that followed saw floral style becoming increasingly ornamental, leading into the Rococo period of the eighteenth century and its trend towards prettiness and charm. Then came the Georgian period, with a strong French influence, before the less inspiring Victorian era when creative taste appeared to be at a low ebb.

Figure 8.1 will help you identify the characteristics of each of the above periods. The chart explains the flowers, type, and color best featured for the period along with the style of container to be utilized.

Renaissance
- Flowers alone used in picture frames, as fabric motifs, as details in paintings, in festivals, and as adornments in the home.
- Flowers and foliage as well as fruit and vegetables frequently grouped together as decoration.
- Favored flowers include lotus, jasmine, iris, tulip, rose, hyacinth, and lilac.
- Flowers arranged in classically shaped urns and vases, tall and lavishly decorated compotes, or elaborately woven baskets.

Baroque
- Flower arrangement increasingly ornamental. Style was virile, blustering, and bold.
- Large flowers often featured; branches of large-leaved foliage strong in form and warm in color.
- Dutch and Flemish artists favored massive containers of metal, glass, and porcelain.

Rococo
- Style in this period reflected prettiness and charm.
- Ceramics, tapestries, and fabrics from this period show many bouquets, so we may assume that this form of floral decoration was very popular.
- Floral arrangements became denser; elegance was enhanced with greater height than width; the beauty of individual flowers was highlighted.
- A typical French arrangement of the day would have included delphiniums, blue hyacinths, white roses, and pale pink hydrangeas displayed in a compote, an alabaster urn, or Dresden ware.

Figure 8.1. Features of floral design during European historic periods. Explains the history and background which influences styles of design.

Georgian • The French influence remained strong: containers such as silver wine chalices, ginger jars, baskets, epergnes, Wedgwood urns, and tureens were popular.
• Plants characteristic of the Georgian era included candytuft, anemone, larkspur, dahlia, chrysanthemum, narcissus, statices, salvia, sunflower, and Queen Anne's lace.

Victorian • Not a popular era in floral design. Color and design fell prey to conflict and clutter.
• Artificial flowers of soft material appeared, carefully arranged with feathers, dried fruits, and shells and preserved under glass.
• The posy, still in fashion today, appeared in this period: a little bunch of various flowers, tied and placed in flared vases or made into a nosegay with lace edging. Flowers in posies included forget-me-nots, steaonatis, and other miniature flowers.

Figure 8.1. (cont.)

Now let's take a look at the four different categories spoken of earlier—traditional, contemporary, Oriental, and European—and see how they can be creatively used to enhance the themes we choose for special events.

The Traditional Style

It's important to have an understanding of the traditional style, because it will always have appeal. It stems from the teachings of the old masters.

The traditional way of styling usually shows flowers and foliage in mass, and this will never be outdated. The shapes featured in the work of traditional artists are the same geometric shapes we use as patterns today. They form the starting point for almost any style. When using traditional styling, we simply need to guard against constant repetition which dulls the thinking and closes the mind to new ways and new styles. It's important to keep the mind open to new ideas and new ways of using the traditional shapes and concepts to create designs for the contemporary word. See Color Plates 27 and 28. Plate 27 gives us an overall look at a room that depicts a very traditional theme; Plate 28 shows the formality created by the fabric swagging in the background. The abundance of blooms in the freestanding pedestal complements the traditional feeling of the centerpiece on this formal table for ten.

Another traditional concept can be seen in Color

Plate 29. These church pews have been lavishly dressed for a wedding with huge bows and flowers. This is an absolutely beautiful look when the traditional style is requested.

It is important to have an understanding of this irreplaceable traditional style. It is useful, appealing, and possibly used more than any other style. Guests love to walk into a room and see flowers en masse; it takes their breath away. Conversation is naturally directed toward the look of the room and the fragrance in the air. The impact of stunning floral design can linger in memory longer than the function itself. The effect of good floral design cannot be underestimated as a component of the event framework. (Refer to Figure 8.2).

View the shape and its usage:

The Traditional Influence

The traditional influence can be seen in the triangular frame (Figure 8.3): flowers are distributed evenly on either side of the central axis.
Ferns and blooms must extend and cascade over the container's edge, adding softness. The edge falls over for effect.
To achieve edge fallover add a medium-sized bowl to the top of the pedestal. This bowl is prepared with dampened floral foam and cascading ferns.
Lowest cascade point.
Transitional edge fallover gives the appropriate balance to the traditional style and influence.

The Contemporary Style

Contemporary designs are characterized by greater flexibility with materials: your imagination can be stretched to the limit. There's greater emphasis on leaves and foliage. Compare the diagram of the traditional arrangement to the contemporary. Figure 8.3 shows the traditional arrangement, in which material is distributed evenly. Similarly, branches and leaves alone can say it all. The contemporary arrangement could be beautifully created with a third of the amount used in the traditional bowl, with the spaces in the design becoming part of the pattern.

The keys to successful floral designing are tech-

Figure 8.2. Flowers in symmetry. The antique pedestal and urn holds a 10-ft. high traditional arrangement which is placed at the entrance of a ballroom. The combination of florals included camellia foliage, asparagus ferns, lilies, stock, carnations, and orchids. The glittered stars and fabric serve as an accessory to the design. The feature is the living statue costumed in royal blue and white lycra to match the design.

nique and details. Place yourself where a guest will sit or stand, and view the work critically. Remember that negative comments can be a demotivator on the job, so avoid criticism unless constructive advice immediately follows. If you can see that corrections need to be made, verbalize them in a positive way: *"It will have better overall look if. . . ."*

Regardless of whether the pattern is symmetric, asymmetric, triangular, or crescent, the look should be full and abundant.

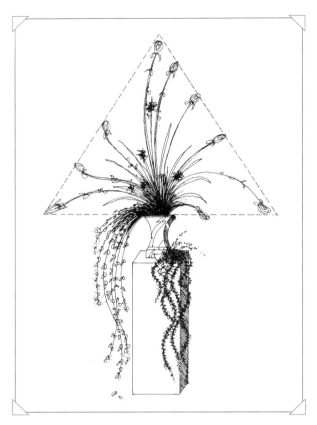

Figure 8.3. Traditional style. Still popular today, this triangular design is accented with a modern edge fallover.

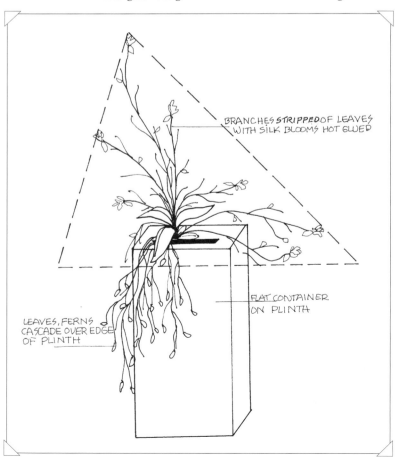

BRANCHES *STRIPPED* OF LEAVES WITH SILK BLOOMS HOT GLUED

FLAT CONTAINER ON PLINTH

LEAVES, FERNS CASCADE OVER EDGE OF PLINTH

The Contemporary Influence

Branches blackened with silk blooms hot-glued for effect. The shape remains traditional, yet the look is quite contemporary in feeling (Figure 8.4)

The balance is achieved by adding gold and distinctive leafage to the base of the vase with edge fallover repeated with the leaves.

Edge fallover is created.

This contemporary feel applied to the look of today is a real plus in event designing and work. In terms of product quantity it is economical, but because of the time spent in preparing the branches being used, costs remain on the same level.

The word new often crops up in the events arena, especially when the client writes the brief. The immediate mental response from the events professional is "What's new? What's different? What's original?" The answer is that nothing is so new that it creates a "must have!" response.

The best way of coming up with something new is to look at what's been done, then revise, revamp, and represent it in a way that has not been seen or done before. Chapter 5 will be useful here.

The contemporary look, built purely on the beauty of the branch, offers great scope for ceiling work as well. Refer to Figure 8.5 to view the added use of branches in the butterfly ceiling mobile. To carry the decor key features throughout the room not only should they be arranged around the room but extended into the ceiling where they free fall from a wooden grid with the fabric draping to create ceiling effects. Sprays of 7-ft branches have been strapped and wired to a wooden grid, which is then tied to ceiling hooks or rods with rope or wire. Flowers are wired to the branches for effect, then foam core butterflies and fabric swagging completes the look. To beautify it further, fairy lights can create a fantasy look in the ceiling and a matching floor piece within the ballroom entrance doors completes the look. (Figure 8.6).

In short, acquiring and developing an understanding of the influences of design allows personal growth.

The Oriental Style

The Oriental style (Figure 8.7) comes from the study of *Ikebana,* or Japanese flower arrangement. Ikebana

Figure 8.4. (left) Contemporary style. This is a shift from the equilateral triangle design and is an often applied look of today.

Figure 8.5. Butterfly mobile. The butterflies are suspended by nylon fishing line rather than to silver wire because when lights hit a mobile of this kind regardless of the decor and it is hung with silver wire or rope, these unsightly mechanics will show. Strive to cover every mechanic.

followers are dedicated to the preservation of traditional values and culture. They strive to maintain the ideas and craft of their ancestors. The Japanese teacher or master aligns himself with nature, and the arrangements depict growth seasons and natural surroundings, to say nothing of skill and understanding.

Ikebana style is based on the asymmetric triangle. The placements at the three points of the triangle are known as *shin, soe,* and *hikae.* To simplify the approach to the Oriental tradition, it is easier to think of these as the primary, secondary, and tertiary points and regard the lines between them as supporting lines. Refer to any Ikebana arrangement: the three points of the triangle are clearly defined. Camellia branches and willow broom, for example, can be shaped, trimmed, and persuaded to form these main lines. Practice and patience, coupled with self-discipline and coordination, are the keys to successful Ikebana design.

Where can Ikebana be used? The theme party, *A Night in the Orient* offered a perfect opportunity to display this Oriental influence. The ballroom was dressed in an Eastern manner, and the colors of red and gold provided the dominant look.

Color Plate 11 shows lavish décor, with a 16-ft red glittered dragon, suspended over the heads of the guests, providing a focal point. The corner displays show a decorative prop that has height, style, and simplicity. The tripod effect was achieved through the use of three pieces of bamboo which were drilled, screwed, and glued to provide a triangular frame. The exotic look is reinforced by the simplistic placement of the fan, fabric, coolie hat, and lantern. The line is repeated in the table centerpiece, and the theme is carried through even to the exacting detail in the napkin trim. Space always becomes an important element to the design. The openness is part of the pattern.

The European Style

The most obvious feature of European styling is its use of parallel or vertical lines, or parallelism as floral

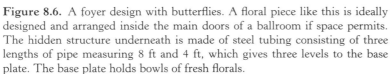

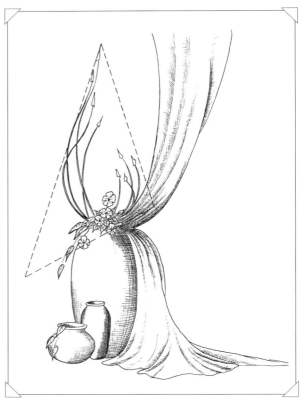

Figure 8.7. Oriental style. An Ikebana look which emphasizes movement.

Figure 8.6. A foyer design with butterflies. A floral piece like this is ideally designed and arranged inside the main doors of a ballroom if space permits. The hidden structure underneath is made of steel tubing consisting of three lengths of pipe measuring 8 ft and 4 ft, which gives three levels to the base plate. The base plate holds bowls of fresh florals.

A design of this style creates conversation as the sheer size of it is a talking point in itself. It measures eighteen feet in height which gives a towering effect. This is balanced by the eight foot dimensional width. The decorative base is made of rocks, bark, slate, small ponds of water, flowering plants, and groupings of flowers plus floating flowers. The butterflies play a dominant role in this specialty design.

presenters often call it. It is built on a series of lines, which can be repeated on different levels. This European influence is developed according to the design requirement, and relies strongly on division of materials and groupings of colors. It is very beautiful when executed properly.

It can be very simple or very elaborate, and can also be arranged with just a few flowers or flowers en masse, but either way the repeating pattern of vertical lines on a table or throughout a venue is strong and striking. See Figure 8.8 which shows the verticals arranged on a park bench.

Table 8.1 provides a valuable comparison of the four types of floral categories.

To Summarize

It's no easy task staying abreast of the reading matter related to any industry, but time spent reading and researching is always worth it. Designers who stay open to new ideas and spend time experimenting find that their skills improve and their performance sharpens. Maintaining a reputation for quality or creativity and workmanship in this way energizes any professional.

Designing and arranging flowers for an event can be both great fun and a stimulating experience. It does entail hard physical work and mental exertion as you study the theme and create the décor. Of course, some events cry out for flowers; others do not. Remain flexible in this area. Flowers can set the mood or create an atmosphere, especially when the imagination is given free rein.

Special event planners or producers do not need to worry about actually caring for, conditioning, transporting or arranging flowers for the event, but it is an undoubted advantage to know what should and could be done to give all blooms their maximum life expectancy. Knowledge is always power.

The Floral Workroom

The florist generally becomes part of the set up/load in process when florists work as part of the event team. Of course, the quantities are subject to change according to the size of the job, but the basic necessities follow:

Floral Workroom Checklist

- Garbage bins and plastic drop sheet
- 20 buckets—small, medium, large
- Flower preservative
- Preferably own trolley/cart

- Four jugs and water sprays
- Box of gauge 22–20 wires
- Chicken wire
- Floral foams and dry foam
- Urns and pedestals
- Glue gun and glue sticks
- Bowls and trays
- Floral tape and pot tape
- Leaf gloss and *Design Master*® sprays
- Flowers required
- Foliage and accessories required
- Cutters, scissors, stapler
- Battery-operated drill
- Cloths for wiping down
- Own hot water urn, tea, coffee and cups etc.
- Instructions on arrangements
- Silk florals if required
- Any floral accessories
- Trestle work tables—rented or owned
- 8 ft × 4 ft plywood and risers (create good worktops)
- Contact numbers of all suppliers
- Contact numbers of all florists
- Checkbook or cash

Figure 8.8. European style. This is a blending of both vertical and horizontal lines.

Table 8.1. Design Comparison Chart

	Background	*Focal Point*	*Midground*
Traditional	• Shape is formal. • Foliage and flowers are extended to fit the full frame of the triangle, asymmetric triangle, or circle. • Flowers are used in abundance, cascading freely over the vase	• The focal flowers are placed directly in front with one point of interest. • The three-dimensional flowers are featured at the heart. • Large open blooms are best used in this area.	• Forms vary in this midground area. • Smaller flowers and softer foliage are used as a filler in this transitional area of construction. • Avoid packing in foliage just to fill it.
Contemporary	• Framework is linear in outline area and ideally used with low budget events. • Less background material is used to frame the geometric shape of the triangle, circle, asymmetric triangle. • The outline can be split: i.e. arrangement is designed in the two sections of the container, while maintaining total look	• This area can also be divided in terms of two interest points instead of one. • Fewer flowers are required at the points of interest but choicest quality predominates. • Fabrics can be included at the focal point, picking up colors of the flowers used.	• This midground area is far less full than a traditional piece. • Clear-cut shapes of either triangles or circles are obvious because restraint is shown in this stage of design construction. • Use foliage that is clear in form and avoid small blustering branches.
European	• Vertical lines are apparent—from one straight line to four or five. • Parallel lines are featured at varying lengths. • Fresh and dried can be combined, even silk flowers can become an option.	• The contrast is in weight and a feeling of calmness. • The focal point or points come to rest. • Stems are cut much shorter, and are accentuated by clumps of leaves with a variety of moss, vines, and leaf.	• Forms are reduced to create space—in effect, the midground is almost non-existent. • Groupings of leaves are formed en masse. • Clusters of grass and layering of the fresh materials is clearly seen.
Oriental	• The Sogetsu study of Ikebana is based on three main lines: *shin, soe,* and *hikae* (primary, secondary, and tertiary). • The triangle is in frame silhouette and all branches are arranged within. • Variety of branch material is used and trimmed to beautify. • Restraint is important with this style—know what to leave out.	• One rose or many can be arranged to form the heart of this Oriental influence. Large distinctive form is used as a feature. • Strong colors are used in this area and add stability as the area of design.	• Softer form is used as a back-up to the principal area. • Textural compatibility is high on the priority list. • Distinctive leafage • Sometimes accessories can be added to repeat a theme concept.

Set Up a Workroom

See Figure 8.9 for an example of a standard breakout room measuring 20 ft × 16 ft.

The following are a few general workroom guidelines:

> **Workroom Guidelines**
>
> • Allocate the product into its specific area
> • Set up an administration area

> • Arrange tables to one side for completing work
> • Other side for water buckets and floral foam
> • Centralize the 4 ft × 4 ft worktops on the in-house or rented trestles

Flowers either arrive directly at the floral studio for the event or are directed to the venue per your instruction. Whenever possible, the flowers should be sent directly to the function, especially if the job is away from your home city. Where the blooms are sent also depends on whether the preparation of the florals must be done on- or off-premise. Often the venue will decide this. Remember to plan this with the producer and consult with the venue coordinator.

The choice of the florals for event and party use will be influenced by availability, but first grade plant material is a must for high standard floristry. Florists realize the importance of treating the flowers before use and allowing correct conditioning time to ensure maximum life span. Flowers have to withstand transport and movement to the venue as well as the lighting within the room. The less flowers are handled the better. Even with slight handling, delicate blooms can be damaged by bruising. Tender loving care is vitally important.

There are no gimmicks with treatment. It's not necessary to rush out and buy flower food pills or mysterious solutions guaranteed to extend the life of blooms. There is, however, a product called *Crysal,* sold by floral wholesale suppliers, which is recommended for event flower use.

Timing the delivery of florals requires experience and planning. The more delicate the bloom (especially roses and tulips), the more it requires careful observation. Often these flowers need to be received as early as two days before the job to allow opening. If they are received on the day of the event, time is too short to allow conditioning and opening. Gladioli, lilium, and the aratum lily should be received into the florist's studio four days prior to the event and then transported to the location. The length of time between actual picking and placement in deep water can be quite considerable, so avoid delay in treating the flowers upon arrival into the workroom.

Heat is another element that draws life-juices from flowers. Sun shining directly on flowers through glass windows in the workroom or venue set-up is to be avoided; as is a venue or hotel breakout room without air conditioning. Spray-mist the flowers morning and afternoon to keep blooms glistening.

Drafts
Avoid having flowers stored in drafty rooms, hallways, or doorways in venues. If the venue set-up is in the open, try to keep them at even temperature. With proper care and treatment their life span is extended. It is important to keep flowers looking their best. They are such a visual element in event design that guests tend to focus on them. Tabletop arrangements are viewed up close and always discussed.

Another tip: if foliage is yellowish or limp, it is a good indicator that the blooms are not fresh. Flowers and leaves should be crisp to the touch and with additional care and conditioning, maximum life span is assured.

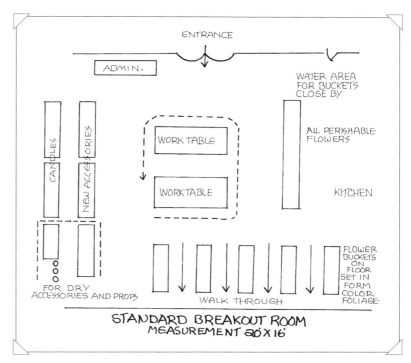

Figure 8.9. Standard breakout room. Your workroom is an essential component when working on site. Assure that its layout is functional.

Care
Flowers usually arrive into the workroom or allocated destination in large, long boxes. Alternatively, arrangements can be made to have them delivered to the location in containers of water protected by cardboard wrap and strapped: an innovative approach to transporting perishable product from grower to designer.

Be Prepared
Before flowers and foliage arrive, have all the buckets prepared in advance. Buckets should be in the following sizes:

6″ (15cm) bucket. For mini roses and small stemmed blooms i.e., lavender, hyacinths, or similar flowers

10″ (25cm) bucket. Holds stems approximately 12″ (30cm) in length, suitable for shorter roses, tulips

15″ (38cm) bucket. Holds most other blooms (Gerbera, Australian native, and lizzianthus)

20″ (51cm) bucket. Exotic anthirriums

24″ (61cm) bucket. Plastic garbage bin is ideally used for all tall fresh materials such as gladioli, long stemmed roses, carnations, lilies, strelitzia, delphiniums, and similar flowers

Tubs 10″ (25cm deep). 24″×16″×10″ (61cm × 40cm × 25cm) in measurement; suitable for soaking and carrying Singapore orchids

Bins. Suitable for holding the masses of foliage, ferns, and grasses

Transporting

Transporting fresh product can be a trial unless you are prepared to carry large batches to the job. Ideally wooden boxes are made specifically to hold, say, six buckets. As flowers come off the truck they are moved onto trolleys rather than having someone carry one or two buckets at a time into a specific area. Bunches may need to be wrapped singly in newspaper to protect them against damage. It is easy to have all florals treated in the floral workroom, bucketed, and then transported.

Large sheets of newspaper are indispensable. If bunches are rolled into a sheet of newspaper, this avoids damage to the head of the bloom. Once flowers are unpacked, sort them by type and stem length: gladioli together, roses together, and so on. Select the tallest and heaviest material such as palms, flax, willow, etc.

Conditioning the Florals

In a flower shop, conditioning is important, but for events work it becomes a priority. This conditioning of the perishable bloom prolongs its lifespan to the maximum. Certainly some floral materials last longer than others, and for event or party work it is wise to use flowers with lasting qualities (even though all blooms respond to care). You will find this information invaluable when dealing with your florist, or even when discussing floral art with your client.

The Method

Scalding

Leave the stems in up to 5 inches (12cm) of boiling water for a count of 20, then immediately place in a bucket filled with tap water for up to three hours before arranging. This treatment allows the stems to draw water more readily and kills any bacteria that may be present. It is most important to treat and condition prior to use.

When preparing flowers for scalding, hold the stems firmly but take care to protect the flower heads from the steam. Ensure that the petals are not crushed in the process.

Burning

This is an important process for flowers with soft stems or blooms, such as poppies and poinsettias, that bleed a milky fluid from the stem when cut. The milky fluid is the very food that prolongs its life, so the flow must be stopped as quickly as possible. Otherwise, the stem will block up with fluid and water cannot be drawn into the flower head.

The best way to burn the stem is by holding it over a flame or gas jet in the kitchen. If you are regularly dealing with large quantities of flowers, you should buy a portable gas jet to speed up and simplify this process. You'll find that it is money well spent.

Cutting

This technique has been developed from Ikebana. Have a shallow bowl of water on hand and recut the stem under water before positioning it in the arrangement. This lengthens the lifespan of the bloom by removing air bubbles from the stem, thus allowing the water to be drawn more freely towards the head of the flower.

Hints for Successful Conditioning

- Whichever method of conditioning you apply, the stems must go into deep water immediately after the treatment. They should be left in water for four hours or overnight. By then the flowers should be crisp and ready to arrange.
- Keep your jars, vases, and buckets clean. After use wash them in warm soapy water with bleach to kill bacteria. Dry them off and store until the next time you need them.
- Buy a water spray with a fine mist from the hardware store or nursery. Even while flowers are standing in their buckets, spray the head of the bloom as well as underneath the leaves. Several plants drink through their leaves, so there is real value in doing this. Once your arrangement is complete, spray it well to prevent premature wilting and help extend the lifespan of the floral material.

Conditioning Foliage

Foliage absorbs water through its surface tissue and therefore needs to be immersed in water. Most foliage should be immersed for several hours or overnight, allowing time for a thorough drink. However, ferns, geraniums, and other delicate leaves should not be immersed in this way. It's really a matter of experimentation, but generally leaves that feel hardy to the touch can be left in water without fear of waterlogging or leaf damage.

To ensure that your plant materials are correctly conditioned, it is important to follow the procedures outlined in this chapter, as well as the treatment chart in Figure 8.10. Why take time arranging

Type	Scald	Burn	Cut	Additional Care and Comments
Abelia			√	
Acacia			√	
Acanthus			√	
Agapanthus			√	Spray the heads of the blooms well
Ageratum	√			Strip it of its excess foliage to allow it to drink freely
Allium			√	
Alocasia			√	
Alpinia			√	
Alstroemeria		√		Remove excess foliage following burning method. Leave to condition in tepid water.
Amaryllis			√	
Anthirrium			√	After recutting, immerse these blooms for 7 minutes in lukewarm water before arranging.
Arum			√	To color, crush colored chalk, dip cotton into it, and touch the lily.
Aster	√			Clean excess foliage, scald, and allow to condition.
Azalea			√	Recut all stems on a slant.
Baby's breath	√			To open, leave in boiling water for 20 seconds then plunge into cool water. Add ¼ cup (60ml) of bleach to water to keep it white.
Banksia			√	Cut and slit the end of stem to allow free flow of water.
Berries			√	Hammer the stems so that they absorb more water. Strip the branch of its foliage.
Blossom			√	Spray the blossoms with hair spray.
Boronia	√			
Bougainvillea	√			
Bouvardia	√			
Calendula			√	
Calla lily			√	
Camellia			√	Submerge camellia branches for 2 hours under water.
Candytuft	√			Remove excess foliage from base of stem, scrape, then scald for longer life.
Carnation			√	Some say to add lemonade to the water—who knows?
Cattleya			√	
Chrysanthemum	√			Scrape ends before scalding, then scald and stand in deep water. Spray the back of the bloom and underneath the leaf.
Cornflower			√	Strip it of its foliage halfway down the stem.
Cyclamen			√	After recutting, place in warm water to condition.
Cymbidium			√	
Daffodil			√	Arrange in shallow water as these draw water easily because of the hollow stems.
Dahlia	√			
Daisy	√			Remove excess foliage under the water level.
Daphne		√		
Delphinium	√			On the giant delphinium pour water into the stem and plug.
Dendrobium			√	Submerge the orchids and allow to soak in warm water for three minutes. Spray regularly.
Easter daisy	√			Spray well to keep the small blossom daisy developing.
Erica			√	

Figure 8.10. Conditioning treatment for flowers—a quick and easy reference to ensure the longevity of your floral materials.

Type	Scald	Burn	Cut	Additional Care and Comments
Eucharis			√	
Forsythia	√			
Frangipani			√	Keep sealed from air.
Freesia			√	
Fuchsia			√	
Gardenia			√	Keep sealed in airtight box with dampened cotton balls over stems.
Gerbera			√	Wrap in paper singly to straighten stems for four hours before arranging.
Gladiolus			√	Remove the two very top florets to keep florets developing on stem.
Gypsophila	√			
Helleborus		√		
Heliconia			√	
Hibiscus			√	
Hydrangea	√			After scalding, submerge under water for 30 minutes.
Iris			√	
Jonquil			√	
Larkspur	√			
Lavender			√	
Lilac			√	After recutting, submerge under water for 50 minutes.
Lilium			√	
Lily			√	
Lily of the Valley			√	
Lupin			√	
Magnolia			√	
Marigold	√			Remove excess foliage under the water level.
Narcissus			√	
Nasturtium			√	
Nerine			√	
Peony	√			Place in warm water to open the heads quickly.
Phaleonopsis orchid			√	Let the orchid float on top of cool water before use, but if holding stems keep air—sealed.
Poinsettia		√		If a leaf is removed, singe that area so that the white fluid is retained.
Poppy		√		
Protea			√	
Queen Anne's lace		√		
Ranunculus		√		
Rose			√	Remove thorns to allow greater intake into stem.
Statice			√	
Stephanotis			√	To hold, place in airtight box. Soak in water 30 minutes before use.
Stock	√			
Strelitzia			√	
Sweet pea			√	
Tuber rose			√	
Tulip			√	Leave to drink in cool water then wrap single stems in newspaper to straighten stems.
Violet			√	Tie in groupings, soak under water for 30 minutes. Spray often.
Watsonia			√	
Wisteria			√	Submerge underwater for two hours before arranging.
Zinnia			√	

Figure 8.10. (cont.)

Do	Don't
• Select two, maybe three types of flowers	• Select seven or eight varieties for an event
• Tie in all supporting urns, columns, or stands	• Mix the style of vases, urns, or large containers
• Concentrate on one major floral presentation if budget is low	• Use a number of urns of flowers in a room if budget is low—less is more
• Continue to search for a new approach with an old way	• Close off the mind due to personal preference
• Test it before you reject it	• Introduce floristry at random just for the sake of having "something there"
• Learn to select the design category of the past to fit the events	• Use four or more ideas in one event
• Stay with one idea to strengthen the theme	
• Guard against constant repetition	• Avoid repetition without interest
• Keep mind open to variety and form	
• Find or have pedestals or columns made that complement the scale of design	• Do huge arrangements in urns/bowls that won't hold the floral materials
• Detail to impress	• Leave unsightly foam or decayed leaves on blooms
• Spray with water: morning, noon, and prior to the function if possible	• Wet the candle wick when spraying the water mister
• Search for inspiration	• Take creativity for granted. Work to source it through research
• Do what you do best while learning new ways and new methods	• Try to be too clever and overextend when skills are not developed
• Delegate tasks to those equipped to handle them	• Expect the truck driver to swag a piece of fabric

Figure 8.11. The dos and don'ts for floral and design work—An excellent checklist to achieve maximum results.

Figure 8.12. Floral layout for a ballroom. Such a diagram helps you place your florals and achieve maximum balance in your venue.

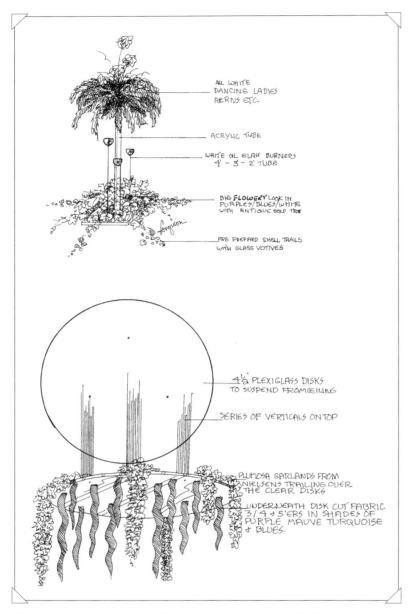

ALL WHITE
DANCING LADIES
FERNS ETC.

ACRYLIC TUBE

WHITE OIL GLASS BURNERS
4' – 3 – 2' TUBE

BIG *FLOWERY* LOOK IN
PURPLES/BLUES/WHITE
WITH ANTIQUE GOLD TRIM

PRE PREPARD SHELL TRAILS
WITH GLASS VOTIVES

4½' PLEXIGLASS DISKS
TO SUSPEND FROM CEILING

SERIES OF VERTICALS ON TOP

PLUMOSA GARLANDS FROM
NIELSENS TRAILING OVER
THE CLEAR DISKS

UNDERNEATH DISK CUT FABRIC
3/4 & 5'ERS IN SHADES OF
PURPLE MAUVE TURQUOISE
& BLUES.

Figure 8.13. Centerpiece and ceilingpiece construction. Utilizing this type of line design assists with the construction of the basic materials to create a masterpiece.

flowers and foliage into a beautiful design, unless you and your client receive the longest possible lifespan?

Floral designers have the benefit of working with a beautiful but perishable product. Let's return the compliment and spend some time to ensure that our plant materials live as long as possible. Refer to the do and don't chart for florals (Figure 8.11).

A layout for a ballroom that features florals. The use of flowers in a ballroom would be ideally displayed as shown in Figure 8.12. Flowers can be massed and cascaded off every pedestal in the room. Use your imagination and fill it in stylishly. Figure 8.13 displays a drawing of a centerpiece and construction for a ceiling. Refer to the look of the Casino in Color Plates 7, 8, and 9.

Chapter 9

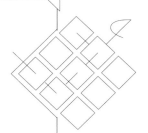

Table Talk

This chapter title says it all for tables that are dressed in style for any special event. The table style and dressing can become conversational. Think back to how many times you have heard it said . . . "and the tables look fabulous!" Unlike the wedding or more formal occasions it is possible to go beyond flowers as many of the tabletops in this book show; for example, tables can go beyond the norm when you cover them with a floor-length cloth. In the case of the tables in Color Plate 30, it's blue satin. The look is extended to the chair covers by using matching fabric. Nine-inch satin bows decorating the chairs contrast with this and complete the look.

Tables

Before the table centerpiece is designed and placed, the table shape must be selected. Tables are available in standard sizes for the round, the rectangle, the oval, and a square which can be created by placing two rectangular tables together. From the rectangular tables, a U-shape, hollow square, or cross can be created.

The U-shape is often selected for use in conference style functions or for lunches where there will be a speaker. The hollow square opens up a few options. It can be arranged in a room with all guests facing into the center or for variety it could be put together on the outside walls of the ballroom with the dance floor in the center. Naturally, breaks are made to allow guest

and waiter access. A most interesting shape is the cross in Figure 9.1. This is an open style for a formal dinner, but could even be used for informal lunches or dinners. Opening up the options like this puts the standard rectangular table to good use.

Linens

The choice of table linens is the next decision to be made. Tablecloths come on a rental, sale, or made to order basis. Linen companies usually rent the items, however, some firms will sell them. If specific colors or fabrics are called for, it may be necessary to source the requirements and have the tablecloths manufactured to style and size. The range of fabrics that are suited for tableware is quite sizeable: polyester, cotton, heavy lamé, tissue lamé, printed chiffon, patterned silk, striped and self-pattern brocade, velveteen and crushed velvet, and lace. It is important that when the cloths are laid down on the table for any function, all seams flow the same way. For example, if there is a center seam, the seams must all flow in the same direction.

The size of the cloths are reasonably standard. The most useful and popular sizes are round floor length cloths (130 in. diameter); the three-quarter size (120 in. diameter); square cloths (90 in. and 84 in. with the 60 in. usually used as an overlay). Rectangular cloths that fall to the floor measure 132

Figure 9.1. Cross table layout—a very interesting design concept for that different dinner.

×90 in., compared to a standard rectangular cloth often used in hotels. The most favored today is the floor length round because it achieves a glamorous look and also covers the table legs and/or any unsightly fittings.

Overlays are also a plus if the budget allows this double clothing. An additional square cloth made of either matching or contrasting color and fabric is positioned over the floor length round cloth. An excellent tip is to place the floor length cloth on the table, followed by a 60 in. square of clear plastic, and finally the matching or contrasting 84 in. overlay. If a glass of wine (especially red) is spilled the stain won't go through to the bottom cloth, which of course is the floor length size. This can save considerably on dry cleaning, not to mention having a crisp, clean cloth to reuse if back-to-back jobs have been booked.

Napkins are an important table accessory and they can be dressed in a variety of ways but the two styles used most often are a stylish fold that is dressed (trimmed) and detailed or the standard catering fold. Figure 9.2 shows three different types of folds.

Figure 9.3 is an example of a buffet design showing a lush look with full skirting and decorative touches.

Tabletops

Figure 9.4 shows a glamorous style of centerpiece. The container is made of plexiglass, otherwise known as perspex. The base is quite heavy to avoid movement and the clear rods are firmly positioned. They vary in length and diameter, giving the vertical effect of the glass votive and flame. The top rod

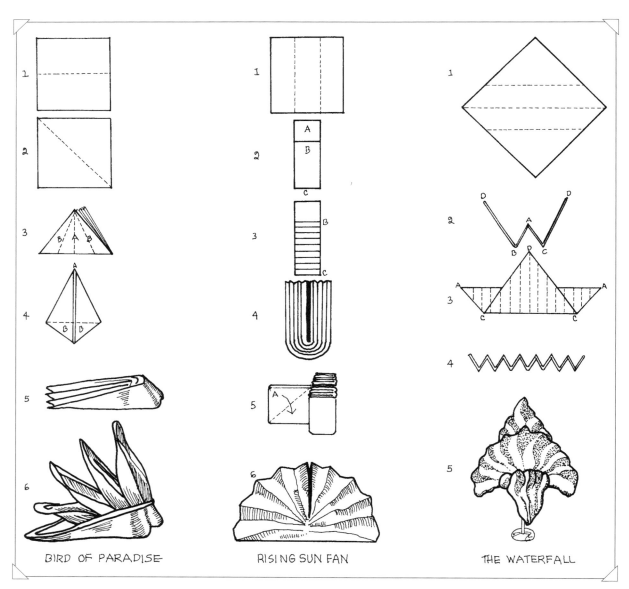

BIRD OF PARADISE   RISING SUN FAN   THE WATERFALL

Figure 9.2. Napkin folds. Trimming or folding your napkins adds that special touch to the table setting.

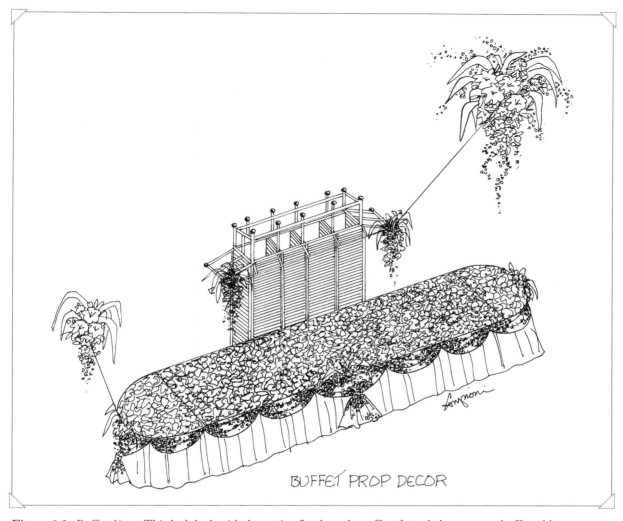

BUFFET PROP DECOR

Figure 9.3. Buffet décor. This lush look with decorative floral touches offers formal elegance to a buffet table.

holds a small plastic container and dampened flower foam to hold the flowers and foliage firmly in position. The shape of this formal design is all round and is naturally viewed from all sides. The combination of fresh florals include asparagus fern, leather fern, and touches of camellia teamed with yellow glass house roses arranged through the design.

The glass votives are attached to the rod with double-sided sticky tape as opposed to hot glue. Votive candles are placed on the tabletop as well to complement the look. The color combination for this scheme is black and gold.

Figure 9.5 shows the full room set for this gala evening where the color combinations are black and gold throughout. A key feature of this particular scheme is the fantasy trees featured in the background of the photograph. They are made of three sheets of 8 ft × 4 ft plywood, cut into a fantasy shape, and silhouetted with masses of fairy lights. The shading of the trees is metallic gold, a scenic paint available from specialty paint or craft stores. The ceiling features many drops of fairy lights which

have been attached to a light aluminum frame to form this special effect.

Figure 9.6 shows a billionaires' breakfast in complete contrast to the gala look. The materials selected for this specialty design are very, very simple and easy to acquire. The design includes a dried branch which has been painted black, gold foil covered chocolate coins, paper money, black satin ribbon, and touches of camellia foliage and fern. The styling of this particular design is easy to arrange but you will need time to give it the required finish. The ribbons and coins have been hot glued.

The photo of the melon and grass shown in Figure 9.7 displays a style which can be used when the budget is restricted. In cases where a minimum figure is allocated for the table setting, the emphasis must be on fewer flowers and more skill, and that is exactly what this photograph offers. It includes seven pieces of dried grass that have been turned and twisted to sit firmly in the dampened floral foam and two full blooms, one sitting on either side of the small foam core hand-painted cutout of the water-

Figure 9.4. Glamor Centerpiece made from plexiglass rods and glued votives. The flowers are arranged on the center rod, which is heavier and thicker to hold the weight of the abundance of flowers and the bowl with a dampened floral foam. This bowl is secured to the top with standard florist's tape. In a ballroom, you can create two styles with this container: Style 1, which you see above, and Style 2, which can be created by eliminating the center rod with the florals. Naturally, the same color flowers and accessories are incorporated into both looks to give the required unity. Neither of these styles obstructs the guests' vision across the table, nor do they interfere with conversations.

Figure 9.5. Fantasy lights room décor. Fairy lights decorate the outline of these designer trees and fairy light ceiling mobiles complete the ambience. The overall look of this ballroom features a full black and gold décor scheme for a corporate event. Note the centerpiece in Figure 9.4, which is on the left of the shot. The tablecloths are in black floor-length lame with black fitted chair covers and gold sashes. All flowers used with this scheme strengthened the look: yellow roses, iris, and glasshouse sim carnations—plus asparagus ferns, which helps to soften the table centerpieces. The fairy lights create a stunning look when suspended from the ceiling on an aluminium frame that holds the drops. A technical lighting operator attaches them to ceiling hanging points and ensures that they work! Thirty sets were used in this ballroom ceiling. The fantasy trees, which are 12 ft high and 8 ft wide, have small holes drilled into the plywood frame through which individual lights are pressed into position. The wiring is taped at the back to secure them. The tree's painted finish can be in black with gold outlining the frame. Another outline of lights (as shown) enhances this.

Figure 9.6. Billionaires' breakfast centerpiece—a novel way to design using chocolate or real coins. Paper play money is the norm (unless your budget allows!) The dried branches are sprayed black and secured in a standard florist's bowl with dry floral foam. The gold covered coins are suspended from ribbon. Hot glue the coins to the ribbon and tie them neatly onto the branches. Create a lavish look with paper money, coins, and asparagus ferns at the base to give a fuller look to the table. This can also be done in a much bigger style and used as a buffet piece and/or arranged as a pair and placed on either end of a freestyle setting.

Figure 9.7. Melon centerpiece. This melon is made from foam core and painted on both sides. The looping of the grass gives movement and the cut lemon gives a fresh scent. This style is simplistic yet stylish and ideally used when the budget is more economical. One feature is that it can be made in advance because the only fresh blooms are the open tiger lilies, which can be added at the last moment. If fresh fruit is to be used, (e.g., lemons, oranges, limes, passionfruit, and grapefruit) it can be cut, wired, and covered—ready to be placed. Before the guests walk in, spray the fruit with water or glaze it with an odorless cooking oil to give a moist look. After the event, keep the watermelon cut-outs as they can be revised and represented again in another complementary scheme. It is wise to build up your collection of table props and accessories as they can become a profitable part of any function.

Figure 9.8. Twin vertical centerpiece. Specifically designed for a long buffet table, its use is ideal for a tropical feast.

melon. A slice of lemon placed on either side of the watermelon gives an overall look to the design which is nestled into moss and short clusters of fern.

Figure 9.8 is a photo of a twin vertical designed specifically for a buffet table. The measurement is quite exaggerated in length and exceeds 7 ft with a height of 4 ft. It is styled as a double vertical arrangement. The base is made from a heavy piece of timber measuring 7 ft long by 9 in. width. The base securely holds flat trays filled with floral foam. The trays are strapped to the base itself. The collection of flowers includes: asparagus fern; moss, camellia, gum, ivy, clusters of hydrangea, bottle brush, cut fruit, wisteria vine, and a foam core cutout.

The twin verticals are suspended and arranged on solid rods of plexiglass and the flowers used are tropical flame, palm leaf, the solid form of rubber leaf, and trails of fine asparagus fern. The dried blades of Australian grass link up to the other vertical line with similar material used throughout the design.

Figure 9.9 shows a combination of a high and low style used in the same ballroom. This is a very versatile look when the high style arrangements are used on the tables farthest from the stage and the low style is utilized on the tables closer to the stage so the guests' vision will not be blocked in any way. The high style arrangement shows a combination of assorted foliage with deep blue iris positioned in the center of the table on a steel stand. A contrasting but complementary low style extends three feet in length but is no more than nine inches in height and the flowers used are iris, orchids, stock, roses, touches of delphinium, and assorted foliage.

Figure 9.10 incorporated black plastic mesh with the striking bloom of the tiger lily family supported by branches of camellia foliage. The flowers themselves are displayed in a two-tiered effect with wild grasses placing emphasis on the design.

Figure 9.11 suggests a badminton party. Sporting events open up a whole range of floral designing for seated or buffet tables. This particular style is displayed and utilized for the buffet. It is arranged on a wooden base with the rackets secured firmly to that base and the fine tubing of plexiglas/perspex is incor-

Figure 9.9. High and low ballroom style centerpieces. A versatile look offers fullness to the outer room walls and good sightlines towards the middle of the room. This was a luncheon setting for a small corporate group. The outside tables displayed the tall arrangements of blue iris and white anthirriums with ferns and other assorted foliage. The low tables were styled with a long, but low, design based on European influences. This style shows groupings of blooms with blocks of color—an ideal look for the oval table that was used. In this case no covers were used as the chairs were appropriate in style for the seetting. The programs on the table were styled as a guest souvenir.

Figure 9.10. Mesh centerpiece—a simple solution that incorporates a client's particular product. This style was used for a Master Builders' formal dinner. The wire mesh, which was purchased from a hardware store, was glamorized with gold spraypaint. The perspex rod, or a wooden dowel stick as an alternative, suffices to hold the wire at the top. Just a few flowers and leaves top this 3-ft design. The base is completed with matching flowers and foliage, wild grass, and more wire mesh.

Figure 9.11. Badminton centerpiece. The florals represent the outdoor feel of the garden court while the shuttlecocks on perspex rods give the movement of a sporting event. Centerpieces such as this become part of the guests' conversation. If the budget is not high, avoid "shotgunning" the decorations by scattering or spreading them around the room. It is better to make the tables more of a feature because this is what the guests view over the dinner period. Again, this style can be pre-prepared, ready to add fresh blooms. Only one racquet is required to create the look; however, utilize two or more for the large style that would be found on buffet tables or food service stations.

Figure 9.12. Sneaker/shoe centerpiece—a fun design appropriately made for a good time party.

porated into the design to show the shuttlecock in flight. Roses and ferns are featured and a black and yellow look is achieved through the use of black rackets, blackened shuttlecock, and bright yellow roses.

Figure 9.12 shows shoes in a simple style but certainly one that would create conversation across the table. Now the secret here is to go out and buy a new shoe. Don't even think of anything else! The new shoe can be painted in a fluorescent color or painted in stripes, polka dots, or stars—your choice. Have fun with it. Add a new sock that has been wired firmly in position and nestled amongst the moss on the mirror base. The length is provided by an aspidistra leaf that has been razored and pinned into a ripple effect.

Figure 9.13 is an arrangement that tends to create an amazing look in a room when there are 20 to 50 tables to complete. This particular tabletop with its gilded palm leaves will carry the entire room simply because of the sheer size of it. It is designed on a black steel stand, the foam is placed on top of the stand, and the 5 ft gilded palm leaves are arranged in the traditional circular fashion creating a pleasing effect from all angles of the table. Soft fronds of asparagus spill over the edge and draw the eye to a

collection of seasonal blooms—roses, gerberas, and iris which complete the table setting.

When all designs and accessories have been placed on the tables, the following points should be checked on your final walk-around:

Final Walk-Around Checklist

- All tables are positioned for guest sight lines to the stage
- No chairs have been removed for rehearsal or use by staff and not replaced
- All linens are even
- Every guest has a napkin
- Pieces of foliage do not trail over a flame or guest plate
- No wilted flowers
- All foliages are clean, crisp, and glossed
- Candles are lit 15–30 minutes prior to guests' entrance
- Menus, place cards, and cutlery are in line with guest seating

Figure 9.13. Gilded palm centerpiece. An excellent centerpiece to fill a large room. Gilded in either silver or gold, lighting plays a major part to emphasize the richness of texture. This centerpiece is over 6 ft high and wide, so it towers over the heads of guests. Palms like this are purchased fresh from market, then undercoated with basic white on both sides. The top layer of brilliant gold *Design/Master* spray will provide a luxurious finish to the leaves. They can also be painted any other color and stored for reuse, but be sure to pack them flat and weigh them down; otherwise the top of frond will turn and become less attractive. Gold lamé floor-length cloths dazzle with effect for this gala look.

Chapter 10

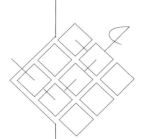

Themes, Themes, Themes

The following pages on themes, themes, themes will provide some inspirational thoughts that can be used for events requiring atmosphere and fantasy. Specific themed layouts like this will act as a springboard for your creativity.

Each themed party will give you the title of the theme with a brief description of what is to be achieved. This is followed by the suggested colors used in the decorations for the room, the use of tablecloth and chair covers, plus table combinations and themed accessories to give a total look.

A Night in Alcatraz . . .

Foghorns, flashing beacon lights, and misty blue fog will surround the guests as they enter into an evening where escape is impossible.

The clanging of the prison gates are repeated as the thumping beat of Jailhouse Rock echoes around the walls of this themed venue. Waiters dressed as prison guards scurry around serving drinks. Laughing guests are given their prison numbers, their fingerprints are taken, and they pose (reluctantly?) for mug shots for the "wanted" poster.

Steel window frames, fencing, and signage all set the scene while the guests await the arrival of Al Capone, the Birdman, and other known criminals. In this company, it might be a good idea to hold on to your wallet!

Colors:
- Black, white, grays

Set Decor:
- Interior walls in sectioned "bars"
- Prison gates at entrance
- Stage backdrop in scenic art
- Paper mache boulders
- Cutouts and outsize picks, shovels, and spades
- Signage—DANGER, HIGH SECURITY, etc.
- Spotlights circulating the room

Linens:
- Gray and white striped cloth
- Matching chair covers

Tabletops:
- Vases of reeds and weeds
- Loaves of bread filled with mock files, screwdrivers
- Clusters of potatoes, peeler, handcuffs, and chain

Accessories:
- Visiting/privilege cards
- Printed pardons
- Foghorns, batons, handcuffs
- Waiter's cap and jacket
- Newspaper clippings on prison news

Figure 10.1. Alcatraz. This diagram features wall design, caged dance floor, sample signage, and props.

Champagne and Chandeliers

This is a cocktail party with a difference! The bubbles are not only in the glasses—a bubble machine keeps the air alive with a constant float of bubbles.

Delicate lighting and glittering chandeliers create a soft, sophisticated atmosphere. The rest is up to the champagne.

Set Decor:	• Huge cutouts of champagne bottles highly decorated and freestanding are massed on the stage • Two huge bowls of long stemmed white roses with silver swagging and lights • The bubble machines continue the theme • A central chandelier which is massed with fairy lights creates a focal point.
Themed Tabletops for the Alternate Seated Dinner:	• Centerpiece will be styled with champagne glasses, votive candles, white roses, and fairy lights or • Champagne bottles can be utilized on the table with candles and white roses
Optional Themed Accessories:	• Piano player and Blues singer • Specialties tailored to suit the client • Silver lamé tablecloths for the buffet tables • Material chair covers

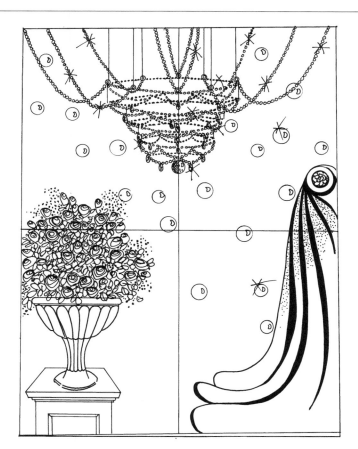

Figure 10.2. Champagne and chandeliers. Utilize these designs to create your themed venue.

The Fabulous Fifties

Happy Days are here again as the '50s are recreated in the atmosphere of a cheerful diner. Go back to the days of oversized Cadillacs, ice cream sundaes, poodle skirts, and rock guitars.

Celebrities on the Wall of Fame gaze down at the guests, who are tapping feet and drumming fingers to the bold beat of fifties rock music. They can join in and jive as full skirts swirl to the Big Bopper, or look on and clap while they bop till they drop. See Color Plates 31–36.

Colors:
- Red and white checks or
- Black and white checks

Set Decor:
- Diner booths are created around the room
- Scenic art backdrop of a drive-in
- Soda and ice cream sundae bars
- Foam core cutout of guitars with poodles and sundaes
- Signage: The Comets, Fats Domino, etc
- Jukebox cutout
- Records and music notes in maxi size

Linens:
- Betty Boop floor length cloths or
- Checks in color

Tables:
- Cutouts of jukeboxes with carnations
- The *'50s* cutout on foam
- Flowers in colors of check cloths

Accessories:
- Shoulder spray
- Boutonnieres
- Bobby socks
- Neck scarves

Figure 10.3. Fabulous Fifties. Stylized signage and oversized props assist in filling the venue walls.

Australian Adventure

Suitable for any venue with either seating or buffet arrangements

1. *"Wonderland Walkabout"*
   - Backdrop of central Australia
   - Aborigines and didgeridoo
   - Rocks, trees, and soil
   - Wooden floor for two aboriginal dancers
   - Aboriginal artifacts

2. *"Great Barrier Reef"*
   - Backdrop of sea, surf, and sand
   - Underwater scene created
   - Fish dining formally
   - Gorgeous mermaid (actress dressed in costume)
   - Treasure chest of corals and jewels
   - Sunken ship

Note:
   - Photographic board allowing guests to be photographed in the scene

3. *"Bushland Adventure with Crocodile Dundee/Rainforests"*
   - Stuffed crocodiles, etc. if available
   - Massive upside-down trees/vines created into a swamp atmosphere with arranged foliage
   - Actor portraying Mick Dundee

Note:
   - Photographic board allowing guests to be photographed on site

4. *"Animal Forest/Ayres Rock"*
   - Background
   - Huge rocks
   - Gum & grevilleas trees

Option:
   - 2 koalas, 1 wombat, 1 kangaroo (2 hour time block for animals with permission required. Current cost of $2,000)

5. *"Stage"*
   - Sydney Opera House & Harbor Bridge 30 ft–40 ft
   - Stage face: Surfers, sun, and umbrella
   - Model basking in sun (optional)
   - Band performing
   - Juggling act & stilt walker

Actors will feature in each vignette to provide a conversation and entertainment aspect for your guests. Material swagging can also be incorporated into any venue ceiling for illusion and enhancement.

Figure 10.4. Australian adventure. This conceptual art of the Great Barrier Reef displays elements which can be used for making props or scenic canvas backdrops.

A Night in the Orient

From the moment guests walk past red-lacquered bamboo and red and gold silk swagging, they enjoy a fantastic oriental experience. The Chinese chefs prepare a banquet fit for emperors, while the fortune teller opens the door to the future for intrigued patrons.

Silk lanterns cast a soft light over the noodle maker, the calligrapher, and the doll maker as they ply their crafts. Guests stroll past on their way to the bar and serving area, which look for all the world like an exotic Eastern market. See Color Plate 11.

Colors:
- Red and gold

Linens:
- Red full length lamé cloths
- Gold lamé chair covers

Theme decor:
- Scenic art backdrop of dragons
- Rickshaw and fans
- Bamboo painted in red lacquer
- Silk lanterns
- Red and gold silk swagging
- Drops of gold mylar
- Chinese umbrellas as ceiling hangings
- Urns of peacock feathers
- Exotic orchids

Accessories:
- Eastern good luck scroll
- Fans as souvenirs
- Waiters in happy jackets
- Fortune tellers, doll maker, weaver, etc.

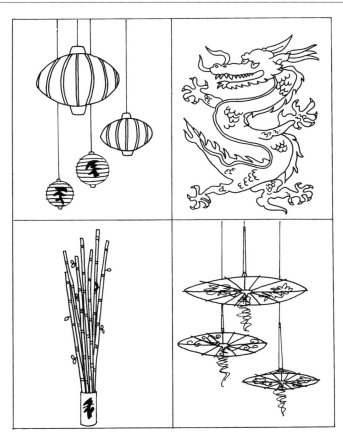

Figure 10.5. A night in the Orient—displays ideas for ceiling mobiles, freestanding cutout dragons, or even large bamboo entrance/doorway or stage pieces.

Paris by Night . . .
an Invitation to the Moulin Rouge

Guests arrive to the sounds of lilting French melodies from the roving musicians as the ladies are given their black velvet choker or wristlet of fresh flowers.

Then romance gives way to the excitement of Paris and the cancan girls. Everyone joins in the mood of frivolity, cheering as legs kick, skirts swirl, and the music intensifies. Laughter and bonhomie continue into the night, accompanied by mouthwatering French food and wine and fabulous entertainment.

The focal point is the imposing cutout of the Eiffel Tower soaring above the heads of the crowd. Pedestals, palms, cascading ferns, and ostrich feathers all set the mood. See Color Plate 20.

Colors:
- Silver, purple, hot pink

Set Decor:
- Moulin Rouge signage with windmill
- Decorative cutouts of cancan dancers
- Fabrics and feathers
- Cutout of the Eiffel Tower
- Masses of potted plants
- Flower carts filled with blooms
- Urns of feathers

Linens:
- Silver lamé floor length cloths
- Overlays alternating in purple and hot pink
- Silver chair covers
- Chair sashes in purple and hot pink

Tabletops:
- Miniature Eiffel towers, mirror, roses, candles
- Silver bowl of roses in pink alternating with silver bowl of iris in blue/purple

Accessories:
- Velvet chokers or wristlet
- Cigarette holders
- Bowler hats
- Boutnnieres

Figure 10.6. Paris by night. The Eiffel Tower could be constructed as a stage piece with the flower cart or feathered urn in the room's corners, while the can-can dancer can be made from core flute and positioned on the walls as a focal point.

Riot in Rio

The *daiquiri bar* is dressed for the occasion as guests mingle in the pre-drinks area of the venue. The waiters, clad in colorful shirts and cummerbunds, serve drinks created with flair to delighted patrons.

As guests enter the ballroom the mood is hot and spicy encouraging the toe tapping and hip swaying to start to the pulsating beat of the reggae band, bongo drums, and steel drums.

Palm trees tower over the partygoers, outsized birds swoop from the ceiling, and lush bright blooms are found in clusters all over the room. It's not long before there's a smile on every face and an animated conversation at every table—yes, mon!

Color:
- Greens dominate with a hot multicolor mix

Set Decor:
- Backdrop of scenic art in tropical foliage
- Huge tropical birds
- Decorative fruit cutouts (Watermelon, banana, and others)
- Green tissue lamé through the ceiling
- Mobiles of birds, fruit, and fabrics

Linens:
- Green floor length lamé cloths with coordinating chair covers or
- Fruit patterned cloths with coordinating solid color chair covers

Tables:
- Two-tiered design of tropical leaves with a variety of fruit, exotic orchids, and candles

Accessories:
- Flowers for the ladies' hair
- Strings of colorful beads

Figure 10.7. Riot in Rio. Bring on the drums and the Samba dancers. Make everything colorful and larger than life.

An Invitation to the Australian Outback

There'll be no dogs, dingos, or flies, but you will enjoy a cool ale and hearty food at the Gooloogong Hotel.

The bushland and outback setting will make the guests feel at home as they witness the "swagman steal the jumbuck and chat with the bushrangers." (Translation: Watch the sheep-rustling hobo steal sheep and talk with bandits.) Step into a simpler time as you take in the general store, post office, pub, and Aussie outhouse. Jack Doolan, together with the Ned Kelly gang, creates general havoc while the bush band plays on. Guests enjoy the shrimp on the barbie with cool ale at the Gooloogong pub.

Colors:
- Earth tones and deep green

Set Decor:
- The pub is the stage for the band
- 3-D scenes of local buildings
- Water tank, windmill, bales of hay
- Drums of reeds and weeds, logs, old pots, water bags
- The infamous crocodile (stuffed, of course)
- Gum trees with lamps, cockatoos, koalas, and bushland ferns fill the surrounds
- Telegraph poles feature across the dance floor
- Cutouts of Australian birds

Linens:
- Deep green hessian floor length cloth
- Deep green hessian sashes for chairs

Tabletops
- Aussie hat with fresh flowers
- Billy can, coals, wood, and flowers
- Dried flowers in pottery vase
- Mini windmill with Australian natives

Accessories:
- Fool's gold and gumleaf momento
- Baby koala bear
- Costumes for staff
- Box of Australian and New Zealand Army Corps (ANZAC) biscuits

Figure 10.8. Australian outback. From the city to the country, feature elements that represent the theme.

An Italian Affair

The romance of Italy is captured in the ripe fruit on the vine, the crusty bread, and intimate lighting. Guests enter the vineyard and are escorted through a walkway lined with cypress trees and tiny twinkling fairy lights.

Friendship and laughter are fostered in the inviting informality of an Italian ristorante. Guests relax over wines and cheeses at tables clad in red and white checked cloth, while the warm flickering light from candles in Chianti bottles dances over happy faces. See Color Plates 12, 13, and 14.

Linens:
- Green floor length cloths
- Red and white check overlays

Tables:
- Chianti bottles and candles
- Italian lamps with clusters of vegetables (onions, garlic, rope, and twine)

Set Decor:
- Wine kegs and ruffle ferns
- Huge palms and pots as decor
- Clusters of clay pots
- Italian rugs
- Wine flasks and bottles
- Pedestals of grape vines, masses of foliage, bunches of grapes
- Topiary trees with lemon hangings
- Displays at base of plants
- Potted plants

Accessories:
- Small baskets

Figure 10.9. An Italian affair. Feature your tables with Chianti bottles, candles, and votives. Walkways or room focals are presented by freestanding potted plant designs or lavishly decorated columns. The wine barrels and signage add to fill the wall space.

Viva Las Vegas!!

Guests circulate amidst the 14-ft high decorative palm trees. The waiters serve cocktails before the ballroom doors open to the glittering world of Vegas. Bold signage seems to explode from the walls: *"Sands, Flamingo, Circus Circus, Plaza, Caesars Palace, Las Vegas,"* etc.

The scenic art backdrop to the stage features the infamous Vegas strip and the sound of slot machines, wheels, and jackpot bells resonate throughout the room. High rollers and showgirls (sight performers) rove the room while fun is maintained with the croupiers, play money, dice, and deck. It's all fabulous fun, all glitter and glitz—a breathtaking whirl of excitement.

Color:
- Range of multicolors—black acts as a background color on the walls and trims.

Set Decor:
- Signage of clubs or hotels
- Vegas cowboy and girl—12-ft high in cutout ply-wood
- Huge $$ signs
- Backdrop of Vegas scenic art
- Huge playing cards

Linens:
- Black floor length cloth with optional overlay of green felt playing cloths

Tables:
- Fun money with dice and playing cards
- Roulette wheels in mini steel
- Packs of cards

Accessories:
- Arm bands Vegas style
- Gambling aprons and eye shades
- Dollar note books
- Rolls of tickets
- Paper money

Figure 10.10. Viva Las Vegas! Neon lights and masses of signage recreate the Vegas strip. Ensure that signage is exact in style and color.

The Gatsby Era

Ah, the Gatsby era! Whether you are drawn to the heady sophistication of beaded and bobbed flappers, or fascinated by machine-gun-toting gangsters, the twenties has an appeal all its own.

The 1930s saw the advent of fashion design in art deco style: bold, potent, and full of energy. That's the theme of the Gatsby party—a time of high style, high-society parties, and flashy cars. Glitzy, glamorous, and gutsy: this is a theme that few can resist.

Color:
- Full white throughout with touches of black

Linens:
- Floor length white damask cloths
- Cotton chair covers in black and white stripe or an alternate of half the chairs white and the other half black
- White full length satin cloths with white overlay and black border

Set Decor:
- Opulent fashion cutout figures
- Busby Berkeley scenic art backdrop
- Screens depicting the '30s era
- Pedestals and ferns
- Urns of white ostrich feathers
- Pedestals with fabric feathers, fern, and lights
- Floor lamps
- Window frames lit from behind

Accessories:
- Orchid corsages
- Wristlet of flowers
- Necklet of flowers
- Misted fog throughout room

Figure 10.11. The Gatsby era. Backlit window frames are a great feature to set the mood while silhouetted dancers on the walls and art deco room dividers create interest throughout.

An Evening on Broadway

There's nothing like an evening on Broadway to make you feel like a million dollars. Suddenly everyone's got stars in their eyes and a spring in their step. The music is irresistible, the decor is a knockout, and the pace never lets up.

It's dazzling, it's captivating, it's entertaining, it's festive! Put on your top hat and tails, put on that glittering gown—it's time for a night on the town! See Color Plate 37.

Set Decor:
- Huge musical notes
- Keyboards
- Top hats and canes
- Fred Astaire and Ginger Rogers cutouts
- Gold and silver fabric
- Lamps
- Huge musical instruments outlined in lights

Linens:
- Gold floor length cloth alternating with silver floor lengths cloths *or*
- White floor length cloths with printed musical notes
- Coordinating chair covers

Tables:
- Keyboards
- Glittery musical note
- Keyboard cutouts with roses *or*
- White roses and candles

Accessories:
- Small musical instruments

Figure 10.12. Evening on Broadway. These are examples of easy designs to be made as oversized flats to feature on stage back or surrounding walls.

Night on the Frontier

Travel back to a time of rough-hewn horse rails, bales of hay, and travel by wagons. Anything goes in a frontier town, and the saloon is the place where it all happens.

You wouldn't be surprised to witness a real Western showdown, but while you're waiting, sit right down and join in a night of laid-back fun and toe-tapping Western music.

Colors:
- Tan, mustard, and earth tones

Linens:
- Floor length wild west print cloth
- Black chair covers with coordinating color for sashes

Set Decor:
- Scenic art of saloon interior
- Scenic art of teepee
- Bales of hay, oats, and barley
- Drums of potatoes
- Cutout of horse and Indian
- Decorative funeral parlor and coffin
- Kegs, bales, horse rails
- Wagon and wagon wheels

Tables:
- Cutout of cactus, boot, and hat
- Votive candles in mini pumpkins
- Clusters of grasses
- Candle holder of wire netting

Accessories:
- Whipcrackers
- Beads and leather bags
- Cowboy hats
- Cowboy neck scarf (bandannas)

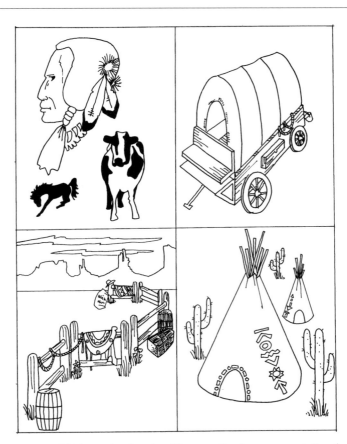

Figure 10.13. Night on the frontier. The use of real or representational props for a Wild West function adds to the fun and creates much interest.

An Invitation to the King's Treasury

Sumptuous treasures spill from chests and guests marvel at stolen crown jewels or ancestral treasures. Jewelled tiaras, glittering coins, and gleaming gems convince guests that they truly have entered an Aladdin's cave.

Even the pedestals are gold, topped with waterfalls of gilded ferns and ivy. Centerpieces are bedecked and bejewelled with clusters of jewels around a striking golden candelabra and swags of fabric cascade from the walls and ceiling.

The band's stage and ceiling is enveloped with gold lamé and colored silk. On either side of the stage, huge jewelled urns complete the scene set for a great night's entertainment.

Colors:
- Rich red, royal blue, and yellows

Set Decor:
- Pedestals, gold lurex swagging, lights, flower urns, and cascading ferns featured around the interior walls as room decor
- Six-foot ceiling chandelier suspended over the band
- Zigzagged swagging in gold lurex
- Treasure chest of jewels positioned on stage
- Urn topped with jewels

Linens:
- Floor length gold lamé with red velvet overlay
- Gold chair covers with red velvet sash

Tabletops
- Box of jewels and fresh roses
- Vase of yellow blooms with strings of pearls
- Formal candelabras and fresh blooms
- 36 in. high gold candelabras with flowers, pearls, and fabrics

Accessories:
- Gold hair bows for staff
- Gold silk corsage for the ladies
- Gold boutonnieres for the gentlemen
- Strings of beads

Figure 10.14. Invitation to the King's treasury. Here we see ideas for centerpieces, entrance ways, and jewelled urn props to be used either on stage or positioned in groups around the venue.

An Evening at Ascot

There's nothing like the buzz of excitement that surrounds a race meeting! Guests enter the world of Royal Ascot when they wander past the scenic art backdrop of the famous racecourse, and exclaim at the life-size plywood horses.

 It's all glamour and sophistication with splashes of vibrant color at tables decorated with the inspiration of racing silks—bold spots, rainbow checks, and dashing stripes. Everyone's a winner here! See Color Plates 25 and 26.

Colors:
- Black and white

Linens:
- Black and white spots, pinstripes, wide stripes, checkerboard—mix the patterns
- Chair sashes to match the cloths

Set Decor:
- Handrails around room
- Scenic art backdrop of Ascot
- Life-size horses cut of plywood
- Huge urns of roses at the entrance
- The winner's horseshoe arch

Tables:
- Mini cutout horses on turf with crinoline and roses or gold cup and roses

Accessories:
- Corporate notebooks for the men's betting slips
- Handmade flower wristlets with ribbons and pearls

Figure 10.15. Evening at Ascot. The racing horses can be on painted canvas backdrop or made into freestanding three-dimensional props. The striped and dotted table cloths in black and white give emphasis to table settings.

A Night of the Blues

We all love the fizz in our champagne glasses, but at this party the guests are actually surrounded by wonderful shimmering bubbles. Delicate rays of blue and mauve highlight the constantly floating iridescent spheres from the bubble machine and the sparkling discs suspended from the ceiling.

These discs, in a variety of sizes, are created from foam core and covered with foil. They rotate slowly as the blues pianist plays.

Masses of sparkling fairy lights, strung through bare branches, add an air of sophistication.

Colors:
- Blues, mauves, and silver

Set Decor:
- The silver discs suspended
- Foam core champagne bottles
- Foam core cutout of champagne glasses
- Bare branches in huge urns
- Clouds of clear or opaque balloons
- Floor chandeliers and candles
- Music notes and scrolls

Linens:
- Full length silver lamé with mauve overlay or white net with silver metallic stripes
- Coordinating white chair covers

Tables:
- Silver chalice filled with glass balls
- Champagne bottle and flowers
- Masses of champagne glasses and roses
- Clusters of clear balloons and roses

Accessories:
- Shredded cellophane
- Silver fabric through the ceiling
- Drops of silver mylar
- Blues singer and pianist

Figure 10.16. Night of the blues. Emphasize the room with lots of champagne, bubbles, and bluesy music. Feature colors of blues, mauves, and silver.

Big Band Swing

Long satin dresses sweep the floor as guests swirl and dance to the fabulous music of the Big Band era. Close your eyes and you can hear the music now: that unmistakable sound of swing that sets your heart racing and brings a smile to your lips.

The room becomes a luxurious nightclub, with clever white airtubing to give a vaulted effect to the ceiling around the stage. Cigarette girls move around the room, smiling pertly at guests; waiters with hair slicked back tend to every need while the band plays on. Huge urns of flowers bedeck the room and complement the satin tablecloths and gleaming candelabras.

Set Decor:
- Eight freestanding screens with Broadway celebrities
- Silhouettes depicting the city skyline
- The stage holds big band instruments plus musical notes and clefs
- Two huge bowls of fresh white flowers

Tabletops
- White roses, glittered musical keyboards, and black satin cloth
- Lavish centerpieces with 36-inch-high candelabras

Linens:
- Table covers to enhance decor
- Material chair covers

Accessories:
- Air tubing is the alternate decor
- Fresh white boutonnieres
- Floral wristlets or corsages

Figure 10.17. Big band swing. Stylize the stage behind the band with city skylines and the walls with freestanding city swingers. Again, large cut props bringing music into play.

A Brazilian Carnivale

There's something about the tropics that makes people want to smile, sing, and dance. The throbbing samba beat, the hot pinks and tropical blues, the baskets of succulent fruit, and the huge fragrant blooms all beckon your guests into a world free of care. See Color Plates 38 and 39.

Whether you're dreamily swaying to "The Girl from Ipanema" or tapping your foot as you watch sinuous dancers move to the Samba rhythm, this Brazilian carnivale is totally irresistible.

Theme Decor:
- The stage is set with Brazilian signage
- Huge baskets painted in color with matching feathers embellish the room
- Brazilian/tropical parrots and birds
- Glittered freestanding palm trees
- Huge paper flowers, cutout fruits
- Lurex swagging through the room

Tables:
- Centerpieces of fruits, flowers, and candles
- Huge paper flowers

Linens:
- Hot colors in pinks, blues, etc.

Accessories:
- Fresh flower and decor fruit hairpieces
- Wristlet of flowers
- Costumes for staff

Music:
- Latin/American band
- Disc jockey

Entertainment:
- Choreographed dancers feature with Samba rhythm dressed in full festive costume
- Feature artist

Figure 10.18. Brazilian carnivale. Oversized props in multicolors bring this carnivale to life. Feature fabulous signage and huge paper flowers. Ceiling mobiles have excellent potential.

Chapter 11

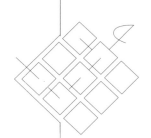

Synopsis of Other Events

The following case studies are events that have been designed, directed, and produced by specific companies. Each particular example shows the originality and individuality that it is possible to achieve for a client. One case from Malaysia also shows that special events are not just a party or celebration, they can be the full working production to launch a specific product. All these cases have involved meticulous planning and execution.

Nescafe and Guinness

Richard Dutton
Red Archer, Kuala Lumpur, Malaysia

Red Archer, an event management company set up in 1992, is headed by its director, Richard Dutton. Richard has had over nine years experience in the advertising industry, having worked with various advertising agencies in Malaysia. He also brings to Red Archer the added advantage of 6 years with Alexander Proudfoot, an international productivity consultant.

Red Archer has created, managed, and supported events for various clients including Pepsi Cola International, Nestle, Guinness Anchor Berhad, Unilever, Measat Broadcast Network Systems, Godfrey Phillips, Cold Storage, Standard Chartered Bank, Intel Asia Sdn Bhd, and many others.

The Guinness Stout Market Impact Promotion

The Guinness Stout Market Impact Promotion, conducted in Malaysia for the past three years, is aimed at reinforcing Guinness Stout's status as the leading brand in the malt liquor market. Red Archer has been the appointed event manager responsible for the implementation of the promotion.

The objectives of the promotion are:

- To build the Guinness Stout franchise in Malaysia
- To increase consumption among the long-time brand loyalists
- To create trials among the competitors, loyalists, and among nondrinkers

Research findings were taken into account in the development of the strategy to be employed. The key findings were as follows.

1. Guinness Stout has been acknowledged as an acquired taste. At first taste, the strong and bitter taste could be difficult to handle. However, after three separate tastings, the drinker finds the taste far more palatable and appreciates the full-bodied flavor of Guinness.
2. The general marketing of Guinness is very channel-driven. On ground marketing activities usually target a particular channel of distribution. This allows programs to be tailored to suit the characteristics of the channel and the customers involved, which in turn, leads to more effective and successful programs.
3. In the multi-racial Malaysian society, the major consumers and potential consumers for Guinness Stout were the Chinese. The Malays are automatically eliminated from such programs because the consumption of alcohol is prohibited by the Muslim religion. The other main racial group, the Indians, were simply too small in terms of numbers to target.

Based on all the background information, the following strategy was developed to achieve the objectives desired in the prevailing market environment:

Promoters. Teams of attractive female promoters would be recruited and trained to visit all identified refreshment outlets in the country to interact with customers and promote Guinness Stout.

Outlets. In West Malaysia, there are 12,000 refreshment outlets. The strategy was to cover each of these outlets at least twice during the project (24,000 outlet visits in nine months).

Outlets are classified as MIP (Market Impact Promotion) outlets and non-MIP outlets. MIP outlets are the identified top 10% high-volume outlets within the channel where the market share of Guinness Stout is low, i.e., below 30%. Different activities were conducted in both the MIP and non-MIP outlets.

Promotion. The team of promoters would spend approximately 15–25 minutes in non-MIP outlets, depending on the crowd present. They would carry a hand-held table game to be played with the customers. Each customer who purchased two glasses of Guinness Stout would be entitled to play the game.

The game was a simple game of chance and the customer would be guaranteed a prize. He only played to determine the size of his prize. If he won, he would receive a grand prize which could be a Guinness travel bag, a Guinness wall clock, or even a Guinness radio cassette player. If he didn't win, he would still walk away with a lighter, a keychain, or a pack of playing cards.

In the bigger MIP outlets, the team of promoters would spend approximately one hour. A special game stall was set up for games to be conducted. The games played and the prizes given out were the same as in the non-MIP outlets. The difference was in the higher visibility and branding in the outlets and in the time spent. (Figure 11.1)

The fact that all participants were winners was critical to overcome Malaysia's strict gaming laws.

Figure 11.1. Guinness Stout promotion. Malaysian promotional staff conducts special taste testing exercises at shopping centers and special venues.

Implementation. In implementing this program, separate areas of responsibility had to be planned and organized up to and including the implementation stage. Red Archer's various areas of responsibility are outlined below.

Red Archer was responsible for the recruitment and training of promoters. Promoters were required to be young Chinese women with attractive looks and personalities. Language requirements were also imposed because of the different local dialects spoken in the geographical areas to be covered.

Candidates were recruited using various methods such as advertisements placed in various newspapers, banners at selected new Chinese villages, and networking within the hotels and food and beverage industry. Interviews were conducted with all candidates before the most ideal candidates were chosen for training.

Red Archer conducted comprehensive training, which covered all job-related areas such as product information, sales techniques, and the mechanics of the promotion. Grooming and deportment areas

were also included to ensure that a professional and memorable impression was created for the brand. A total of 18 promoters were hired to work in six teams of three promoters each.

Red Archer also conceptualized the promotion games and developed the relevant props and equipment employed. This was done with the target audience in mind. Games of chance with gambling elements have traditionally appealed to the target audience and was a major factor in the development of the games.

The nature of the market and the target outlets meant that the promotion hours were severely limited. The ideal time of outlet visit was between 7 P.M. and 12 A.M. and because such a large area needed to be covered, an average of 15 outlets needed to be visited each night. This meant that time spent in getting from one outlet to the next had to be kept at an absolute minimum. Set up and tear down of equipment and props could not take longer than a few minutes for the system to work.

With this in mind, the entire promotion package

was designed in a compact manner, which allowed maximum mobility and minimum time and resources spent for set up, dismantling, and travel between outlets. All the promotion equipment was packed into four bags, which were lightweight and mobile. It took five minutes to set up the whole display and another five minutes to dismantle and pack up. This ensured that no time was wasted during operations.

Designs also ensured that maximum brand exposure was created via the game equipment, point of sales materials such as banners and posters, and uniforms worn by the promoters.

The next major area involved the securing of outlets and planning of itineraries for the campaign. As the target was to cover 100% of the refreshment outlet universe in Malaysia, there was no necessity to select outlets. The main task involved scheduling the visits to ensure maximum impact and minimum travel time between outlets. A tentative outlet visit itinerary was developed for all six teams based on all the above criterias.

Based on the itinerary, the Guinness regional office was responsible for the securing of the outlets. All the outlets were visited by the sales staff to confirm the dates and times of the promotion. After this, some fine-tuning was done before the final outlet visit itinerary was obtained. Merchandising of the outlets was then conducted. Point of sales materials such as event banners and posters were put up in all the outlets, detailing the date and time of the promotion in order to generate pre-publicity and to ensure a good crowd and atmosphere for the promotion.

On promotion nights, the salesperson in charge of the area and the team of three promoters would implement the promotion jointly. Red Archer would be responsible for monitoring the operations and ensuring that the prescribed mechanics were adhered to. Any on ground decisions that needed to be made were the responsibility of the salesperson in charge.

After the promotion, the salesperson and the promoters would generate separate reports, which were submitted to Red Archer. The two reports served as check and balances for each other and ensured that all the necessary data was obtained. The performance was then reviewed with Guinness headquarters and any action plans decided would be communicated through Red Archer.

Response. The promotion was generally very well received by all the parties concerned. A summary of the feedback follows.

The Guinness MIP was very well received with the Guinness sales force. They managed to use it as an effective sales tool in their negotiations with the outlet owners on the basis that any incremental orders by the outlet owner would be offloaded very quickly with the promotion being implemented. It also served as a means to create goodwill between the sales staff and the outlet owners.

The outlet owners were especially pleased with the program due to the coverage target of 100% of the outlet universe. By setting such a wide coverage base, many outlets in the outskirt areas and lower volume outlets were covered by the promotion. These outlets may have been in existence for years without any company ever having considered doing activities there and they were especially appreciative of the attention. The promotion was a major event for them. Although the volume in these outlets was not the largest, the goodwill created for the brand was immeasurable.

The customers are the most important targets of the promotion. In terms of volume generation, a sales target was set at 65 pints for MIP outlets and 8 pints in non-MIP outlets. On a national average basis, the sales targets were achieved comfortably. However, upon closer analysis, it was found that the volume generally comes from certain areas and types of outlets. The customers are more responsive in the outskirt and rural areas as opposed to the urban cities. The urban crowd tends to be more aloof to activities of this nature while the promotion is a major event in the lives of the rural crowd.

However, when compared to the normal average sales of the outlets, an increase in sales volume of all outlets promoted was detected during the promotional period.

Start Your Day with Nescafe Classic (SYDWNC)

Nationwide sampling program. The SYDWNC sampling program was implemented for a 4-month period from May to August of 1996. This was a nationwide sampling program designed to build the business franchise of Nescafe Classic throughout Malaysia.

Nescafe Classic has been the clear leader in the instant coffee market in Malaysia. However, a sampling program was needed because the growth in this particular category of products had been slowing down and consumption volume needed a boost. Also, new consumers needed to be introduced to the product to build the long-term business prospects.

The objectives of the sampling program were:

- To build the business volume of Nescafe Classic
- To increase the in-home penetration of the brand
- To counter any potential activities by the competitors' brands

The program was skewed to target mainly consumers of competitive brands throughout East and West Malaysia. Within this universe, sampling was targeted at both urban and rural areas.

Figure 11.2. Nescafe taste sampling. This is an outdoor taste testing at one of 240 outlets in Malaysia.

The sampling methods can be divided into two broad areas, wet and dry sampling. Wet sampling refers to the serving of pre-prepared drinks to consumers while dry sampling refers to the distribution of the miniature product packs for consumers to take home for consumption. Both kinds of sampling have their respective merits and faults.

Schedules and venues. In terms of the scale of operations, a target of 500,000 samples, both wet and dry, were to be distributed.

The strategy was to employ mobile sampling teams who target identified venues where sampling can be conducted. By cross-referencing the targeted number of samples with the duration of the project, the crew strength and the crews' daily targets were determined.

A population spread analysis of the whole country was also conducted as part of the preparatory process to ensure that our scheduling and resource allocation would be ideal to ensure all targets are achieved.

The types of venues targeted consisted of transient audience venues such as bus depots, train stations, commuter rail stations, petrol stations, wet markets, toll booths, and others and captive audience venues such as shopping complexes, coffee shops, government and office buildings, and factories. (Figure 11.2)

A list of potential venues was then developed and approached to get consent. In Peninsular Malaysia alone, a total of 410 venues were approached for permission to sample. These venues were selected based on the traffic of people, the accessibility to resources such as water and electrical points, and legislative approval requirements.

Our applications were approved by 240 venues. A schedule could be developed at this stage.

During the project, each venue was visited an average of 2.3 times each. This was skewed towards certain geographical areas where the population was large and brand share needed strengthening.

Resources. Once the schedule was confirmed, the resource requirements could be determined. Each mobile sampling unit had to be equipped with the following items:

• Manpower
• A van for transportation

- A sampling trolley complete with Nescafe branding
- A household coffee pot
- Product-related items such as Nescafe, creamer, sugar, etc.
- Serving-related items such as cups and covers, stirrers, etc.

In terms of manpower, each sampling unit included a supervisor, a driver, and four sampling crew members. All these team members were recruited and specially trained by Red Archer prior to the implementation of the project.

All product- and service-related items needed to be regularly replenished as the sampling program continued. Therefore, points of replenishment locations and times were worked into the schedule.

Operations. The implementation operated as follows.

Based on the schedule, the sampling unit arrives at the specified venue and makes contact with the person in charge of the venue. In an area covered, several booths are set up at various points in the vicinity. This allowed a higher number of consumers to be sampled at a particular venue, and also eased the traffic flow at any particular booth when it was very crowded.

Once booths are set up at the identified areas, wet samples are prepared. This involved locating water and power facilities to boil water. Coffee samples, creamers, and sugar are then added to prepare the coffee for wet sampling.

Once the coffee is ready, the crew invites people in the crowd to try a cup of coffee and also distributed dry samples to ensure that the prospective customer would take the product home and try it. The crew also talked with people about Nescafe and any feedback was included in the reports on the project.

The supervisor's role included monitoring the crowd and response levels to determine whether to shut down operations early or to extend operations in a particular venue. Flexibility was an important factor to ensure none of the resources were wasted through strict adherence to planned schedules.

When the supervisor decided to shut down operations in a particular venue, all equipment and materials are packed up and the whole team proceeds to the next venue on the schedule. The daily plans for each team included an average of 6.5 venues per day. Different amounts of time were spent at each venue depending on factors like expected crowd, expected target audience, and date and time of visit. Also certain special events such as Big Walk events and parades were given priority as sampling venues.

Results. The total number of samples distributed during the project exceeded the target of 500,000.

This was achieved from overwhelming response in certain venues which exceeded expectations.

In terms of the actual reach of the program, the family members of those sampled must be taken into account because presumably the dry samples distributed were also consumed by family members as well as the sampled person telling family members about the program.

The computation of reach can be done as follows:

Sample number:	500,000
Average members per household:	5
Total reach potential:	2,500,000
Less 20% for duplication:	500,000
Net reach:	2,000,000

The magnitude of the program can be better understood when compared to the population of Malaysia which is approximately 17.5 million people.

The reach therefore consists of approximately 12% of the total population.

Great Events Are Great Art

Janet Elkins
President, EventWorks, Inc., Los Angeles, California

A great event is like a great piece of art. As the painter blends every stroke on the canvas to create a seamless illusion, Los Angeles-based EventWorks integrated a number of elements to create a beautiful evening which took its cue from the world of art.

MCI Communications Corporation's guests enjoyed this masterpiece of event planning in September, 1994. Playing off of the venue, EventWorks developed an upscale evening which immersed guests in an environment which was in itself a piece of art.

The Monterey Peninsula Museum of Art at La Mirada was the setting for the evening. The museum, attached to a historic adobe structure with a storeyed past was the setting for a cocktail reception among its exhibits and gardens. To reflect the historic figures who frequented the museum property during its diversified history, EventWorks placed two costumed characters—a Charlie Chaplin look-alike and an actress to represent one of the founding citizens of California—inside the museum to interact with guests during cocktails.

Guests then moved to the rear of the museum property, where a first class, 80' × 120' tent structure was erected by HDO Productions to house dinner. Inside the tent structure, the art theme was brilliantly realized with a design concept which synthesized beautiful decor with live characters to bring great masterpieces to life.

Moving from the museum to the tent, guests had the opportunity to enjoy cocktails in two park style settings of ficus trees, park benches, fountains, and planter boxes overflowing with fresh blooms. These settings were designed to conceal the tent's electrical logistics.

Beautiful, classical imagery was used at the tent entrance. A pair of gold candelabra dripping with dozens of multi-faceted crystals flanked the doorway on pedestals. The candelabra held a gorgeous array of florals and greenery which dripped down to the ground. Fabric swags (complementing the color scheme of the overlays used inside on guest tables) swept from the pedestals through gold gilded frames to the ground.

In creating an environment which was a piece of art, special recreations of great artwork were assembled around the buffets. Costumed living statues posed in front of realistic backdrops to recreate the masterpieces Whistler's Mother and American Gothic. Huge, ornately gilded gold frames were placed in front of the buffet displays, with the comprehensive effect becoming a life-size recreation of the pageantry of the masters.

These settings further allowed guests to glimpse what the painter may have seen but not had the canvas or desire to paint. The three-dimensional backdrops of props, artifacts, and antiques extended beyond what was depicted in the original painting—the scene extending to either side of the huge gold frame for a surreal and whimsical effect. To enhance the overall impact, these settings were elevated on risers.

Whistler's Mother herself was viewed as an actress in an exact costume replica posed on a rocking chair. The scene extended beyond the frame with a series of vintage, antique props including end tables, curios, chairs, greenery, and an assortment of period artifacts.

The famous portrait of a farm couple, *American Gothic*, came to life as costumed models stood in front of a three-dimensional, white farmhouse building facade. The farm scene also extended beyond the frames with a red water pump, wood watering trough, hay bales, greenery, and an assortment of farm implements. (Figure 11.3)

The art theme was incorporated in the food service tables as well. Menu cards for the evening were rendered in calligraphy and placed in gold gilded frames along the buffet surface. Fabric swags corresponding to the guest table linens softened the buffets.

A stunning view of the room as a whole was dominated by the integration of centerpieces and ceiling treatment. Centerpieces were suspended from the tent ceiling, making the structure appear to be a fantasy garden setting. All white florals—Casablanca lilies, roses, tulips, dendrobium orchids, and astilbe—sprinkled amid an orb of fresh greenery descended from the tent ceiling to just above the tabletops. Green garland (smilax) and two stands of white twinkle lights totalling one hundred lights were wound around the cables of the suspension system to mask the mechanics.

The florals and greenery of the suspended orb dripped to inches above the tabletop, where they met a table-based centerpiece which reinforced the art motif. The table florals were seen through a gold gilt frame, with a gold paintbrush attached to the frame extending three-dimensionally.

Burgundy linens to the floor dressed each table, with burgundy napkins at each setting. A beautiful justus pattern overlay with a pattern of muted, swirling colors covered the linens. Gold Chevari chairs encircled the tables to complete the look.

To complement the main decor elements at the art recreations and guest tables, EventWorks enhanced the tent structure with fabric swags on the ceiling, entrance, and stage. The poles and ceiling within the tent were treated with pleated white fabric swags which was both aesthetically attractive and concealed the tent's mechanics.

Fabric colors and patterns were coordinated to add continuity to the environment and blend it with the beautiful natural settings surrounding the museum.

Environmental lighting took the edge off of the growing twilight, replacing it with the subtle glow of a muted palette. Ambient and theatrical lighting helped to reinforce the wonderful environment of the evening. Theatrical lighting techniques enhanced and complemented the appearance of the entrance, two large displays, and stage treatment, emphasizing warm, rich, bright colors. Centerpieces were double pinspotted for added impact. The lighting package included generator rental and power distribution, which was a necessary and appropriate precaution in this venue.

A Special Event
The Floral Opening of a Casino

Lena Malouf, CSEP
Designer Decorator for the Gala Dinner

The Opening of the Reef Casino in Cairns Queensland, on April 18, 1996 was a special event and its success was due to one primary factor—planning.

In 1994, Venables Creating Entertainment in Sydney Australia, alias Paul Venables and Sarah Ploughman, first mentioned the possibility of my services being required for the decor of the opening night gala dinner. In June 1995 we mutually agreed

Figure 11.3. "Great Events Are Great Art." An excellent example of still life brought to three-dimensional life. By Janet Elkins of Event Works, Inc., Los Angeles, CA.

on an underwater theme with the colors depicting the location—the tropical reef with its shimmering blues and greens.

The action from here was to Plan the Work, then Work the Plan. This enabled the design and decor proposal being presented to the client to be close to the anticipated budget. The aim with a gala event of this size is to prepare the look without restriction. Design the venue as it should look for such a special evening. In this situation, a casino opening, it is

preferable to give the client (in this case, the producer) the option to reject the creativity. The success rate is often high because of the careful preparation of the visuals and prototypes. Having samples of table product accessories, fabrics, and fresh florals available for the client's inspection is a big plus. Yes, it is work, and it is costly but with an open design budget, the absolute best can be achieved.

Frankly, it is damaging to reputation to have an

open budget and not match it with expertise and skill. The client must get value with style.

In this case the areas allocated for decor of the large marquee were:

1. A 200-foot walkway
2. The walls and side pillars
3. The ceiling waterfalls
4. Tablecloths, napkins, and chair covers
5. Tabletop centerpieces and accessories for an expected 1,250 guests
6. VIP gift presentations.

After regular meetings with Venables Creating Entertainment, layouts for presentation began. Conceptual art of the overall job—drawings of the table tops and samples of glass votive, shells, cording, meshing, and fabrics—were presented to the producers. This was well received and the budget guidelines accepted.

Because the budget was extremely healthy but necessary for a job of this size, it took time to find table fabrics and matching chair cover fabrics. These fabrics were supplied by Rose Brand, Inc. from New York. Glass table trims (hand blown glass baubles) came from Perth (Western Australia), with glass candle votives from Melbourne (Victoria) and Perth, and shells from Coolangatta (Queensland) and Adelaide (South Australia). The fresh flowers came from New Zealand, Tasmania, Darwin, Melbourne, and Sydney, and finally all non-perishable florals from Knud Nielsen in Alabama.

At this point, all the required components were available. In order to achieve this, constant communications with suppliers was essential. Hours were spent at the drawing board sketching styles, lines, and patterns for the 7-ft. high tabletop design. These were designed to tower over the heads of the guests to give the feeling of sitting under an umbrella of flowers. These specialty designs were to be placed on the outside tables within the marquee, which had a beautiful crystal clear ceiling.

Because the entertainment component was very lavish for the evening, it was important that the guests' viewing should not be obstructed in any way. Therefore, the 72 center tables were designed to display a different style and size from the 44 double outer table designs, so guests would not be inconvenienced by a cumbersome tabletop arrangement.

For a job of this size, selecting, shipping, and maintaining the lifespan of perishable flowers can be a nightmare, but because of my strong connections in the floral industry, the growers in Singapore as well as the other Australian states, shipped direct into Cairns. This was an advantage because it avoided the double handling of going through local markets. The growers also agreed to cut as late as possible thus ensuring the absolute freshness of the blooms.

Foliage, however, is a different story and for special events work, delicate greens are avoided at all costs. Asparagus and coarse ferns, exotic leaves, miniature palms, and mosses were selected for this job because it allowed my floral team of ten to start basing up the arrangements six days prior to the event.

As the head designer, I had to decide whether to take two or three key people from my team and hire local florists or take my trained team and hire go-fors or unskilled locals. I chose the second option, and in this case it was necessary.

My regular team included Julie Sidie-McIntyre, my personal assistant, Angela Morrison, Paul Hurst, Richard Go (AIFD), Monica Goebel, and Ian Murphy.

I tend to be pedantic about tabletops, have been for years, and will probably never change because guests view the tabletop very, very closely so every detail of its design is to be considered and finished as a designer piece. Beautiful tabletops do become conversation pieces. Also, the florals can make or break an event regardless of how good everything else in the venue looks.

With this specialty work it is also advisable that the producer and client view a full prototype of the table and tabletop completely finished prior to the event. This allows them to eliminate any of their dislikes. Fortunately, in this case, all parties concerned loved the look and the adjustments were minimal.

At this stage, Venables forwarded the elevation dimensions and table layouts so the prototype for the ceiling could be designed. It is also imperative to meet with the technical people in this regard. Again, do a prototype and, with the producer and technical team, discuss the ways and means of suspending the units well prior to the function so that problems are avoided once on location. It is essential that decor doesn't interfere with lighting placements. Chameleon Touring Systems of Sydney, Australia were contracted for this job since they are familiar with this style of work.

This pond, or plexiglass ceiling disc, was featured with masses of ferns and shimmering waves of fabric. Along with this, waterfalls of fairy lights with every single globe covered in green and royal blue cellophane provided a magical look throughout the marquee. These were then suspended over the heads of the guests.

The planning of the work continues with setting out the necessary master charts for:

1. The non-perishable product ordering, supply, and delivery
2. The perishable product ordering, supply, and delivery

3. The task analysis of every single task to be executed
4. The action sheet for who, when, and what task
5. Determining the work hours to fit the allocated budget
6. Detailing the load out and return trucking to Sydney.

This was a very exciting project, but good communication is essential and the bi-weekly meetings with Venables and/or their assistants, plus the regular training sessions I conducted in-house, were vital and enhanced the overall success of the event.

A major consideration was that we were able to set up our workroom in an available building 100 yards away from the marquee. Originally a restaurant, this space was now rented for floral designing and was set up with pre-existing sinks, stainless steel benches, refrigeration, and air-conditioning. These working conditions made it possible to meet every deadline expected and certainly negated any stress or strain in the tropical heat.

Following an event like this, it is necessary to get the team together and ask the group what they found workable, nonworkable, totally impossible, and what changes they would like to see made to be even more effective on future jobs. In this case, the same meeting was also conducted with the producers.

Our business philosophy of neverending and constant improvement rises to the surface with a gala event such as this and nothing is taken for granted because in this industry we are only as good as our last event.

Refer to the two casino photographs, Color Plates 7 and 8. One photograph shows the room in its completed stage of dressing. The full decor color was in royal blue and kelly green to interpret an underwater look. Notice on the right of the photograph the towering arrangements on the perspex containers with the glass votives and the center tables clearly showing the lower style design. Hanging from the ceiling are the perspex discs loaded with ferns, garlands, grasses, and slivers of lamé fabric in blues and greens.

The table linens and chair covers add strong color to the room because each table alternates between the royal blue and kelly green. To complete the decor, the side walls of the marquee were dressed with fabulous garlands from Knud Nielsen, USA. The base of the arrangement became a conversation piece because it was loaded with shells, cord, meshing, moss, and fresh flowers.

These arrangements show a style similar to the VIP arrangements that were sent to the guest's rooms. The colors for the VIPs were colors other than royal blue and green and contained profusion of fresh seasonal flowers. These arrangements were large, lush, and lovely because there was a healthy budget for each arrangement. Wouldn't it be great to have a function like this once a month! Even once a quarter would be sufficient!

Qantas Australian Grand Prix

Lech Sobecki
Event Affairs, Melbourne, Australia

We were excited to be heavily involved once again in this year's Qantas Australian Grand Prix. Our involvement was based around the presentation of a number of corporate marquees including the prestigious Formula 1 paddock Club which hosted such guests as the Prince of Monaco and the Premier of Victoria, Mr Jeff Kennett.

The objective was to depict the characteristics of Formula 1 Grand Prix Racing by giving visual expression to the movement, speed, excitement, and worldwide passion of the sport while taking into consideration requirements of both the Australian Grand Prix Corporation and the Fire Brigade Authorities.

To achieve this, custom printed material was manufactured in the official colors of the Qantas Australian Grand Prix, including the checkered flag design and then specially treated to attain the required fire retardant qualities. Lengths of the material were then suspended along the roofline of the club, designed to decorate and soften the rough finish of the ceilings and at the same time, allow a free and uninterrupted flow of water from the sprinklers in case of emergency. The result was a magnificent array of color throughout the venue which projected the professional image of the event.

In addition Event Affairs was also commissioned to enhance the Checkered Flag and Grid Clubs. Once again lengths of custom printed fabric in the official colors of the event were suspended across the ceiling to present soft lines. Checkered fabric was then draped along the rear wall of the marquees to add interest, color, and identity.

We were proud to be associated again with the Shell/Ferrari Racing Team. This association included decorating No.1 Spring St—Shell House; Novotel on Collins, 333 Collins St; ANZ Gothic Chamber, and the Shell Track Marquee.

Decorating No.1 Spring Street began with the suspension of polymesh banners on the exterior flag poles of the building as a highlight to passersby. These banners were red and featured both the Shell and Ferrari Racing Team logo which was used as a basic theme throughout the venues. The materials used to produce the banners required no hemming and ensured that fraying was kept to a minimum.

Once inside the building, the guests were greeted by a colorful, visually exciting display within the foyer of the building beginning with two rotating banner displays. From the entrance, guests were welcomed in either direction by impressive displays enriched with color and character. To the right, guests were treated to an adaptation of the Australian Grand Prix complete with Grand Prix backdrop, bridge, track, and model Shell/Ferrari Formula 1 Racing Cars. To the left of the entrance was a cascading array of fabric custom printed in the checkered flag design.

The overall enhancement was completed with freestanding Shell/Ferrari Racing Team banners strategically placed along the window wall of the building.

Our mandate required us to provide highly visual yet unobtrusive displays within the Novotel complex which presented a uniform image with the other venues. To achieve this, Shell/Ferrari Racing Team banners were suspended in the entrance to the hotel which were not only inviting to guests entering the hotel, but were seen by passersby on Melbourne's busy Collins Street.

A display depicting a pit stop image was placed in the hotel restaurant lobby. Custom printed fabric was draped along the ceiling of the lobby with freestanding banner displays adding the finishing touches to the design.

The adaptation of 333 Collins Street to subtly blend the ornate setting with the mood of the Grand Prix Racing was certainly exciting. Through the use of fabric draping and the suspension of Shell/Ferrari Racing Team banners, the design highlighted the rich appearance of the venue while incorporating the excitement and stature of Formula 1 Grand Prix racing. This effect was capped off with the use of the Hyper Simulator as a centerpiece to the room for dramatic effect. (Figure 11.4)

An array of Shell/Ferrari Racing Team banners was utilized throughout the ANZ Gothic Chamber to provide a unified image with the other venues and

Figure 11.4. Qantas Australian Grand Prix. This is known as a *Hyper Simulator* utilized as a central room or foyer centerpiece creating dramatic effect.

enhance the richness of the chamber. Through strategic placement a wonderful colorful effect was achieved while capitalizing on the space available.

Once again, uniformity was maintained within the Shell Track Marquee. Shell Ferrari Racing Team banners were suspended to follow the line of the ceiling and placed between checkered flags draped with an attachment at the midpoint of each section. As an additional highlight to the ceiling, red and yellow fabric was molded around checkered fabric in a plaited design and draped along the central point of the ceiling adding color and vitality. Banners were utilized around the perimeters of the marquee adding color throughout the venue but without obstructing the flow of either guests or staff members. The overall enhancement of the marquee was designed to be welcoming, uncomplicated, colorful, and festive while allowing guests to move freely and enjoy the sporting extravaganza that is Formula 1 Grand Prix racing.

This year we were pleased to be associated with the ANZ with the presentation of their trackside marquee. Four rows of custom printed checkered fabric were draped to follow the billowing lines of the ceiling of the marquee and extended the entire width of the roofline, then cascading down the walls for wonderful impact. Blue draping was added to the corners of the marquee to provide color and identity. Banners of the host ANZ were suspended around the perimeters of the walls successfully blending both the event and the host in a harmonious display while projecting their professional image. To complete the image of the marquee, centerpieces representing the winners' trophy were elegantly displayed on a trophy pedestal featuring flags of the event and the host. The centerpieces added the final touch to what was certainly an elegant presentation.

Another new venture this year was the visual enhancements to one of the syndicated corporate suites. The challenge was to unify both the upper and lower decks of the suite while creating a look of individualism in each area. Through an elaborate display of richly elegant fabric draping uniting the colors of the event with the Checkered Flag design, an image presenting sleek flowing lines which softened the harsh finish of the ceilings and camouflaged their low clearance levels was created. For diversity, the upper level of the marquee was based on the checkered design with color highlights and the lower level on the corporate colors of the event incorporating the checkered design. Overall a look of consistency was achieved through the entire suite, while offering diversity and individualism.

Overall our involvement included the premier Corporate Hosting venue, six marquees, and four city sites.

An Arty Party

Pamela Wheat,
Producer Special Events, ICMS Australasia,
Sydney, Australia

Winner of Meetings Industry Association of Australia's Award of Excellence 1997. ICMS Australasia has been established for 31 years and is one of Australia's largest conference and event management companies.

This event was for a German pharmaceutical company, one of the exhibitors at an International Medical Congress held in Sydney. During the Congress there was one free night during which many exhibitors planned to hold parties and invite selected delegates. However, these delegates would have to choose between six or more events. This competition obviously made every single one of these exhibitors want to have the biggest and the best party, not to mention the most memorable!

The Background

The client visited Australia five months before the party to find a venue with a capacity for 250–300 guests. The theme had to be artistic and encapsulate Australiana for the international guests. There were two venue possibilities: the Museum of Contemporary Art at Circular Quay in the heart of the city and an empty shed in Darling Harbor near the city center. Two proposals complete with costs were designed with each venue in mind.

The Museum of Contemporary Art was chosen for An Arty Party, a concept I had long wanted to create, but had not yet had the opportunity. Basically it was a walk-around party. Guests were to arrive and enjoy drinks and canapes on the terrace overlooking Sydney Harbor, the Harbor Bridge, and the Opera House, with a performance outside on the lawn. Inside the room they would be surrounded by performances, both theatrical and culinary. The performance was not to be intrusive, but simply to be there if guests wished to watch with lots of opportunities for networking and no formalities whatsoever.

One entire section of the room was to be filled with an enormous 18-ft high 24-ft wide scaffolding scrim-covered stage divided into five sections. Two hours of continuous performance would be devised and musically choreographed. A computerized lighting program involving rear and front lighting, fog, and gobos were to create amazing images behind the scrim, enhanced with stunning effects achieved with the use of props such as confetti, torches, and balls. The company, Stretch Mk1 were engaged to create a performance behind this scrim. It involved masks, music, acrobatics, mime, dance, and magic.

Two other small stages would be used for individual performances and a stage for the dance band set up and draped off to be revealed later in the evening. Unusual street theatre performers needed to be found to interact with the guests. Some food was to be cooked at special stations, while others would be waiter/tray service.

At this stage, the client started designing invitations while I began the production process. Guest numbers had now increased to 350 and one month later to 450! Floor plans now had to be redesigned to allow the maximum number in the room. Together with the venue and caterers, it was decided 450 would be the limit!

The next challenge was to design and test the scaffolding stage. It had to be safe and strong enough to hold performers on two levels as well as rigging for an aerialist. The external walls needed to be covered with both external and internal drapes both to beautify and to prevent light spill from one section to another. However performers had to be able to move from one area to another and have a hidden backstage area. A stage was constructed in the lighting studio and tested for different lighting techniques. Performers then tested some of their effects and devised the choreography.

Meanwhile, the search continued for interesting, talented, and unusual performers for other areas of the room. To change their appearances, for example, a beautiful double-bass musician was fitted in a full white bridal gown complete with veil. Period costume used in the movie *The Piano* was utilized for the female saxophonist. A blues jazz duo was dressed in Pierrot costumes complete with blue painted faces and wigs. A street theatre group of five performers was engaged and we commissioned a new piece called *The Pillars of Society*. (Refer to Figure 11.5)

Meanwhile a 60s style band who could perform a repertoire sufficiently well known to the guests from more than 80 countries was hired to get guests up and dancing.

Aerial sculptures, giant moving structures of aluminum and fabric which changed shape by tugging on a rope, were also incorporated.

Due to the increased number of guests, the adjoining cafe was used for three caricature artists seated at tables who would sketch the guests when they sat down with their glass of wine or plate of food.

The menu was devised with the caterers. It combined the practicality of tray service plus the visual effects of waiters cooking noodles in enormous

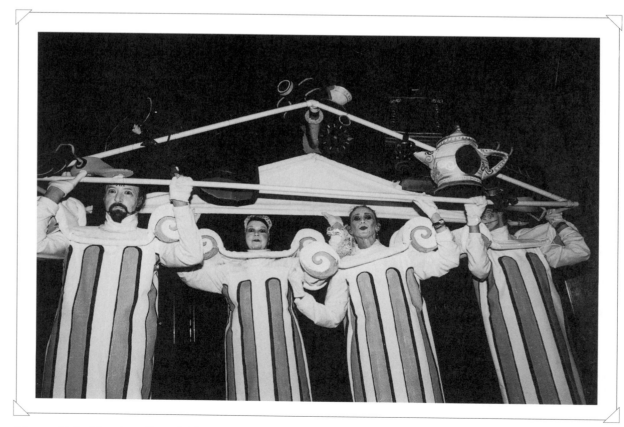

Figure 11.5. "An Arty Party." These five street-theater performers were commissioned to represent *The Pillars of Society*—a very flamboyant and fun aspect. (Photo Courtesy of Jan Kuczenawy.)

woks, and other freshly shucking oysters. Later in the evening these food stations would change over to dessert and coffee stations with an espresso machine set up to serve all variety of coffees.

An Aboriginal dance troupe was engaged to perform on the lawn during the pre-dinner drinks period.

The Execution

Bump-in and rehearsal schedules were written. A minute-by-minute running sheet was produced showing events happening simultaneously: outside on the lawn, on all five sections of the scrim stage, the two small cameo stages, the band stage, and in the cafe plus the wandering elements.

The venue had many restrictions since it was the cafe area of a public museum. It was open for coffee and lunch until mid-afternoon, and the foyer of the museum was open until 5 P.M. There were no dressing rooms as such and access to a meeting room could only be gained after 3 P.M. This meeting room had to be set up for our make-up artist, hairdresser, and all performers! It was also on the sixth floor and security guards were required to operate the elevator to take crew and performers to and from the performance area. Permission, (which would have been preferable), could not be obtained to set up an outside tent for performers.

Access to the venue was only from 7 A.M. on the day of the event, and guests were to arrive at 7 P.M. The building of the scrim stage was the first priority and had the greatest potential for delay. However, all went well according to plan. By midday the lights in the scrim stage were being set up. Luckily the lighting company was able to work on the trussing and other room lighting from 7 A.M. Lighting and sound also had to be set up outside for the Aboriginal dance performance. By 3 P.M. all stages, draping, sound, and lighting were completed and at 4 P.M. the performers rehearsed.

All was now ready for the guests' arrival for pre-dinner drinks on the terrace.

Luckily the weather was good but a wet weather contingency plan (which involved guests having drinks in the main foyer and the cafe) was still available as backup. Guests enjoyed champagne and canapes while watching the Aboriginal dance performance on the lawn. Immediately after the performance was finished the doors opened into the main room.

There is no doubt that guests were more than impressed at their first sight of the venue. While watching the tableaux taking place behind the scrim, they were able to choose from the oyster bar and/or the noodle bar. Street theatre included silent men with bonsai plants instead of heads and miniature, but moving, garden gnomes. *The Pillars of Society*

greeted the guests, music was provided alternately by the double-bass playing bride and the blues singers and occasionally crossed to the ambient music from the scrim stage. Some guests immediately positioned themselves in the cafe in order to have their caricature drawn as a memento of the evening, while others were happy to take in their surroundings, chat with their colleagues, and occasionally try transforming the aerial sculptures from domes and bells into flowers or butterflies.

The delicious array of dessert and espresso coffees served from the food stations created yet another area of interest!

At 10 P.M., the performance on the scrim stage finished dramatically with an amazing aerial act. Suddenly guests heard music from the band stage and *The Shy Guys* were revealed. The lead singer moved onto the dance floor and the guests began to dance. Once they started, they didn't want to stop!

The Result

It was an extremely successful evening. My client had achieved her objective of an unusual and memorable event with an artistic theme and lots of opportunity for networking. The event had been produced to budget and ran smoothly. In her thank you letter she stated: *"One thing is clear—the* **Arty Party** *was a major contribution to the overall success of the Congress."*

1997 Johnnie Walker Classic

Romaine Periera
International Corporate Events (ICE),
Sydney, Australia

For the first time the Espirit Award for **Event of the Year** has been bestowed to an Australian company. Winning this award and being acknowledged by our international peers certainly is a great motivator which will spur us on to bigger and better events. With the 2000 games and all its challenges ahead of us, global focus is set on Sydney and Australia. Therefore we needed to make a point that Australia has come of age and would be able to mix it with the best in the world. High expectations need a great deal of passion and dedication. Therefore it is important for Australian special event professionals to be heading the list.

The Event

The **Johnnie Walker Classic** is shared jointly on the Australasian golfing calendar and the European Tour and is renowned as one of the most lucrative events in professional golf with minimum prize money of UK£700,000, It is also one of the most widely televised golf events in the world, receiving live TV in the United States, Europe, Canada, and Australasia.

For the first time in seven years the JW Classic left its Asian homebase to take part in an exciting venture agreement between the Australian and British governments—the New Images Program. The staging of the prestigious tournament officially launched the first of many sporting, cultural, and economic interactions between Britain and Australia.

International Corporate Events (ICE) was assigned the task of concept designing, producing, and project managing every facet of this complex event. This involved the:

- Design and production of all evening events
- Design and production of printing, invitations, flags, and banners
- Public relations
- Hotel arrangements and hospitality personnel
- Airport arrangements
- Golf course VIP hospitality arrangements

Australia's Gold Coast, An international playground was chosen as the venue to play host to this prestigious premier golfing event. Its VIP guests ranged from Lords and Ladies, to Ambassadors and High Commissioners from each country, to leading political figures and international sports stars, not to mention the top golfing pros such as Ernie Els, Fred Couples, Nick Faldo, John Daly, Colin Montgomerie, and Bernhard Langer, just to name a few. **ICE** embraced this event with all its complex diversities and with a yearning to prove our worth.

The Opening Ceremony at Hope Island Golf Course

Precision timing was required on our first assignment as we went to a live audience of 5000 guests on-site and a potential TV audience of some 500 million. Lord McFarlane and the Premier of Queensland opened the 1997 Johnnie Walker Classic followed by the appearance of a band of more than 100 Scottish Pipers marching in formation on cue! A 25 ft balloon replica of Johnnie Walker was inflated in the distance to mark the 18th hole. As the pipers neared our guests, the national anthems were heralded and the culmination of the formalities was the great thunder of a surprise air display performed with split second timing by the Formation Aerobatics Team of the Royal Australian Air Force. Their display sequence included several popular maneuvers finishing with the spectacular barrel roll and bomb burst. The Wow effect was achieved and we took our first breath!

The Welcome Dinner at Sheraton Mirage Gold Coast

The Sheraton Mirage allowed us to create an informal BBQ surrounding for 300 guests. The lagoon-style pool was home to the largest Johnnie

Walker banner immersed to its base and spot-lit to highlight the importance of this event. A synchronized swimming team performed during pre-dinner cocktails, followed by a spectacular seafood buffet set for individual tables and featuring the best of Queensland produce.

The Pro-Am Dinner at Washington Waters Park

The Pro–Am was designed to acknowledge and award the up-and-coming golfers on the circuit. The brief was to produce an opening celebration unseen on the Gold Coast before. This evening had to be different. It had to take in the diverse cultures of our guests, and our concept and design could in no way offend any of these cultures or nationalities. Therefore we had to ensure that all colors or symbols were authentic reproductions and commemorated the message of good will. Sounds easy in theory but was a nightmare for the design artist!

A 150-ft × 75-ft tent was set up overlooking Washington Waters Park. Pre-dinner drinks were hosted on the waterfront while an entertainment spectacular featured a dozen bare chested, bronzed drummers in silver lamé harem pants who heralded the commencement of a water ski display. This display incorporated a pyramid formation and other flame-lit sequences and a finale performed with the backing of a spectacular pyrotechnic display.

The drummers were now positioned at the front entrance of the tent which was completely covered by a wall of 12-ft pillars of helium balloons. At a given moment the balloons were released simultaneously to reveal the inner contents, thus marking the beginning of the dinner for 500 guests.

The Gala Night at Conrad Jupiter Casino Ballroom (850 guests)

The venue selected was the ballroom of the Conrad Jupiter Casino. We decided to create a Thai royal theme and chose to create the set of the inside of the Royal Palace. The entrance to the building needed a major statement of the theme so we framed the entrance with two life-size elephant statues complete with gold dressing and created an antechamber as a hallway. Twelve international models were flown in to participate in a choreographed display of Johnnie Walker product presentation and to create a live feature in the antechamber. For this section they were draped in gold lamé which made them a real life prop set on risers.

The ballroom was draped in black fabric containing thousands of twinkling fairy lights covered with black sharks tooth gauze to create the night sky. One mile of fairy lights were used to create a star curtain over 400 ft long. There were 85 tables, each pin spotted to highlight the floral centerpieces and set on imported Thai silk tablecloths with the JW logo embossed into the fabric. Chair covers were deco-

Figure 11.6. Johnnie Walker Classic 1997. Aerial Laser Performance. A three-person performance over the guests at the Conrad Jupiter Casino, Queensland, Australia.

rated with a similar Thai silk bow—a long journey and many hours of preparation for the 850 bows which needed to be individually tied. Royal china and crockery with the gold JW logo were specially flown in from London for this evening. Our concept started to take form with its 150 ft × 18 ft, three-dimensional replica of the Thai Royal Palace—fit for any king or queen.

This evening gala for 850 guests commenced with the sound of an antique Thai gong as our guests entered the flickering ambiance of the evening. Many oohs and ahs later they were seated and the first entertainment feature began—a three-person aerial laser performance (Figure 11.6) dressed in full head and body suits made of mirrors to reflect the maximum impact of the laser (Figure 11.7), followed by our models dressed in elaborate, traditional costumes reflecting the various Asian cultures. After a set formal dinner menu another fabric laser performance followed and the finale was a cabaret performed by Mary Wilson and the Supremes and the Four Tops, closing with a nine-piece dance band, The Enormous Horns. Dancing went on until the wee hours of the morning and many memories were created for our guests.

The Farewell at Sheraton Mirage Gold Coast
What better day than January 26, Australia Day, to bid farewell to all our international VIP's and to showcase the natural beauty for which Australia is famous.

The theme was A Taste of Australia and the venue was the Sheraton Mirage Ballroom and its equally large foyer. The foyer was utilized for pre-dinner drinks. We took on three phases of Australia. The entrance was a corrugated iron barn where the 400 guests were met by staff attired in Australiana bush outfits complete with Akubra hats, as they proceeded into a manmade rainforest created with six hundred tropical plants and the floor completely covered with wood bark walkways (Figure 11.8). The sounds of tropical birds and waterfalls echoed throughout the forest to enhance its ambiance! A camouflage net canopy was entwined with vines to cover the ceiling. The ballroom was designed with backdrops lining all walls and special FX lighting to create its depth. Each table featured a centerpiece of Australian blackboy plants set in hessian baskets filled with moss and pin spotted for more effect. The tablecloths were made up of very large Australian flags. The napkins were folded into a replica of the

Figure 11.7. (left) Johnnie Walker Classic 1997. The amazing full head and body suits of the Aerial Laser Performers are made of mirrors to reflect the maximum impact of the laser.

Figure 11.8. (below) Johnnie Walker Classic 1997. The man-made rainforest created in the Sheraton Mirage Gold Coast Hotel, Queensland. Note the ceiling and the wood bark floor.

Opera House. An Australiana style hat and a pin clip of the well-loved Koala was placed at each setting for our guests. Entertainment commenced with an Aboriginal dance troupe set against a backdrop of Ayers Rock which disappeared at the end of the performance by creative lighting to reveal a backdrop of the Sydney Harbor Bridge and harbor activity at night. The last evening was by this time in full swing. The guests were going to party and party they did to the beautiful voices of Vernie Varga and Martin Nievera flown in from the Philippines and finally back for an encore, The Enormous Horns.

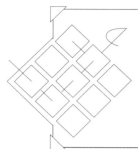

Suggested Readings

Berlonghi, Alexander, M.S. *The Special Event Risk Management Manual.* Alexander Berlonghi. 1990.

Deal, Terence D. and M.M. Key. *Corporate Celebration.* Berrett-Koehler Publishers, Inc. 1998.

Goldblatt, Joe Jeff, CSEP. *Dollars and Events: How to Succeed in the Business of Special Events.* John Wiley & Sons, Inc. 1999.

———. *Special Events: Best Practices in Modern Event Management,* Second Edition. John Wiley & Sons, Inc. 1997.

Goldblatt, Joe Jeff, CSEP, and Carol McKibben, CSEP. *The Dictionary of Event Management.* John Wiley & Sons, Inc. 1996.

Kahan, Nancy. *Entertaining for Business.* Crown Publishing Group, Inc. 1990.

Radice, Judi, with the National Restaurant Association. *Menu Design #5.* Pbc International. 1993.

Reynolds, Renny. *The Art of the Party.* Penquin Studio. 1992.

Surbeck, Linda, CSEP. *Creating Special Events: The Ultimate Guide to Producing Special Events.* Master Publications. 1991.

Wigger, G. Eugene. *Themes, Dreams, and Schemes: Banquet Menu Ideas, Concepts, and Thematic Experiences.* John Wiley & Sons, Inc. 1997.

Special events magazines on subscription. Magazines available from:
Special Events
P.O. Box 16868
North Hollywood, California, 91615-6868

Index

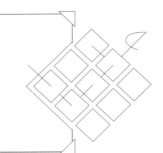